DP DISPLACED PERSON

MARGARITA MEYENDORFF

DP
DISPLACED
PERSON

BARONESS PUBLICATIONS

Baroness Publications

P.O. Box 299
Rosendale, NY 12472

www.margaritameyendorff.com

ISBN: 978-0-9975868-0-0

DEDICATION

This memoir is dedicated to my parents, who passed on to me their histories, their creativity, and the rich Russian culture and language without which my life would not have been fulfilled. Спасибо, Мама и Папа. . .

Disclaimer:

Some names and identifying details have been changed
to protect the privacy of individuals.

CONTENTS

INTRODUCTION

In the wake of the 1917 Russian Revolution, when many immigrants were looking for ways to cross the ocean to escape from the war in Europe, a shipful of refugees attempted to cross the Atlantic Ocean, heading for America. Through his binoculars, the ship's navigator spotted a raft with a person who appeared to be flailing. The ship drew closer and the crewman threw a lifeline out to the raft. The man was holding onto a suitcase. The captain called out, "Let go of the suitcase!" to help save him, but the man yelled back, "I cannot let go of the suitcase. I am Baron von Meyendorff and my entire family history is in this suitcase!"

This anecdote was related by my cousin, Baronessa Elena Nikolaevna, daughter of my uncle, Baron Nicholas Meyendorff, when she gave a television interview in her home city of Salzburg, Austria.

It was not clear which Baron von Meyendorff Elena is speaking of; there were many. Was it my father, Baron George Meyendorff? He crossed the Atlantic in 1949 and he was certainly hanging onto a suitcase filled with Meyendorff history. What other journeys did that suitcase take, clutched in Meyendorff hands? Was this the suitcase stuffed under a bed in our family's numerous apartments in America with all the rest of the Old World memorabilia? Was this the suitcase I carried with me through my various journeys? Why was I so reluctant to open it? I was curious about the contents, but not yet prepared to look inside.

Years after our family's Atlantic crossing in 1949, when I was finally settled and able to pull the suitcase from underneath my bed, dust off the top and open it, I found a treasure of memoirs, notes, poetry, photographs, letters, and journals, both from my father, Baron George Meyendorff and my mother Margarita Angelika Ulk–a Pandora's box of invaluable information that unveiled the mysteries of the family histories. This is the foundation for my memoir.

Chapter One

Clarkstown Country Club

SPRING, 1950. "ТЕПЕРЬ МЕНЯ ВЕЗИ." ("Now pull me.") I sat in the little red wagon in the driveway of the Clarkstown Country Club, a seventy-two acre estate situated on South Mountain Road in Nyack, New York, our first home in America. My cousin Andrei and I were in front of our apartment: newly renovated elephant stalls (yes, elephant stalls, but the elephants were no longer in them) that housed several other Russian immigrant families, many of whom were relatives, displaced persons who, like us, had just arrived from war-torn Europe.

I was already in love with cousin Andrei, with his beautiful red hair. Andrei obeyed my every command. Photos of me at age three show a little girl, half-waif but also half-princess, with luminous hazel eyes and light chestnut hair tied up with a large bow. Andrei pulled and I sat like a little titled ruler in my red wagon royal carriage, and together we set out to explore our alien surroundings.

My three-year-old memories of the Clarkstown Country Club estate come in flashes, but they are vivid images of a small exotic world: The renovated elephant stalls had large wooden doors with slatted windows that looked like they once were bars from which elephant heads and trunks would sway, begging for peanuts. In front of the stalls, on the far side of the driveway, peacocks strutted in the meadow, their iridescent feathers fanning out in full display. Beyond the meadow was an enchanted pond filled with very green frogs and bright orange goldfish and mysterious mossy stone stairs leading upwards... to nowhere.

Near the renovated elephant stall apartments was a little house where an ugly, mean, scary old woman lived. She was always dressed in black. Everyone called her "the Baba Yaga," the Russian fairy-tale witch. Occasionally I would see the Baba Yaga sweeping outside her door. If any of us children got too near her, she would yell and wave her broom. This sent us screaming towards home, afraid that the house would revolve on chicken legs, or that she would put a spell on us and we would disappear.

I watched the volleyball parties, reserved for adults and older kids who knew how to play, and I would squeal with glee when I could fetch the ball that rolled near me. One winter day there was a wonderland highlight: a toboggan party that took place on the long hill on the property. All the relatives, my brothers, and my wonderful Andrei attended, and there was much whooping for joy as we swooped down the snow-covered slope–a bit of the old Meyendorff Kumna estate transplanted to Nyack.

There were at least three other DP (Displaced Persons) families living on the estate. My father's older sister, Aunt Tessia, lived on the second floor of our building with her husband, Alexander Lopuchin, and their seven children, my second cousins. Aunt Sandra, my father's twin sister, lived with the Lopuchins. There were the Rodziankos (a most famous name from the beginnings of the Russian Revolution) and the Novikov family, who also lived on the second floor. The Novikovs had a son, Lyona, a year younger than I was, and we played together. On the second floor there was also a small Russian Orthodox Chapel.

My father, my mother, Aunt Alina, Andrei, and I lived on the first floor, where the elephants were once housed. My stepbrothers Kurt and George, who were already attending Nyack High School, lived on the second floor with the Lopuchins and the Rodziankos. The rooms were cluttered with second-hand furniture and partitioned off by curtains to give an illusion of privacy; a small votive candle lit the Russian Orthodox icon hanging in the corner of the main room. The second floor apartments had bedrooms with large bathrooms attached, but they had no doors. The reason for the doorless bathrooms was never explained. It was worrisome, and made for nervous trips, cramping, and worse. Andrei's mother, Aunt Alina, who was responsible for procuring the renovated apartments for her relatives arriving from Europe, discovered huge Kama Sutra drawings depicting pretzel-like sexual positions painted on the walls. She painted over these erotic images of entwined nudes in anticipation of the new immigrants' arrival.

My family knew little about Pierre Bernard, our elusive and eccentric landlord, who lived in the Tudor-style mansion with a stone porte-cochere above the driveway at the entrance to the estate. Cars would take the long winding driveway, pass under this stone covered entrance, and continue to our buildings within the property. As a child, I saw Bernard's home as a castle, complete with turrets on both sides. The mere mention of his name conjured up an image of a mysterious old wizard, which was not far from the truth.

As our first home was influenced by Bernard's philosophies and experiences, I must expound on his extraordinary life, which gave root to our life in America.

According to Robert Love's book, *The Great Oom*, Pierre Arnold Bernard was a pioneering American yogi, scholar, occultist, philosopher, mystic, and businessman; he also had a notorious reputation as a con man, seducer, and philanderer. Bernard reclaimed an ancient yoga discipline that was banned in Victorian India and packaged this discipline to the Americans. He called his organization the Tantric Order, and it became a secret society based on the idea that physical human experience is a pathway to spiritual enlightenment–the beginning of what we know today as Hatha Yoga. He was dubbed "The Great Oom," "Omnipotent Oom," or "Oom the Magnificent".

In 1918, Bernard received the Clarkstown Country Club–a seventy-two acre estate in South Nyack with a thirty-room mansion–as a gift from a disciple. He made it his home and began to build his empire. His yoga practice, with its emphasis on difficult physical poses and breathing techniques, was considered foreign and exotic and was not well accepted in the United States. However, the yoga wound up having mesmerizing effects on Bernard's disciples. And those disciples increasingly tended to be bored, wealthy young women who found themselves invigorated by whatever Mr. Bernard had to offer. There are many photographs in Robert Love's book showing nymph-like nude young women frolicking in the waters, or perched on rocks at the estate. Bernard was known to have jokingly told a journalist "not to overlook the opium dens and the orgy rooms." Bernard's reputation as an exploiter of women and perpetrator of "free love" led to his imprisonment in 1910 for allegedly enticing a woman for the purpose of sexual intercourse. Charges were dropped after three months.

Bernard was rather like the Hugh Hefner of his day, but with more exotic philosophies and some genuinely healthy and spiritual practices. He became extremely wealthy and shifted his attentions to more conventional businesses, including building a baseball stadium, a dog track, and an airport on the estate. He supported boxing matches, gave lavish all-night dinner parties, entertained his guests with outlandish schemes and projects, and had his own traveling circus with five elephants living on the property.

In the early 1900s, there were many celebrated visitors to the Clarkstown Country Club who shared Bernard's vision of well-being: the Vanderbilts, the Goodriches, Broadway stars, musicians, lawyers, teachers, wrestlers, Leopold Stokowski, and a very young Pete Seeger. Bernard's library at the estate was said to have the best Sanskrit collection in the country, and to contain some seven thousand volumes of philosophy, ethics, psychology, education, metaphysics, and related material on physiology and medicine.

In the 1930s, the Depression put an end to Bernard's empire, and by the beginning of the 1940s, Bernard was selling off his possessions, renovating the elephant stalls into apartments, and renting rooms in his mansion and in the numerous outbuildings on the property.

My cousin Michael Lopuchin, who was sixteen years old at that time and lived with his family in one of the second floor–apartments on the estate, told me that he had met Pierre Bernard. Michael and his friends wanted to put up a volleyball net on the property for their family tournaments, and they went to Bernard for permission. Michael's impression of him was of "an elderly man who was very kind and curious." Bernard greeted the young men at the door of his diminished kingdom and a lively discussion followed. Their volleyball request was granted with great enthusiasm (after all, Bernard was all for physical exercise). However, he had no idea who they were; no idea that he had Russian Displaced Person families living on his property in renovated elephant stalls. A manager called Mr. Max handled all of his affairs.

Years later when I was in the seventh grade at Nyack Junior High School, which was built partly on the old Bernard property, I would be reprimanded by the teacher for daydreaming and staring at the Tudor-style building where Bernard had lived. I would recall the castle images and tell my classmates that as a child I had lived on that adjacent property in renovated elephant stalls and seen peacocks strutting around. They didn't believe me.

Chapter Two

Baron George Meyendorff

IN 1893, WHEN MY GRANDMOTHER, Baronessa Elena Pavlovna (nee Countess Shuvalova) was expecting again, my grandparents already had eleven children. The officers in my grandfather Baron Bogdan Meyendorff's regiment began making bets on the sex of the twelfth child. Elena Pavlovna was very upset that the officers were holding bets at her expense and asked if they would stop. But Bogdan said that he couldn't tell his officers what to do in their free time. On July 16 1894, at their Kumna estate in Estonia, Elena Pavlovna surprised everyone and gave birth to twins. As soon as she could catch her breath, she had a telegram sent to the officers that all bets were off, that she had a girl *and* a boy, and the money had to be returned. The boy, the younger of the twins by a few minutes and the last of thirteen children, was my father, George Meyendorff.

As a child, my father enjoyed the privileged aristocratic life to which he was born. He ran with his sisters and brothers in the Meyendorff house on Pervaya Liniya (First Line Street) on Vassilisskom Ostrove, not far from the Winter Palace in St. Petersburg. He played music, put on performances in the family theatre, and painted. He was well taken care of by his older siblings. His nickname became Liulik because his twin sister Alexandra could not pronounce Yurik, a diminutive for George in Russian. The name Liulik stuck for the rest of his life among his closest relatives and friends, including (many years later) his wife Rita, my mother.

In 1892, cousins to my father's family with the thirteen Meyendorff children, moved to St. Petersburg from their estate in the south of Russia. Every other Saturday–"субботники," they called them, the family visited my grandparents and their thirteen children at the big house on "Первая Линия." One of the cousins, Aunt Manya, wrote a memoir of her life in Russia entitled *Memories*. In her book she mentions how she and her eight brothers and sisters called my grandfather "Uncle Bogdasha" and my grandmother "Aunt Mimi" (although her first name was Elena). Aunt Manya also spoke of how creative all the thirteen children were. She would walk into Uncle Bogdasha's room where all the children would gather. Someone would be reading, another would be drawing, someone else arranging photographs, while the others were playing chess or checkers, the little ones playing hide-and-seek. The children were always busy.

As Liulik grew older, he attended the Cadet Military Academy, across the street from his home on Pervaya Liniya. During his student years, he had a chance meeting with Czar Nicholas II at a Christmas party at Tsarskoe Selo, the Czar's Village, the country palace of the Czar and his family outside of St. Petersburg. At the party, he found himself face to face with Czar Nicholas II. The Czar asked him, "Well, young man, how are you doing in school?" As it was unthinkable to say anything good about yourself, especially to the Czar, my father responded, "Not so very well, Your Excellency." Somewhat later the Czar found him again, and said, "Young man, I just talked to your father, and he said you are doing very well in school. You must always tell the truth to the Czar."

Growing up in the aristocratic milieu of St. Petersburg in the early 1900s, young Baron George Meyendorff rubbed shoulders with many socialites at parties, balls, and concert evenings. One of his encounters was with Count Felix Yusupov, with whom he played tennis on several occasions. Yusupov was a very wealthy Russian aristocrat, a prince and a count whose family owned no less than four palaces in St. Petersburg. My father remembered Felix as a very flamboyant character–he often wore cosmetics and costumes and was known for his bisexual escapades–who became notorious for his participation in the assassination of Rasputin in 1916. As Yusupov married the Czar's only niece, Irina, and conspired with Dimitri Pavlovich, a cousin of the Czar, they fulfilled Rasputin's prophecy: that if Rasputin was murdered by the Czar's relatives, the Romanov family would themselves be killed within two years. Rasputin wrote a letter to this effect, and it is often referred to as "Rasputin's curse." Because they were so closely connected to the Imperial family, the two conspirators, Felix and Dimitri, were not executed but sent into exile (which ironically saved their lives after the Revolution).

My father remained concerned with the fate of the Romanovs. In 1922, when Anna Anderson was trying to convince the world that she was "Anastasia," the youngest daughter of the czar, and did not perish in the murder of the family in 1918, my father did not believe her. My father told me that when he was about twenty years old, as a cadet at the Military Academy, he had danced with Anastasia at an annual Spring Ball given by the Czar at the Winter Palace in St. Petersburg. Anastasia, who was about thirteen years old and a little plump in her light blue veiled dress, danced delightfully with the eligible bachelors at her coming-out party. My father, one of the eligible young cadets, expertly swirled her across the beautiful parquet floor of the grand ballroom, their eyes meeting at every turn. He never forgot her, and he saw at once that Anna Anderson looked nothing like the youngest daughter of the Czar. Much later, in 1989, with the collapse of the Soviet Union, DNA testing was done on the Romanov family, and Anderson's DNA did not match Anastasia's, confirming that my father was right. (Anna Anderson's DNA proved she was a Polish factory worker, whose wounds– which she had claimed were from the executioners' bullets and bayonets–were in reality incurred in a munitions plant explosion.)

In 1917, with the Bolshevik Revolution raging and Lenin coming to power, the monarchy toppled. The Russian intelligentsia, aristocrats, and landowners fled for their lives. The large Meyendorff family scattered in many different directions, trying to save themselves and their families. They took little with them. Some Meyendorffs were arrested, some escaped, some were exiled, and some were murdered. The Winter Palace in St. Petersburg was looted and pillaged and beautiful paintings were thrown onto Nevsky Prospect, one of the main streets in St. Petersburg. Those who knew the value of the paintings picked them out of the gutters. The lucky ones were able to keep the paintings; others sold them for passage out of Russia.

In 1917, my father escaped to Kumna, the Meyendorffs' summer estate, one hour south of Tallinn in Estonia, an independent republic at that time. From 1917 to 1919, my father, a young White Russian cavalry officer, fought the Bolsheviks for Estonia's freedom from the Soviets. One story he told me was from his time at the Estonian front. He was in charge of a small battalion of men who made camp near a bank of a river. My father decided to take his big grey horse called "Пыль" ("Dust" in Russian) closer to the river to see if there were enemy lines nearby. As he was getting closer to the bank, he saw one campfire, then another, then another. A large Red Army battalion was camped on the other side of the river. He turned his horse back to where his men waited and packed them up in a hurry. Had they not left their camp, they might have been discovered and killed the next morning.

At the end of 1919, when the battles were over and Estonia was able to maintain its independence from Bolshevik Russia, the Estonian government passed the Agrarian Reform Bill, which divided the manorial estates into twenty to twenty-five acre lots to satisfy the needs of the peasantry, giving some of this land to those who had fought for Estonian independence. The Meyendorffs had lost seven hundred and seventy-seven acres from the original Kumna estate, but because my father had fought against the Bolsheviks, he was allowed to keep the manor house and twenty-three acres of the original land.

It was part of this land that my father sold to help his two sisters, my Aunt Sandra and Aunt Tessia, Tessia's husband Alexei Lopuchin and their seven children to escape from Soviet Russia to come to Kumna in 1933-34. My father paid three thousand rubles for each of the adults' passports; the children were free. This transaction was made through the Political Red Cross, an organization headed by Ekaterina Peshkova, who was married to the famous Soviet writer Maxim Gorky (his real name was Peshkov). Well into the late 1930s, Peshkova helped Russian prisoners returning from the gulags and Russians at risk to establish themselves outside of the Soviet Union. After Aunt Sandra, Aunt Tessia, her husband, and their seven children were safely settled in Kumna, my father took a trip to Paris, funded by money left over from the sale of the land. He was severely criticized by his family for going to Paris. How frivolous! Little did anyone know at the time what lay ahead for the Meyendorffs. Perhaps my father sensed that his time in Paris would be his last fling.

Aside from becoming a fine artist like many of his brothers and sisters, my father was a skilled equestrian and raced semi-professionally in steeplechase tournaments in Estonia. He was also an excellent hunter. My cousin Michael Lopuchin, Aunt Tessia's youngest son, remembers my father's unerring aim as he shot two rabbits out of the cabbage patch in Kumna and gave one of them to him for the family's supper.

My father trained English setters for hunting. His favorite dog was an English setter whom he named "Nice" (the single English word he knew at that time) who was so well-trained that when friends and relatives would come to Kumna to hunt, my father would instruct "Nice" to hunt for his guests and bring the kill to them, which "Nice" reluctantly did.

In her memoirs, published when she was already living in the United States, my cousin Tanya Rodzianko, one of Aunt Tessia's daughters, wrote an account of what the living conditions were like for the Meyendorff and the Lopuchin families in the early 1930s, a relatively peaceful time at their Kumna estate in Estonia.

Tanya describes the main, sprawling, wooden house in Kumna as having one floor, a full basement, and a large attic. The central entrance had two wings leading away from the main rooms. Inside the wings were hallways connecting the rooms, with passageways leading to different areas of the house. In front of the outside entrance was a semi-circular driveway where horses and carriages would deliver or pick up passengers. In front of this driveway was a manicured lawn. There were many flower and vegetable gardens and orchards–apple, pear, and plum trees–fields of strawberries, and long rows of blueberry, blackcurrant, and raspberry bushes. The Meyendorffs were quite self-sufficient in living off the land. Aunt Maya, an older sister of my father's who never married, was the main gardener, responsible for growing the vegetables in the summer. She was very strict about her gardens and the children would be reprimanded if they picked the vegetables and fruits without Aunt Maya's permission.

Summers were the most fun, with volleyball matches, tennis matches, ping-pong, horseback riding, swimming, and many other outdoor activities. There were family competitions that included foot races, bike races, races with eggs in teaspoons, scooter races for the little ones, and bridge tournaments for the adults.

These "Family Olympics" were followed by a medal-awarding ceremony and a feast. There were instrumental and singing concerts and elaborate theatrical productions as well. Aunt Tessia and my father would play four-hand piano or separately accompany the singers.

Summers were the time for visits from many friends and relatives of the Meyendorffs: noble families such as the Sheremetevs, the Mukhanoffs, the Schidlovskys, and the Wrangels came for vacations. Aunt Alina Teploff, my cousin, visited from America, and my father's oldest sister, Olga Orlova Deneesova (nee Meyendorff), visited from Italy, where she lived with her son. Life was a constant round of celebratory events, dinners, and parties.

In addition to all the relatives and friends visiting, rooms in the main house in Kumna were rented out in the summer for families living in Reval (the pre-revolutionary name for Tallinn). Every summer, the Lopuchin family had to vacate their rooms for the renters and move into a smaller stone house they called Little Kumna. In the winter, they would move back into the main house.

The family members who lived in Kumna year-round were my grandmother, Baronessa Elena Pavlovna, Aunt Maya, Aunt Sandra, and Aunt Tessia with her large Lopuchin family. Aunt Sonia, another one of my father's sisters, and her husband Uncle Valya, with their daughter Mayuka, lived in the guest house across from the main house. During the 1930s, my father lived and worked in Reval and came to Kumna often to spend time with the family.[1]

History took a drastic turn when Germany invaded Poland in 1939. Not wanting to fight on two fronts, Hitler signed a non-aggression pact with the Soviet Union in which the Baltic countries, including Estonia, would become part of the Soviet "sphere of influence." In October of 1940, Estonia became occupied by the Soviets. It was dangerous for the Meyendorffs and other Baltic/Russian noble families who were living in Estonia at that time to remain. Arrest, exile, or death at the hands of the Soviets would await them if they stayed. One by one, they started leaving Estonia for the West.

....

1   From Tanya Rodzianko's memoirs

The Meyendorff family members who remained in Kumna in 1940, the first year of the Soviet occupation, lived in poverty and fear of being arrested. Years later, I asked my father why the Soviets did not arrest him and the others during that year, and he said that the new Soviet government was not fully organized enough to start the persecutions. My brother, George, remembers a moment when he saw Aunt Sandra inscribing a red cloth with a hammer and sickle. Even as a child, he knew what that symbol meant, and when he questioned her, Aunt Sandra said, "We have to eat and we have to live."

In April, 1940, my father married my mother, Margarita Angelika (nee Ulk), an event I will elaborate on in the next chapter, dedicated to my mother.

Exactly a year later, the Baron left Estonia with my mother, Rita, as she was called; her two children from her previous marriage, Kurt and George Marquart; my grandmother, Baronessa Elena Pavlovna; and my Aunt Sandra. They took with them ten suitcases and a bicycle. The Meyendorffs were allowed to leave Estonia and cross Nazi Germany because the German government helped only those families who had German ancestry; two of my great-grandparents were German.

The day of their departure was cloudy. In the gray fog, which seemed appropriate for the occasion, the group headed for the Baltic Station, the main railroad station in Tallinn. There was a long line of tables set up perpendicular to the entrance to the station, where they were required to stop. My brother remembers my mother taking off her diamond engagement ring and giving it to the Soviet officer sitting behind the table, and my father surrendering one of his two hunting rifles. They boarded the train, never to return to Russia and Estonia.

Chapter Three

Margarita Angelika Ulk

IN 1874, MY MOTHER'S FATHER Jaan Ulk was born in the small village of Paistu in central Estonia. Born into a wealthy landowner family, Jaan Ulk chose to study at the Railroad Engineering Institute in St. Petersburg instead of staying and working on the estate. Jaan became the first Estonian to graduate from the Railroad Institute and in 1902, he was sent to southern Russia with his new bride Margarethe to work as an engineer for the Russian railroad.

Margarethe Berta Karoline Keyll, my mother's mother, was born in Riga, Latvia on May 2, 1882, a descendant of Saxon farmers who were invited to live in Russia by Catherine the Great in the 1700s. Part of Margarethe's family lived in Moscow, where her brother was a famous composer and a piano tuner for Knabe pianos. (Without knowing this, I bought a Knabe piano fifteen years ago and still have it in my living room).

Although Margarethe was born in Latvia, she lived in southern Russia most of her adult life, until her untimely death at age thirty-seven in 1919. Jaan and Margarethe had two children. While taking a trip together in 1905, Margarethe, who was expecting their first child, went into labor. They stopped in Debaltsevo, a little village near Krivoi Rog, Russia, where her son Zhenya (Eugene) was born. Two years later, my mother, Rita, was born in Hartzisk.

Hartzisk was situated near the Ukrainian border in southern Russia, which was officially called Malorossia and considered the bread basket of Russia and

Eastern Europe. (This area, now considered part of Ukraine, is the center of the Russian/Ukrainian crisis that began in 2013.)

Tchaikovsky's Little Russian Symphony was inspired by the Malorossian countryside. The beautiful steppe stretches out for hectares upon hectares from Rostov-Na-Donu in the south to Moscow in the north, laden with rich dark soil known as black gold, which fed the Russian people for centuries. There are the long winding rivers that supply nourishment and water to the fields before flowing south to the Sea of Azov and finally into the Black Sea. The mighty Don River, a subject of many a romantic and historical novel, flows near here and into the Azov. The wooden peasant houses ("*izbi*"), with their intricate designs on the shuttered windows, are clustered in small villages. The "*izbi*" are surrounded by muddy paths after a rain, leading to groves of birch trees and dense forests; the Russian peasants work on their wheat, barley, and rye fields. The churches with their bell towers ring out the chords of their faith to rich and poor alike; the crucifixes on the multicolored starred onion-shaped domes form the unique architecture of the Russian landscape.

This area, the Novocherkassk region in southern Russian, near the Sea of Azov, was also noted as the home of the Cossacks, a special ethnic group of soldiers known for their military prowess and most often used as cavalry by the Czars. The Cossacks were notorious as fierce swordsmen, known for their horsemanship and their regalia. Their uniforms–fleece hats, tunics with ornamental cartridge loops, colored *бешмет* (waistcoats) and wide breeches–have come to epitomize the popular image of the Cossacks.

This is the Russia my mother loved, and where she lived for fifteen years.

On October 25, 1917, the Bolsheviks, discontent with the economic breakdown and the autocratic system in Russia and weary from the wars, seized power in St. Petersburg. The political and social chaos of the October (Bolshevik) Revolution escalated, ousting the much more civilized Kerensky-led Provisional Government, which had orchestrated an essentially nonviolent transfer from the monarchy when Nicholas II abdicated on March 15, 1917. After the October Revolution, the brutal Lenin regime took over. Not only were the Romanovs doomed, but all former titled and wealthy families were in grave danger. The southern part of Russia where the Ulks had settled became a focal point of conflict among many contending armies which included Czarist loyalists, different factions of Ukrainian nationalists, partisans of both the White and Red Armies, and the Bolsheviks. Landowners were hung or shot; their estates burned to ashes. Peasants were run off their fields. The fields were left barren, and as a result, Russia experienced widespread starvation. The Estonian government urged their citizens to come home to avoid the disaster, and in 1922, offered Jaan Ulk a job promotion, which he accepted. With his son and daughter, Jaan Ulk packed up and moved to Taganrog, a Russian port city situated on the north shore of the Sea of Azov. For one year, they were able to live in Taganrog before they were forced to leave Russia forever. In 1923, the small family moved to Reval in Estonia.

During that time period, my mother kept a journal, which, in a fortunate turn of circumstances, I acquired and have been able to draw upon for this book.

Chapter Four

My Mother's Journals

IN 1967, MY BROTHER, GEORGE was on a business trip to London and decided to look up Koka Andreev, a professor at Cambridge University who was once a friend of our mother's when they both attended the Technicum College in Tallinn, Estonia. Because World War II scattered people all over the world, it was not unusual to visit friends and relatives in foreign countries to catch up on history and interesting stories of survival. George was curious about Andreev, having heard so much about him from our mother Rita.

Andreev invited George to his home, handed him a sealed envelope, and made an unusual request: that George promise he would not read the contents until after our mother's death. My brother kept that promise until our mother died on December 7, 1979. Inside the envelope were three journals that Rita had written while she was attending the Technicum in Estonia. The journals included entries about Rita's mother and Rita's love for Russia, but mostly they were preoccupied with her unrequited love for Koka. In 1927, Rita had sent the journals to him as a last effort to win his love. Koka had kept these journals for forty years.

In 2000, George sent the journals to me, thirty-three years after receiving them from Koka. The journals were written in Estonia and cover only five months of our mother's life, dating from August 9, 1927 to Thursday, December 1, 1927, but as I read through the journals, hanging on every word, tears streamed down my face. I felt my mother revealing herself as if she were speaking to me alone.

As if we were two young women sitting in a café renewing a friendship, I became acquainted with a mother I never knew.

For the purpose of this memoir, I translated my mother's journals from Russian to English.

The first time Rita tried to commit suicide was when her mother died of kidney failure in 1919 in Harzisk, Russia. Rita was twelve years old. She took some matches, scraped off the chemicals that make them light up and put them in a glass of water. She was about to drink this cocktail in her room when the door to her bedroom opened, and the spectral figure of her mother walked in. She said in Russian, "Стоит ли?" ("Is it worth it?") and the ghost went out, closing the door behind her.

Eight years later, in Estonia. . .

August 10, 1927, 5:30 a.m.

How wonderful my mother was–smart, generous, happy, and unbelievably kind. How incredible my childhood was to be surrounded by her love, her kindness, and her care. I see this vision in front of me: It is dusk and I am curled up on the couch in the living room. In the dining room close by, Mama is playing something sad on the piano. Later we sit for a long time on the couch, embracing each other and her hand is caressing my cheek, my hair. I love her hands, my favorite hands, and I kiss them.

All this is gone now. I will never again feel a mother's love. Never. Sometimes I so want to feel the kindness, the caring and love from people and to tell them about the injustice. When we were visiting Uncle Fedia in Moscow, I was always on the verge of tears when I saw how kind Aunt Zina was to him. I also wanted this kindness but I know this is not to be. Papa? Yes, he loves me very much and I love him, but I don't know how to get close to him. He is so uptight, my "Papchik". It's all right. It's not worth thinking about. It just makes me sad. And this sadness is not only about the past but also about a mysterious happiness, something very beautiful and something very dark. If I could climb up a huge mountain, I would yell out, "How do I live?"

Or if I could simply just go away, somewhere far, far, away, and there on the steppe where the wind and the sky and the sun meet, I would stretch out my arms and I would tell the world that I have both sadness and joy in my heart; that I want to live; that I have the strength, but that I have no life. So many questions and no answers. I have to answer for myself, by myself. Yes, by myself. I am utterly alone. Alone with my thoughts. And hopes. And sadness. . .

August 13, 1927, evening

Today, Elschen's husband, the doctor, received a letter that his uncle shot himself. How awful! A person lives and all of a sudden he's gone. He's gone! Death is not a good thing. It's one thing if I die, then it doesn't matter, but how awful it is when someone close to you dies.

I remember when I was a little girl, I would imagine my mother dying and I would become so afraid. These thoughts would come to me usually when my mother was out for the evening or in the middle of the night when I awoke. Then I wanted to jump out of bed and climb into Mama's bed and cry out of fear of losing her. I would take her scarf, the one she would wrap herself in when she was cold and I would kiss it and cry. The later it got the more frightened I became for her. It was silent and dark. My brother Zhenya would sleep and I would wait. Suddenly I would hear the key turning in the American lock and immediately I would feel peace and happiness. My mother, all dressed up and happy, would come into my room and with tears of happiness, I would throw my arms around her neck. "Mama Darling!"

I stopped writing in my journal for a moment and remembered that all this happened a long, long time ago. Mama is gone. Her grave is far away in Russia. No one is taking care of her grave, no one is decorating it. How I want to go there! To come to the grave, to cry a little, to tell Mama how much I miss her; to tell her everything, everything...

In 2001, I was dancing with Lynn Barr's dance company in Urbino, Italy. By chance, I met a Russian woman in the street who on impulse gave me a cassette of beautiful Russian songs. There was one song in particular which I fell in love with, called "Россия" (Russia). Later, when I had returned home, I learned the song on the guitar and on the piano, and sang it at several concert events. In

2012, when I finally read my mother's journals, my heart skipped a beat. My mother was in love with the same song in 1927! Eighty-five years ago!

August 10, 1927, evening

How I love that song "Россия".

Россия, нищая Россия	Russia, poverty-stricken Russia
В ней избы серые твои	To me your grey "izbi"
Твои мне песни ветравые	And your capricious songs
Как слёзы первые любви	Are like the tears of a first love.

When I think of Russia, my heart fills with such sadness–my favorite, unforgettable Russia. Moscow! Such fascination in that word! I don't know it very well, but no other city is as special to me as Moscow. I see it all in front of me: Kuznetsky Bridge, the Bolshoi Theatre, Red Square, Arbat Street. Churches everywhere, small and large, with ancient cupolas shaped like onions bulbs. Christ the Saviour Church, the Kremlin walls–ancient, covered with moss, surviving the generations. I want to go back to Russia. The forests, the steppe and the rivers are all so different from here. . .

At age eighteen, my mother Rita was beautiful, with large hazel eyes, thick chestnut hair, full lips, and high cheekbones. Even as a teenager in Russia, she was regarded as a catch for the many young men who courted her. Rita loved the attention although in her journals, she berated herself for her flirtatious character. There was Gyorg, Vova, Shura, Zyablik, and Kostja, who moved to South America from Estonia and proposed to Rita in a letter after her first marriage ended in 1939.

Rita, however, fell deeply in love with Koka Andreev while attending the Russian Technicum in Estonia, and considered him to be her first love. Koka, an aspiring writer, was one year ahead of Rita in school. While in Reval, they saw each other as much as they could. When Koka left to attend a university in Prague, Rita, at twenty, found herself alone, pining for his letters, trying not to write to him too often, trying not to bother him, not to make him feel trapped; to give him his freedom.

August 16, 1927, afternoon

I was walking on Glipyanoi and he was walking on Nikolskoi Street and I saw him! I felt like all my blood drained out of me and my heart stopped for a second and then started beating again so hard and fast that I could hardly breathe. He didn't see me and that was good because I was so nervous I probably would not have been able to say a word… I followed him until I caught up to him and was walking next to him. Finally, we were face to face and I made believe that I felt calm. I couldn't read anything on his face except surprise. I waited for him while he dropped off something at his editor and then we went home. What did we talk about? We jumped from subject to subject. He spoke about his journey to Tansal and I listened not believing that Koka is here next to me. Tomorrow we meet again…

August 17th, evening

My dear Koka. I love you. How I love you. Love is a deep bond both spiritual and physical. I am in love. But is he with me? I'm terrified that he will forget me; that he will tire of me. But now I am at peace, basking in the knowledge that he is near. I knew that he would come and see me and he did.

Если ж к пропости приду, и	If I would walk to the edge of a cliff, and
Заглядевшись на звезду	Upon gazing at a star
Буду падать не жалее	I would fall on the rocks below
Что на камни упаду	I would do so without regret

November 3, 1927, evening

My dear Koka. I don't want to write about my love for you, but not to write to you is impossible. How I would love to speak with you. Your photograph is standing in front of me–your face so serious and preoccupied. After reading your letter, the memories poured in and don't leave me in peace. I want to see you in person, my dearest, my love. I want to hear your voice, to look into your eyes, to experience you close to me. I want to relive those cloudy, rainy September and October evenings when we forgot that time and space exist.

My mother filled her emptiness, depression, and frequent headaches by writing poetry, journals, studying and reading Russian literature voraciously: Pushkin, Lermontov, Chekhov, Tolstoy, and Turgenev, to name a few. On the last page of her last journal, Rita lists several books that she had read with a one-line critique next to them. She loves Tolstoy's *Anna Karenina*.

Reading Anna Karenina! Like Kitty and Levin, I want to merge completely with another person, to love, to understand them. Then we can work, think, improve, suffer and struggle together. That would be happiness. For women it could only be this way. Maybe someday I will have this happiness. Koka is not here now. I have never felt so lonely.

September 10, 1927, evening

Last night I went with Irma to the Russian church. The walls were shining in the semi-darkness, the cloth around the curtains moving from the heat of the candles. The choir sang and I was standing and thinking. About what? About life and death. About people. About the love I have for them. About sacrifice. But my heart remained cold. There was a pain and sadness there. In an attempt to pray, I wanted to forget my surroundings and feel God's spirit. But I knew that this would be impossible. I don't have the kind of faith that allows me to forget everything and believe in prayer. My soul is poisoned by doubt. Oh!

November 26, 1927, Saturday

Tomorrow I will be in a play called The City of Kitete. My role is so small that I'm not at all nervous. The rehearsals are interesting. I like the fact that the Russian costume looks great on me and everyone is looking at me with a kind of wonder. Of course that is terrible of me, but I don't care. I'm not thinking of Koka's letter. Of course when I get home, even as I take off my coat, "Is there a letter or not?" All day today I sewed my costume. I'm tired. Again that feeling of disinterest. It's your fault, Koka!

Thursday, December 1ˢᵗ, 1927

Well, Koka, my love, in front of you are my journals, my soul such as it is. You will understand a great deal from them.. Don't feel sorry for me. Everything passes and this will pass as well. There is nothing more. This is the end, the real end. From now we go our separate ways. To quote you, "adherence to the old, to the past, gets in the way of one's freedom and invisibly but perceptibly creates a noticeable burden." With your words, I end my journal and "The Story of Summer, 1927."

In 1928, Rita graduated from the Technicum. One year after her relationship with Koka ended, she had two illegal abortions in Reval. Her beau at that time was Kurt Arved Marquart, a young man from a wealthy German family. Because of the Marquart's social standing, the abortions were performed by the family doctor, Dr. Thal. Rita married Kurt in 1929 while she was attending Tartu University in Tartu, Estonia, first as a student of Mathematics, then switching to the Department of Economics in the Faculty of Law. Education for Rita stopped when her sons were born: my older brother Kurt on June 20, 1934, and her second son, George, on September 16, 1936. After Kurt was born, Rita's husband started sleeping late, throwing dirty dishes out of the window, and then, in bursts of action, sailing on the Baltic Sea every chance he got. After George was born, he stopped getting out of bed at all.

In the summer of 1939, the von Seidletzes, a well-known Baltic German noble family in Reval, held a masquerade ball. Rita dressed as a marquise. She wore a white curly wig with little white braids hanging down to her shoulders. Her costume was a tight-fitting blue ballroom gown that showed off her full bosom and small waist. The dark makeup on her eyes and bright red lips stood out on her white powdered face. She was ravishing. All night long she flitted about in her ball gown and glided past the numerous costumed guests, flirting and glaring at her husband, who was costumed as a turbaned and frocked stranger from India, inspired by Rimsky-Korsakov's opera *Sadko*. Her husband's jealous eyes were darting; he caught my mother's every flirtatious move.

There was a gentleman at the party who was dressed as a baker, complete with a high white baker's hat, shirt and pants, and a white oversized apron. He was handsome, with a chiseled thin face, and despite the comic outfit, there was an air of aristocracy and gentility about him. The baker was there with his twin sister, who had begged him to take her to the masquerade ball. His sister was dressed as a 1920s flapper in a dizzy multicolored dress with a black choker around her neck and a matching headband.

The large ballroom with its chandeliers and floor to ceiling windows was decorated with multi-colored streamers and the portraits on the walls flickered from the lights as if they were old friends observing and enjoying the merriment. The party glittered, fraught with gaiety and celebration.

It was sometime that evening, in the midst of the excitement, that the baker and the marquise caught each other's attention. He was smitten by her beauty; she was swept away by his aristocratic and genteel manner. He was Baron George Meyendorff, a forty-five year old Russian aristocrat residing in Estonia. He was handsome. He was a bachelor. He spoke Russian. He was Russian! Russian! He was my father, and the die was cast.

In 1939, Rita got a divorce from her husband Kurt, and on April 21, 1940, Baron George Meyendorff and Margarita Angelika Ulk married in the Church of our Lady Kazan, a Russian Orthodox Church in Reval, Estonia. The church is still in existence today and is one of the oldest wooden structures in Tallinn.

As Rita entered the church to take her marriage vows, my brother George, then three years old and standing in the back with his older brother, Kurt, yelled out "Mama! Mama!," much to the surprise of the attendees. At the reception, which was held at the Russian Club, George continued his scandalous behavior by sipping from everybody's champagne glasses and singing Russian gypsy songs that he had heard his mother sing at home. One of the songs was called "Dark Eyes and White Bosom."

My mother's position as a divorcee with two children was risque for that time, but the Baron's mother, the Baroness Meyendorff, and the large Meyendorff family were very kind and accepted Rita into the family. Rita was in love, and for the time being, she felt safe.

Exactly a year after their marriage, Rita's dream of settling down peacefully in Reval with her aristocratic new husband was shattered. With the Soviets already occupying Estonia, it was no longer safe for the Baron Meyendorff and his family to stay in the country. In April, 1941, with their possessions packed in suitcases and trunks, the Baron fled Estonia with his new wife, her two sons, my grandmother, and his twin sister, Aunt Sandra. They were heading west. Rita's life was uprooted once again. What happened to her dreams of marrying into aristocracy, into privilege, into security, into kindness and a genteel existence?

One catastrophe after another unfolded for Rita. She survived illnesses, a miscarriage, a stillborn death, and—just before I was born—a second attempt at suicide at the Estonian Displaced Persons Camp in Germany.

In December, 1949, Mama came to America. She was exhausted. How much the displacements had damaged her, I was to discover later, as I grew up, knowing only the instability that would further displace me. We lost each other, and when I finally held her journals, I at last knew my mother—too late. But our conversation had begun, as spectral in its way as her own exchange with her dead mother, when her ghost had appeared to save her life.

Chapter Five

Leaving Estonia

THE MEYENDORFF ENTOURAGE LEFT ESTONIA with their most precious possessions, their best clothes, family records, and photographs packed into suitcases and trunks, heading west towards Germany. At the point where the wide gauge of the Russian tracks ended, presumably somewhere in Poland, my family was transferred to a German train. My brothers George and Kurt were immediately provided with small, paper Nazi flags which, I am sorry to say, they were very proud to have, as they were too young to understand the terrible significance of Nazism.

The Meyendorffs' first stop was a refugee transit camp in a monastery in Neresheim, in southwestern Germany. Here, my mother suffered some sort of mysterious illness that almost killed her. My brother George, who was four years old, ran next to the gurney as she was being taken into the ambulance, pleading in German, "Mutti, please don't die, please don't die." My mother survived this catastrophe and when she was well enough to travel, the family pushed on.

Their next stop was Vienna, where my father found a job as an estimator for a contractor named Otto Smereker, and his company of the same name, which still exists today. The fourth floor apartment that my family found in Vienna had five rooms, a large kitchen, and one bathroom with only a toilet and a sink with no running hot water. Originally the entire fourth floor had been one apartment, but it had been made into two, and the bathtub was in the other one. My parents had a large cooking pot where the boys fit in separately and where, once a week, they were bathed.

My parents had to take in renters to help pay the rent. Two rooms were rented out to Russian university students. One tiny room, formerly the maid's room, was occupied by Aunt Sandra. My grandmother, Kurt and George slept in another room, and my parents slept in the dining room/living room combination that also served as an additional bedroom. There were always eight and nine people living in that apartment. In the common kitchen, the students did their own limited cooking and boiled their own tea water. The circumstances were not unlike a communal apartment in the much-disparaged Soviet Union. The renters were jointly referred to as "*Kolkhoz*," a reference to the equally disparaged communal farming system of the Soviet Union. It was common that after one of the members of the "*Kolkhoz*" had put their teapot on the stove and it began to boil while they were not in the immediate vicinity, someone would yell out, "колхоз кипит!" ("the Kolkhoz is boiling"), and the owner of the pot would run to come and get it. There was some, but not much, turnover among the renters. There were two Olgas. They were called "Red Olga" and "Black Olga" for the color of their hair, to distinguish them. Two other renters, Tatjana Voitishek and Leonid Feodorov, eventually married each other and moved away.

During the summer, my father also worked in a special camp for Russian prisoners of war who were being trained to go back to the Soviet Union and act as spies for Germany. Some of these POWs visited the family under my father's supervision, without guards, thrilled to be among a Russian family. For George's birthday, they made him a model of a German bomber plane, and often the family went fishing and mushroom picking with the Russian soldiers. History shows that nearly all of these POWs turned themselves in as soon as they crossed the front line, and were immediately executed by Stalin's orders. The fact that they came from the West made them automatically "enemies of the people."

Despite the tight living conditions, the poverty, and the uncertainty of their future, the family managed to socialize with relatives and friends who stopped to visit them. In 1944, Uncle Valya, who was married to my father's older sister, Aunt Sophia, visited my parents and took George and Kurt to see *Hansel and Gretel* at the Vienna Opera, an unforgettable experience for the boys. After a few days, Uncle Valya left Vienna to go back to Posnan, Poland, where his family was waiting for him. Poznan was at that time a quaint, colorful city, but its vintage charms could not hold Uncle Valya, who wanted to escape blood-soaked Eastern Europe. Uncle Valya's intention was to gather his family and continue west to America. He was never seen again; presumed dead. After the Yalta Conference in 1945, which gave the Soviet Union political power in Poland, Aunt Sophia and her daughter Majuka were exiled from Posnan back to the Soviet Union to settle in Saratov, on the Volga River, where Aunt Sophia died. Majuka stayed in Saratov, where she settled with a new family.

There were cultural events. In a turn of the century ornate-faced theatre with a velvet and gilded interior and with Nazi flags hanging from the balconies, my parents performed Chekhov's *The Cherry Orchard* for a Russian theatre company. My mother played Dunya, the maid, and my brothers remember her performing Dunya so naturally and with such skill that she was unrecognizable even to her sons. My father, having been roped into rehearsals, expertly navigated the role of the drunk. Many of the rehearsals took place in my parents' tiny communal apartment.

It was here in romantic Vienna that my mother had a clandestine romance with Vladimir Galskoi, a Russian poet. The feelings between them were mutual, but as she confided to my brother many years later, "до постели не доходило" ("the relationship did not reach the bedroom"). After the war, Galskoi moved to Morocco.

World War II was looming and in September, 1942, the first Allied air raids began in Vienna, then a German occupied territory. In 1943, the air raids became more serious, and by 1944, they became a daily occurrence that sent the family running into shelters at all hours. My two brothers made lists of neighbors in the event that a bomb struck a house, so search parties would know who to look for in the rubble. After a bombing, my brothers would run up to the roof to see how the city was damaged. Rubble was also the place to look for wood to use for cooking and heating—another job for the boys. It was after one of these outings to search for wood in a bombed-out building that Aunt Sandra made the oft-quoted comment to my brother George, "Someday, you will be driving in your own car in America and we will all be eating oranges."

On January 18, 1943, my grandmother, Baronessa Elena Pavlovna, died at age eighty-six. There was a proper Russian Orthodox funeral and she was buried in the Russian Orthodox section of the vast Zentralfriedhof cemetery on the outskirts of Vienna. The second largest cemetery in Europe at six hundred twenty acres, it is a famous tourist attraction. The graveyard has a designated resting place for famous musicians (*musiker*) such as Beethoven, Strauss (Johann and family), Brahms, and Schubert, to name just a few. Mozart is represented by a memorial monument, as he died in such poverty that his actual remains are lost in a common grave in nearby St. Marx. The vast graveyard is also ecumenical, including Protestant, Jewish, Greek, Russian Orthodox, Buddhist, Mormon, and Muslim sections.

The Zentralfriedhof cemetery is divided into sections. The original Jewish graveyard (the resting place of such rich and famous Jews as the Rothschilds) is segregated. The cemetery was also the setting for the opening and closing scenes of Orson Welles' film *The Third Man*. Even today, there are more dead people underground in Zentralfriedhof than there are living people in all of Vienna. There are areas reserved for those who donated their bodies to science, and a babies' graveyard where infants are interred. Since 1906, the transportation throughout the cemetery has been by a tram numbered "71." In Vienna, there was an expression when someone had died: "He has taken the #71."

In 1944, my mother gave birth to the first child of my parents' marriage, whom they named Alexander Meyendorff. He lived for only three days. As my older brothers had a different father, Alexander would have been my full-blood brother. After the birth, my mother suffered a depression and then a protracted series of illnesses: blood poisoning and a severe attack of rheumatic fever. During the rheumatic fever, she was unable to move because of her painful joints. A friend of the family, Kotik Semchevsky, helped my mother by "paying" a German doctor–not with money, as they had none, but with a large sausage from the black market. My mother's care improved. In each instance when my mother was taken to the hospital, Kurt and George took special pleasure in bringing Aunt Sandra, who took care of them during my mother's illnesses, to near total madness with their childhood shenanigans.

It was during those first few months that Kurt and George, playing outside of the apartment house, saw a strange man walking up the street. He was old, with long hair and a beard, dressed all in black, wearing a hat, and there was a yellow star on the left side of his coat. He was walking in the street, not on the sidewalk. George described this man to my mother and she replied with a strange look on her face, "That was a Jew, and they are not allowed to walk on the sidewalk." There was no more discussion of the subject. In October, 1942, the Mayor of Vienna, Alois Brunner, declared Vienna "Judenfrei" ("Free of Jews"). At the age of four, my brother knew that anti-Semitism was rampant, but did not know about the atrocities, the concentration camps where millions of Jews were exterminated by the Germans, until after the end of the war. At that time, George was not sure how informed my parents were.

In the summer of 2005, my husband and I visited the Vienna apartment near the railroad station where my family had lived, Graf Starhemberg Gasse 37, apt. 7. We took the old-fashioned iron grated "лифт" (elevator) to the fourth floor. I knocked on the door, but there was no one at home. Years later, my brother told me that the building and the apartment had belonged to the Skoda family, a prominent Jewish-Austrian family of industrialists who had been probably taken to a concentration camp.

On March 1, 1945, under threat of the oncoming Soviet Army, my parents and the two boys were forced to leave Vienna. As the saying goes, they went "from the frying pan into the fire." Because the Germans considered this effort to flee as displaying a "defeatist attitude," leaving Vienna was tricky. My father obtained, with difficulty, the needed documents and tickets for passage on the trains. Aunt Sandra, for reasons unknown, had to stay behind in Vienna and connect with other relatives. Continuing west, now a family of four, they often dragged twenty-three pieces of luggage and a bicycle from one end of each town to another because all the central train stations were bombed. On the edge of town, where there were no buildings or platforms, miraculously, a train would be waiting on undamaged train tracks and passengers would board. It took ten trains to reach Fuchsberg in what is now Germany, where my mother's brother awaited the family. Vienna was indeed captured by the Soviets at the end of March.

It was at the next to the last stop before reaching Fuchsberg that George, who was eight years old at the time, got lost. The family had stopped at NSV (National Socialist Women's Organization), an organization that provided food and drink to refugees caught up in the chaos of war. As they proceeded to find a place to sleep, having been up all night, George discovered that he had left his rucksack, with their big metal pot for boiling water to make tea, at the NSV. Little George must have looked a sight with his rucksack on his back and a big metal pot hanging from it. Somehow he convinced the parents that he knew where the NSV was, and took off to find the rucksack with the pot. It was already very dark when suddenly he heard a voice in German, "Halt, who goes there?" In a little voice, George said in German, "Ich." ("Me.")

Out of the dark, a German soldier appeared and asked him what he was doing there, to which George replied in German that he had been at the train station with his parents, but got lost. The German soldier turned out to be very friendly and told George that he had wandered into the entrance of a Russian POW camp. He summoned one of the prisoners to take him back to the station. When George was out of earshot of the German, he started speaking Russian, which made the poor POW soldier very happy. When they reached the train station, a policeman grabbed George and much to our parents' relief, he was returned to them; the cooking pot was never retrieved. The next day, it took only two hours for the family to reach Fuchsberg, West Germany, where they stayed with my mother's brother Uncle Zhenya (Eugene) Ulk and his family.

In Fuchsberg, Russian, Ukrainian, and Polish refugees, brought there by the Germans, worked in the peat bogs. My father worked there and Uncle Zhenya became Chief Engineer. After one week of eight people living in a single room in a barrack, my father found a room in the hamlet of Darlaten, two kilometers away. Even though there was no electricity, no running water, and only a wood burning stove for heating and cooking, the family stayed here for about six months.

Towards the end of World War II, The UNRRA (United Nations Relief and Rehabilitation Administration) set up several Displaced Persons camps in Germany to help the thousands of refugees stuck in Europe at this time. It was 1945 and winter was on its way. My father decided to move the family to an Estonian Displaced Persons Camp in Uchte, about ten kilometers away. The Estonians were not happy about the fact that my father was a Russian Baron and tried to disqualify the family from refugee status because they were not "pure" Estonian. Nevertheless, the family stayed at the Estonian Displaced Persons Camp for two years. It was here that I was conceived.

Chapter Six

Mourka

AFTER THE EXHAUSTING AND PERILOUS journey from Estonia to West Germany, life for my family became easier in the Uchte refugee camp. They lived in a room that had been requisitioned from its former German owners, and even though the family lived with uncertainty and poverty, the UN organization in charge of the camp did a good job supplying food. According to my brother George, there was not a lot of variety, but at least the family was never hungry.

Despite the conditions, my parents made lasting friends and a lively social community developed among the cultured Germans in the towns and the refugees in the camp. At that time, my parents' best friend was a Frau Haesecker whose husband, a dentist, was at the front lines. Mama explained to her that since the root of her name comes from the German word "Hase," or rabbit, she would nickname her "Zaichik." The name stuck. She used to organize concerts and literature readings at her home. There were singers, poets, and writers in the camp who would take part. Everyone in town knew that "Zaichik" was half-Jewish, but did not give her away.

Sometime in 1946, at one of these community gatherings, my father flirted with one of the local beauties and my mother became jealous. That night, my parents had a terrific argument in their one partitioned-off room. My brothers, feigning sleep, overheard their accusations. Later that same night, my mother tried to commit suicide and overdosed on my father's sleeping pills. My brothers remember seeing my father with a few other people from camp walking her around all night, her feet barely touching on the floor, her body limp. In the morning, she was taken to the local dispensary, where her stomach was pumped out. This was Rita's second attempt at suicide. Her first was when her mother died of kidney failure, when Rita was only twelve years old.

I was born on July 21, 1947, in Stolzenau, a small town that had a hospital, ten kilometers from the refugee camp. Could my mother have been pregnant with me during her suicide attempt?

When the labor pains came on, my mother was taken to the hospital at night in a military ambulance. They placed her on a stretcher in the back of the ambulance and my father sat on a bench next to her. The journey was dark as there were no lights in the back. Because all the bridges were bombed as a result of the war, the ambulance was put on a ferry, which was pulled across the Weser River on a chain.

They named me Margarita, like my mother and her mother. They called me Mourik for short.

Now we had one room for four people and a baby. To make matters worse, I became ill with diarrhea that would not stop. Fortunately, the family had met two elderly sisters who lived in town, whose brother was Uchte's chief of police. One of the sisters was a nurse and she recommended large amounts of carrot juice, which saved me from dehydration and near death.

During this stressful time, George, who was about ten years old at the time, found himself browsing in the camp store. He had no money to buy anything; he was "just looking" when he saw a bowl full of tiny religious medals. In his mind, he felt that if the family had one of these medals, it would bring us good fortune and solve all of our problems. George picked up one of the small medals and put it in his pocket. He then proudly presented the medal to my mother with his childish assumption that everyone would understand what a wonderful thing he did. When my mother asked him where he got the medal, George confessed that he stole it. The magical thinking was dismissed, and to George's dismay, my father took him back to the store to face the humiliation of confessing to the theft and returning the stolen medal.

It wasn't long after my birth that we moved from the Estonian refugee camp to a Russian Displaced Persons camp in Fischbeck, near Hamburg. Here there was a Russian Orthodox church, a Russian school that my brothers attended, and generally more living space for the family. We lived in barracks for a short time until Prince Volkonsky, the civilian camp commandant and a friend of the family, gave us use of part of his apartment in the former administrative building. The family called it the Kremlin. In the Fischbeck DP camp, there was regular food distribution of meat, vegetables, flour, and Hershey bars from America. Toward the end of the stay, my mother worked in the kindergarten and my father as a bookkeeper, saving up money for their eventual exit from the camp.

Besides the obvious difficulties of basic survival for the Meyendorff family, there was an underlying tension between my parents about my mother's sons, George and Kurt. There were arguments about how the boys should be treated. They were not my father's sons, and although my father did his best to take care of them, his love and caring were often in the guise of duty, something that he owed them as their stepfather.

This was particularly true with my older brother Kurt. Uncle Liulik, as the boys called my father, devised different ways to make Kurt miserable, all presented as a desire to prepare him for life. At age thirteen, my father put Kurt into a machine shop ten kilometers from where we lived, so he could learn a "*remeslo*," a trade. The boys felt that Uncle Liulik had a talent for doing "*gadosti*" (nastiness) disguised as good intentions. When a small amount of butter was available, my father unfairly announced to my brothers that only sick people, mothers, and babies received butter–an announcement never forgotten and not taken lightly by my brothers. Eventually, butter became more available and the misappropriation was forgotten. My brothers do not remember a single kind or gentle word from Uncle Liulik at any time in their childhood. Having gone to a military academy as a young man, my father's idea of bringing up children was stern and militaristic. My mother spent a lot of her declining energy protecting her sons, creating a tension between her and my father. In 1948, a year after I was born, Rita had a miscarriage and slipped into another depression.

A stealthy wedge formed in the family, creating tension and unhealthy feelings. My mother sided with the boys because they were mistreated by my father. My father, who clearly loved me, tried to spoil me, and in so doing alienated my mother from me. Perhaps she felt it unfair that I was treated differently from my brothers. Perhaps she was jealous of my father's affection for me. It's hard to say. In later years, she didn't hesitate to remind me how spoiled I was and how miserable she was.

There was also the issue of religion. My mother was Lutheran and had promised my father that she would convert to the Russian Orthodox Church when the boys were old enough to leave the house. But she never did. This was a source of anger for my father, who at one point wanted to take me away from my mother and have his sister, Aunt Tessia, raise me in the Russian Orthodox faith. Years later in our home in Nyack, I found a letter from a Russian Orthodox priest, a family friend. The letter, which was written at the DP camp, was addressed to my father reprimanding him for even thinking of taking me away from my mother.

As the years went by, this family dynamic followed us and raised its ugly head more than once as we attempted to find a cohesive home for ourselves.

In 1949, four years after the war ended, there were still 850,000 refugees in Europe who needed to be repatriated. It was time for the family to make a decision to leave the DP camp in Germany. My parents knew that there was no future for any of us if the United Nations turned the refugees over to the German government, a distinct possibility. At that time war refugees were generally invited to Argentina, Brazil, Australia, and America. America was our first choice as there were already some relatives settled in the U.S. Also, my parents considered it the most civilized of the four countries and the best for the future of the children. But we still had to find someone to sponsor us once we emigrated, and that was proving difficult. We had written to relatives already in America, but when we had not received an answer, we had our passports made to enter Argentina where the Moukhanoffs, our relatives were ready with affidavits to receive us.

At the end of 1949, at the last minute, my family got an affidavit from Prince Beloselsky, a Russian aristocrat living in New York City, inviting us to come to America. The affidavit gave gardener and maid jobs to my mother and father in the Beloselskys' home in Mahopac, New York, called The Princess Inn. My parents understood that these jobs were fictitious; that they were invented to help bring the family into the United States; that we would be on our own as soon as we stepped on American soil. In Hamburg, Germany, just before boarding the ship, we stood like packages being sent off to a distant land with Displaced Persons identification tags flapping in our lapels and our luggage marked for the Princess Inn in Mahopac, the bogus destination.

In December, 1949, we crossed the Atlantic and anchored in Boston. The United States of America! Land of milk and honey.

From Boston, we took a train to Penn Station in New York City, arriving there at midnight. On the way from Boston, my mother couldn't believe that a little dime could buy us so much milk. From Penn Station we traveled by subway to Grand Central Station, where we stayed the night on benches in the waiting room. In the morning we were picked up by distant relatives and taken to their Lexington Avenue apartment. There we waited for my cousin Aunt Alina and Aunt Sandra, my father's twin sister, to pick us up in Aunt Alina's big black 1943 Packard. We were driven to Nyack, to the renovated elephant stall apartments, our new home, and to the clutch of Russian displaced persons who were already housed there.

My first memory in America was being held by my wonderful Aunt Sandra at a lookout point on Route 9W just past the George Washington Bridge, en route to Nyack, where the family stopped to rest. I was two and a half years old. I had on a white fur "*nanaxa*" hat and a white fur muff that was tied around my neck. I also had on a small dark jacket with a knapsack over my shoulders that housed a little pee pot. This pee pot was my responsibility to carry all the way from Germany. While everyone was looking back at the majestic George Washington Bridge, the ghostly skyscrapers of Manhattan, and the beautiful Hudson River, making their first impressions of America, I was staring at three-year-old Andrei, who was being held by his mother, Aunt Alina. It was in that moment that I fell in love with Andrei–his beautiful face, welcoming smile, and that shock of red hair.

Chapter Seven

NYACK

THE THIRD WAVE OF RUSSIAN immigration to the United States (1945-1955) was a direct riptide of World War II. During this period, approximately 20,000 Russian displaced persons arrived in the United States.

A large number of White Russians (a label for all those Russians who opposed the emergence of the Soviet Union, especially those of aristocratic background) who arrived in the immediate post-World War II era, found it difficult to adapt to an American society that lacked the respect and deference that Russian nobles, princes, princesses, and intellectuals had come to expect. My father took "Baron" as his first name to continue his legacy–and so no one could mistake his lineage. I believe my father upheld his aristocratic title in the hope that his stay abroad was temporary. The idea was that his family must live a Russian life while in temporary exile, until the inevitable fall of the Soviet Union, which would allow us to return to a democratic Russia. This was the basic ideology that held the post-World War II DPs together, even though they represented a wide variety of political persuasions.

From the beginning, my father's unrealistic ideas of returning to Russia created a fantasy world that contradicted the realities of our survival in the United States. My father was fifty-five years old when he came to the States and my mother was forty-two. Perhaps with the right resources, they could have started a new life in the new country, but because my father was ill with mysterious stomach illnesses and my mother was shell-shocked from early life catastrophes that left her mental health very fragile, life became a struggle for survival. My parents' inability to learn the English language well and our below poverty-line existence also made it difficult for my family to start over.

But start over they did.

In the 1950s, Nyack was a quaint, charming little village located on the western banks of the Hudson River. A large number of new Russian émigrés settled here because of the proximity to New York City. They would travel the Red and Tan bus lines from Nyack to New York City, a convenient thirty-minute commute to work and to universities to pursue educational degrees. In 1952, as a five-year-old child, I watched the construction of the massive Tappan Zee Bridge, which connected Nyack to Tarrytown and the rest of Westchester County on the other side of the river. (My brother George worked on the bridge in the summers as an assistant to Nick Umrichen, a construction engineer and a friend of the family). The New York State Thruway gutted South Nyack by cutting a huge swath through the black ghettos and splitting them in half to make way for this first interstate highway. I watched huge houses being lifted up from their foundations, placed on huge boards, and towed by gigantic trucks to different destinations. One such house was placed on an empty lot next to us on Brookside Avenue, where we lived at that time.

Although I was too young to appreciate the many celebrities who lived in and visited Nyack in the late 1950s and early 60s, the little village was teeming with actors and actresses, musicians, and poets. The Tappan Zee Playhouse was a very successful regional theatre where some of the best Broadway plays were produced. Helen Hayes, a famous actress who lived in Upper Nyack, gave out dollar bills for Halloween, and when I was old enough to go "trick or treating," a group of us children would walk the four miles from South Nyack to Upper Nyack to reap the benefits.

Nyack was an enclave of Russian nobility, and as a child, I was surrounded by my Russian aristocratic relatives and other Russian families who sought refuge in the United States. Aunt Tessia, my father's older sister, was the matriarch of her large Lopuchin family and of the growing Russian population that centered around the Russian Orthodox church. Her seven children, my first cousins, were at least ten years older than me. Because my father was the last of the original thirteen Meyendorff children, had married late, and was fifty-three years old when I was born in 1947, all my cousins (those who were still alive) were much older than I was. Out of respect, I called my cousins Aunts and Uncles. It was their children, my second cousins, who were closer to my age, with whom I played as a child.

The many relatives would often convene usually around church holidays, funerals, and weddings. There were tables covered with large amounts of tasty Russian food and drink and there was always a pot of borscht on the stove. My Aunt Tessia made her own "*kvass*," a soda-like drink made from fermented beets. The huge glass bottles filled with beet brine stood under the sink. "*Kvass*" was delicious. After the meal, both children and adults would gather around a large table and play the card game "Pounce." Essentially it was a solitaire where everyone could play off each other. It was called "Pounce" because the game went quickly, with ten or more people "pouncing" cards into the center to reach their goal: to get rid of their thirteen downward-facing cards. A yell of "Pounce" signaled the end of the game. There was always a great deal of laughter and screaming. I loved those warm, loving gatherings. I looked forward to them.

Of course, there was my favorite Aunt Sandra, my father's twin sister, who took me on outings in her tiny Opel. We would go swimming in Haverstraw in the Hudson River or go pick berries or mushrooms in the forest. Aunt Sandra never married, and lived and worked as a clerk on the Tolstoy Foundation in Valley Cottage. She was very independent and traveled alone all over the world, visiting relatives. She had a closet for a room at the Tolstoy Farm, filled with photographs and books. A seven-string gypsy guitar with a multitude of colored ribbons that she brought back from Russia hung in the corner of her room. There was one tiny bed. I loved staying overnight with Aunt Sandra, sleeping together in that tiny bed. My Aunt Sandra was a good friend to me.

Within the émigré colony, there were many famous Russians. Perhaps the most famous was the Tolstoy family. Although I was too young at the time to appreciate Leo Tolstoy's genius and his literary contributions to the world, I played with his great-granddaughter, Masha Tolstoy, who lived in Nyack with her parents, Aunt Olga and Uncle Vladimir Tolstoy. Uncle Vladimir was Leo

Tolstoy's grandson, who escaped from Russia to Paris in 1919 and married Aunt Olga, nee Rodzianko. They immigrated to the United States in 1949.

Alexandra Lvovna Tolstaya, Leo Tolstoy youngest daughter, arrived in the United States in 1929 from the Soviet Union. She founded the Tolstoy Foundation in 1939 and was responsible for helping many Eastern European and Russian immigrants to relocate to the United States via the Tolstoy Farm in Valley Cottage, New York. Vladimir Nabokov and Sergei Rachmaninoff were two of the more notable artists Alexandra Lvovna helped to escape Bolshevik persecution and settle in the United States.

Perhaps because my father did not want to compete with Aunt Tessia's matriarchy, our family went to the church at the Tolstoy Farm, five miles from the Nyack church. It was there that I met Alexandra Lvovna, and was often in her presence in church or at church holiday gatherings. Alexandra Lvovna lived in a modest house near the main house on the Tolstoy Farm, and always had a lush vegetable garden. Because Aunt Sandra's garden was right next to hers, it was easy for me to steal Alexandra Lvovna's beautiful ripe cherry tomatoes, which hung in abundance on the vines.

I have already mentioned Aunt Manya, one of the nine cousins to the thirteen Meyendorffs and the author of *Memories,* her story of her life in Russia. One chapter of Aunt Manya's memoir was dedicated to meeting Count Leo Tolstoy at one of our uncle's estates, named Nikolskoe, near Moscow in 1895. Aunt Manya was twenty-four years old.

Tolstoy would often retreat to Nikolskoe to "rest" from the hubbub of "Ясная Поляна," his famous estate. During one of Tolstoy's visits, the uncle invited Aunt Manya and her younger sister Anna to spend their Christmas holidays there, but under no circumstances were the girls to act like some sort of silly fans; they were ordered "not to bother Tolstoy with any questions!"

Leo Tolstoy had just come back from a walk in the snow when my aunts first met him and their first impression was that of a kind, very tall, older man with a polite smile, dressed in a large kaftan and "валенки" (Russian felt boots made of sheep's wool); he was completely covered with snow. He had come there with his daughter, Tatiana, to write and finish his story, Хозяин и Работник ("Master and Man").

Although Tolstoy stayed up to play Whist in the evening with her uncle and aunt, every morning he would get up early, eat only kasha, and go out for a walk. Aunt Manya and her sister would see Tolstoy during lunch and dinner hours, when they listened but were afraid to get involved in various religious, political, and philosophical discussions. Aunt Manya was fascinated by Tolstoy's genuine interest in mankind and became keenly aware of his ability to delve deep into people's souls and try to understand them. It was this ability and his honesty, she concluded in her memoir, that helped Tolstoy to become the genius he was and to create the extraordinary characters in his novels.

One evening, the two sisters noticed that Tatiana, Tolstoy's daughter, never joined them for the lunch and dinner meals. Tatiana, also called "Tanya," was sitting alone in Tolstoy's study transcribing his manuscripts so that he could reread and change them as needed. The sisters felt sorry for Tanya and asked if they could help her, which is exactly what they did. My Aunt Manya and Aunt Anna deciphered Tolstoy's difficult handwriting and helped Tanya recopy his manuscript for "Master and Man!" And three weeks later, it was my Aunt Manya who, unable to sleep and with great trepidation, carried the precious, finished "Master and Man" manuscript in her suitcase on the overnight train to Tolstoy's publisher in St. Petersburg. [2]

Princess Vera Konstantinovna Romanova, great-granddaughter of Czar Nicholas I (Emperor of Russia from 1825 to 1855) and a third cousin to Czar Nicholas II, spent her first years in fabulous splendor during the last period of Imperial Russia. As a young girl, Princess Vera often played with Czar Nicholas II's five children at the Winter Palace or Tsarskoe Selo, where the Czar's family resided. Empress Alexandra Feodorovna, the wife of Czar Nicholas II, was Princess Vera's godmother. Princess Vera was forever haunted by the tragic loss of most of her family during the 1917 Bolshevik Revolution and World War I.

Vera Konstantinovna immigrated to the United States in 1949 and lived on the Tolstoy Farm, where she worked side by side with Alexandra Lvovna Tolstaya, bringing Russian and Eastern European refugees to the United States. I was about six years old when I met Princess Vera for the first time at the church

....

2   From Aunt Manya's memoirs

on the Tolstoy Farm. She was very kind and courteous, as grand elder Russians are with young children. But from my six-year-old perspective, I could not understand why a tall, older person with dark-rimmed square glasses on her face was called a Princess. I already associated Princesses with fairy-tale beauties. Princess Vera was not beautiful, and was usually dressed in black or grey–never anything a princess would wear.

My young world consisted of going to the Russian Orthodox Church at the Tolstoy Farm on Sundays, and on Saturdays, I attended the Russian school in Nyack, located in the basement of the church on Cedar Hill Avenue. Svetlana Umrichen taught me to read and write in Russian. There were classes in Russian history with an emphasis on Russian Orthodox history. The Russian history class was taught by Aunt Sophia Koulomzin, who founded the Nyack Russian school. Aunt Sophia was the daughter of Sergei Schidlovsky, the vice president of Czar Nicholas II's Duma. She married into the Koulomzin family, also a noble Russian family.

When the Russian school was established, there was space to produce and perform Russian Christmas children's plays. The plays employed the talents of the many Russian émigrés who needed an outlet for their creativity in their New World: directors, set designers, costumers, musicians, dancers. Svetlana Umrichen, who later became like a second mother to me, wrote and directed the plays. Vladimir Odinokov, a set designer for the Metropolitan Opera, painted our beautiful sets. My mother helped with the costumes. We were surrounded by professionals, and unbeknownst to me at that time, my die was cast.

There were three of us who consistently performed together: Tanya, my five-year old second cousin; Svetlana's daughter Mika, my best friend, who was six years old; and me, the oldest at seven.

At seven years of age, I made my debut on stage. It was Russian Christmas and we were performing at a concert hall in New York City. I played the rooster in the *Rabbit, Fox, Rooster* children's fable. Mika was the rabbit and Tanya, the fox. Dressed in a lavish rooster costume, complete with a huge red-feathered tail that swung as I moved, I was front and center on a concert stage singing the Russian equivalent of "cock-a-doodle-doo" (Ку Ка Ри Ку) with a musical phrase that concluded with a high C. In that instant, I looked down at the front row where five black-clad, bearded Russian priests were sitting very upright in their righteousness. They were glaring up at me, ready to pounce with a new depth of disapproval and impose yet another layer of God-fearing guilt. I hit the high C anyway.

The priests' mouths flew open in a collective gasp. There was a minute pause, and then the concert hall burst out in applause and cheers. I stood there resplendent in my red and gold feathers, my plumy tail erect. I basked in the applause and the clapping went on. . . and on. . .

In that moment, I knew I was loved. I was loved for hitting the right note. I was loved for being only seven years old. I was loved for being me. I was loved unconditionally, and all I had to do was to stand on stage. I was swept up in a moment I would never forget, and in a sense, I never left.

Chapter Eight

21 Depew Avenue

THEN MY FAMILY BEGAN THE peripatetic moves, never settling for long, from one apartment to another on different streets and different sections of Nyack and its environs. Often it was unclear to me why we moved. It began to feel as if moving was natural for us, a continuation of being DPs, Displaced Persons. No place could be home for long. There was no upward mobility–at times it was downward movement. Nor was there a geographic pattern–we would move in any direction. All that was permanent was impermanence, a pattern I would continue for most of my life. There were the different streets–Depew, Brookside, Broadway, Gesner, Washington–and the apartments, mostly small and crammed, and then one grand exception: a little house in the country in Rockland Lake. But mostly, there were different addresses, new configurations, and new neighbors, friends, and our constant problems, which always accompanied us, as if in the large suitcase that came all the way from Russia.

The Clarkstown Country Club estate was situated on a hill in South Nyack overlooking the Village of Nyack and the wide, sprawling, picturesque Hudson River. It was a good fifteen-minute car ride from the estate into the village and probably a half hour walk. Aunt Alina's black 1943 Packard was always hauling relatives to and from work, school, shopping, and anything else that was deemed necessary. My brother George remembers how one day my father tried to squeeze the huge Packard between two stone walls. He didn't quite make it and scraped the fender against one wall. When he tried to back up and turned the steering wheel the wrong way, the fender almost fell off. My father's small accident caused a great deal of commotion among the relatives who were afraid to lose their only form of transportation. Peace was restored when Mr. Vladimir Novikov, a good friend, who lived upstairs from us at the Clarkstown Country Club with his family, fixed the fender and hammered out the dents.

After awhile, the Russian families started moving out of the apartments with no doors on the bathrooms and found more convenient and comfortable places to live in the village of Nyack. My family stayed in the elephant stall apartments for a year before we rented a faded grey clapboard house on the corner of Depew Avenue and Piermont Avenue in Nyack. The first Russian Orthodox Church was established in an old garage across the street from the house and became the center for the new Russian community. Diagonally across from our house was a large public park with huge stone steps that led down to the Hudson River. Sailboats and yachts docked on the river and my brothers would take me there often for walks. I loved my brothers Kurt and George. In fact, I worshiped them. Kurt was twelve years older and George eleven years older than I. Both of them were very tall; like giants to me.

I was about four years old when one morning, after my breakfast, I followed my brothers who had gone off to school. I couldn't bear to be without them. I had no clue where the high school was, but that did not deter me from walking out of the house, making my way up the hill on Depew Avenue to the corner, and turning right on Broadway. I was not afraid, as I was walking past familiar landmarks: our little A&P grocery store, the bank a little further up, the drugstore across the street. Suddenly I felt someone grabbing my arm, taking my hand, and leading me to the next corner. It was a policeman who saw a four year old walking alone on the street. He took the initiative to hold my hand and keep me safe until someone collected me. He attempted conversation, but I didn't understand. I was a little Russian girl. I trusted and I stood, excited to watch the cars whiz by and feel the hustle and bustle of a busy street corner—a foreshadowing of future escapes from home to more interesting and unconfined worlds.

My mother was not home; she was already working at Sol Walter's dress factory. It did not take too long for my father to discover that I was missing. He must have looked all over the house, then the park, then started into the village.

And there I was on the corner of Main Street and Broadway, holding hands with a policeman as if it were the most natural thing to do. I was not punished from sheer relief of being found.

Aunt Tzenka Rodzianko lived up the street on Depew Avenue and was the first of the relatives to have a piano in her apartment. Because my father had an expectation that I would someday be a brilliant concert pianist and would make the Russian aristocrats proud, I started piano lessons at a very early age, too early. I hated piano lessons. I wanted to take ballet lessons with Larissa, the beautiful white-haired lady who taught ballet. Instead, I sat in scary Aunt Tsenka's musty apartment watching her as she uncurled my little baby fingers and placed them on the keys. The lessons marked the beginning of many tortured, tearful episodes of piano practice.

When I was fifteen years old and still playing the piano, I was part of a recital at my new piano teacher's house. My father, who was in the audience and was hard of hearing, turned up his hearing aid, and a horrendous high-pitched sound screeched from the device, drowning out the beautiful tones of the Chopin Prelude I was attempting to play. I finished the piece, walked away from the piano, and never touched the instrument again.

Chapter Nine

61 Brookside Avenue

FROM DEPEW AVENUE, WE MOVED to a three-bedroom apartment house on 61 Brookside Avenue. We needed more living space. The rent was cheap because the old green and white stucco Victorian house was situated in the black section of town. The upper part of the street closed off by a wooden wall, forming the boundary where the New York State Thruway was being built, keeping the traffic noise and the dust to a minimum.

The large house was once gracious, with a wide porch in the front and a beautiful etched glass panel door that lead to the entrance foyer. Inside, the steps with the shiny wooden banister led up to our apartment on the second floor. The door into our apartment opened into the hallway on an angle. My two brothers shared the main bedroom; I had the small bedroom/closet space. My parents slept in separate beds in the living room where my father had also set up his art studio. As were all of his brothers and sisters, my father was a gifted artist. He found work in New York City as a canvas designer, and Rosetta Larson, who owned a needlepoint shop on Madison Avenue had several ladies needlepointing my father's designs into chairs and rugs, which were later sold in exquisite Madison Avenue retail stores. Papa was able to paint at home and be the at-home father while my mother worked in the dress factories.

The third bedroom was rented out to Russian immigrants in need of a room. A man we called "The Cossack" lived there for a short while. He had long dark hair and a dark beard. His clothes were always rumpled and he walked stooped over–a Dostoevsky character.

For my fourth birthday, my mother created a beautiful doll corner in my room, complete with a tiny kitchen set and table and chairs. My mother excelled at making nests and she made all of our many homes cozy places to live. I had three dolls: the large baby doll, Kukla; the girly doll, Vera; and the little boy doll, Nikolka. For Christmas, I received another doll, which I named Sergey. I announced at that time that I didn't want any more dolls because "I can't take care of any more children."

Spending time with my brothers gave me a great deal of pleasure, although I was not allowed to bother my brothers in their room while they were studying. Sunday nights were special when the three of us listened to *The Lone Ranger* on the radio for a half an hour. Another game that emerged in our house was bowling. The long hallway between the bedrooms and the bathroom was perfect for setting up the threading spools from my mother's sewing factory as pins and knocking the pins down with a ball.

My brothers were not always benevolent in their game-playing and often enjoyed torturing me in the form of a Hide and Seek game. This was especially true when they had to babysit in the evening. They would turn off the lights and hide and have me look for them in the dark apartment. When I would open the closet door, my tall older brother would lunge out with a coat on his head, monster-like. I would run away petrified and scream for my other brother. He, however, was of no help, hiding behind towels in the bathroom. All I saw was legs. I would be terrified and find myself in tears before the game would stop. One night, my parents came home and I was in hysterics. That game ended in a hurry, but my brothers employed other frightening techniques. On weekends, instead of taking me to films for children, they took me to films they wanted to see at the old Nyack movie house. The classic film *Bridge over the River Kwai* terrified me with bloody fighting and tortures, and when I would turn my head away, my older brother would hold my eyes open so that I could get my eyeful of the violence.

Russian Christmas Eve was always special. Mama would take all of my little second cousins and me through the dark rooms, all of us holding hands and taking time to thread in and out of the rooms to look for the Christmas tree. Finally the living room doors would open and there it was: the beautiful candle-lit Christmas tree in the corner with all the presents underneath. The festivities would begin with sweets and opening presents.

Having Russian Christmas two weeks later than "American Christmas" allowed for extra luxuries. (The Russian Orthodox Church continued to adhere to the Julian calendar, which was two weeks behind the Gregorian calendar adopted by the western churches.) Because Christmas trees were discarded by neighbors who had celebrated earlier, Papa had no problem picking up the most glorious tree out of the garbage with ornaments and tinsel still stuck on the needles. Papa then hauled the decorated tree home and resurrected it in our living room. Some of the presents were found in the garbage as well, and much of the decoration and wrappings. "What people throw out in this country," I would hear him say.

Papa was always feeling sick. There was something wrong with his stomach and no one really knew what was the matter. As a child, I heard many complaints and conversations about his pain, and my father was often angry and frustrated about his health. When Papa was ill, Mama would walk to the factory sweatshop, walk home and then start preparing bland meals for him, catering to his every need. He had hundreds of pills for this and that, but much too often, he ended up on an operating table in a hospital so that surgeons could do exploratory surgery. Too often, Mama and I took the bus to New York City and visited Papa in a hospital. By the end of his life, my father had only a quarter of his stomach left.

My brothers graduated from high school and went to the Lutheran seminary in Bronxville, New York to become Lutheran ministers. My mother missed them and their absence was a source of her depression. While the boys were still living with us, she felt she had some help, a support system. My mother and the boys had a special bond. They were connected by their Lutheran religion and they were "her" boys. My mother hoped that someday George and Kurt would save her from the drudgery of her work at the sweatshops. When the boys departed for the seminary, she was left with a sick husband and a child to take care of after work. Because my father was home most of the time, taking care of me was relegated to him. I became "his" daughter. I missed my mother's affections–they were few and far between. We seldom did things together. The wedge between Mama, Papa, and me deepened.

The lonelier Mama felt, the lonelier I felt.

At four years old, I looked longingly out of the window onto the street. I pressed my nose against the windowsill and smelled the outside cool air pushing its way into the house. I wanted to be outside. My father painted his canvasses and had little time for me. The air in the apartment was thick with the smell of oil paint and turpentine. I would go outside, step on the sidewalk and yell at the top of my lungs for Mika, my little Russian friend who lived many blocks away, to come and play with me. She couldn't hear me.

By age five, I was on Brookside Avenue, out in the street, independent and playing with the black kids on the block. The peeing in the pants began. I didn't want to go indoors to the bathroom because it would take too much time and I might not be able to come out again. I postponed the urge to go until it was too late. When the urgency finally struck me, I would freeze in place and cross my legs–one move and I would dribble through my underwear and onto the sidewalk. When I finally made it home with wet clothes, I was spanked and confined to the dark bathroom.

I continued to pee in my pants. I was even farmed out to my parents' friends the Benzemanns, who lived in Valley Cottage, to try and cure me. I had no idea why I was being sent away, but I had a great time playing with the Benzemann boys who were close to my age. After a week, I was picked up by my parents, and Aunt Nina Benzemann proudly announced to my parents that I was cured. Several hours later there was a phone call from Aunt Nina betraying me with her discovery: five wet panties had been found behind the bureau.

I was seven years old when I was sent to the Russian children's camp at the Tolstoy Farm in Valley Cottage. I didn't want to go; I was forced. Although I peed in my pants less frequently, I still had accidents here and there. I was the youngest child in our little bungalow and was allocated the top bunk. I knew then I was in trouble. In the middle of the night, I dreamt that I went to the outhouse to pee, but in fact, the thought of climbing down from the top bunk and going outside into the dark outhouse was not a reality for me. In the morning, I was mortified as my indiscretion was discovered, and I was punished by not being allowed to go on a swimming field trip. Instead I had to stay behind to clean the outhouses, which were filled with those black, hairy, huge, moving spiders called "wolf spiders" that live en masse and crawl in regiments. They were as terrifying in the day as they were at night. I waited until everyone left for the field trip, picked up my clothes and my little bag with the shampoo and toothbrush, and walked out of the camp. It was several hours later that the counselors discovered that I was missing. I was picked up by my parents on 9W South, walking towards Nyack and home.

I don't know who initiated the doctor games outside on Brookside Avenue, but it wasn't long before I was playing sexual exploration games with the little black boys on the block. We stood by the chain link fence or in the bushes near my yard and I asked to see their penises and they asked to see my vagina. Fair trade. I loved their penises and I touched them. They were so soft and protruding. I loved the penises so much that I put a stick between my labia and made believe that I had a penis too. The stick gave me a great sensation in my vagina and a whole new secret world opened up to me. If I couldn't have chewing gum (gum being a forbidden substance), I could touch as many penises as I wanted.

A white boy moved in with his family next to our house and we become friends. We didn't play doctor, but he had a television set and I was invited regularly to come and watch cartoons. This I loved. But the peanut butter and jelly sandwiches his mother made to accompany the television watching sent me over the top. Life was good.

School was a challenge. Like it or not, speak English or not, I had to start with half-day kindergarten. Liberty Street Elementary School, with its huge black asphalt playgrounds surrounded by chain link fences, looked ominous. Inside, the school was painted a pea green color and smelled of sour milk cartons. There were crowds of kids holding onto metal lunch boxes with fantasy pictures on them and smelling like the sandwiches inside them. Russian food was embarrassing to eat at lunchtime. Nobody brought Russian borscht in a container. But I did. It looked like I was eating blood.

I campaigned for the American sandwiches. With peanut butter and jelly sandwiches on Wonder Bread, I blended in with everyone else. And a bonus: I got toys from the Wonder Bread labels when I saved enough of them. My mother saved Raleigh coupons from her cigarettes and I saved coupons from Wonder Bread. Coupons–only in America!

I was lucky and had nice teachers through third grade at Liberty Street. Thanks to my first grade teacher, who had polio, I learned to read, write, and speak English by the end of that year.

In the 1950s there was an outbreak of polio in the United States and everybody had to get polio shots in school. Father Michael, the priest at the Tolstoy Farm Church, experienced a tragedy when his oldest son Sergei came down with polio. For years, nobody could swim in nearby Rockland Lake. At school, we were called into the nurse's office by groups, and the nurse asked us girls to take off our skirts. Everyone was standing in a slip but I didn't know what a slip was and stood in my underwear. I was mortified.

When I was in second grade, I was bullied on the playground by the older black kids who lived on my block. They would become fickle and I wouldn't know from one day to the next if we were friends or not. I thought I did have one little black girlfriend, Joyce. We played and shared toys. I even went to her house one day. Her house was ugly inside–dirt everywhere–a bunch of black folks sitting around a kitchen table eating greasy chicken; a slick of grease just about everywhere. The smell was so strong it made my stomach heave. But she was my friend–or so I thought.

One day, I was walking home from school and several of the black kids were behind me; yelling, taunting, making fun. Joyce was part of the gang. That day when the black gang followed me, I barely made it to my porch and was about to run into the house, when Joyce got a signal from one of her little cousins to beat me up. And she did. I got punched and kicked. It happened so fast, I felt it was all a big mistake.

One night there was a knock on our apartment door. Two very tall black men stood in the doorway and muttered something to my father. Did my father catch up to Joyce and hit her? Did he reprimand her? My father closed the door, turned to my mother and me and said, "Brookside Avenue is too dangerous. We have to move."

Chapter Ten

Chewing Gum

ALONG WITH PLAYING DOCTOR WITH the black boys near 61 Brookside Avenue, I was obsessed with chewing gum. Gum was a forbidden substance. My parents didn't allow me to chew it. Maybe chewing gum was not an aristocratic thing to do, and we were aristocrats. Maybe it was an American custom and we were Russian, and Russians didn't chew gum. I don't know. All I know is that I am a Russian aristocrat, and for this little Baroness, chewing gum was as desirable as it was forbidden.

I started out with stealing gum from the grocery store on the corner of Main Street and Franklin in Nyack where my parents did their weekly shopping. I loved Bazooka the best. It was big in the mouth and I loved the pink color, the sugary texture and the colorful comics that went with the label. Of course, I couldn't read the comics as I didn't read English yet, but I loved the pictures. I stole the gum, brought it home, hid it under my pillow in my bed and chewed it after my father and I recited the Russian Orthodox night prayer in church Slavonic: "Heavenly King, Comforter, Spirit of Truth, Who art everywhere and fulfilling all the treasure of good and Giver of life. Come and abide in me and cleanse me from all evil. Save me."

Sometimes I fell asleep chewing gum and found the wad next to me in the morning, a big pink cold lump of goo. I promptly put the wad back in my mouth, chewed it a little, drained all the sugar out, climbed out of bed, and finally spit it into the toilet and flushed. All traces gone.

Inevitably I got caught stealing gum. We were in the store, and I swiped the gum and held it in my pockets—one pack in each pocket. Keeping my hands in my pockets for so long aroused my parents' suspicions, and finally they asked me to take my hands out of my pockets and show them everything I had. I was so ashamed. My parents escorted me to the checkout lady. With the Bazooka in my hand and in broken English, I had to confess to the cashier that I had taken the gum without paying for it. Nothing like this had ever happened. *I have shamed my parents, all Russians, disgraced the aristocracy. I have blasphemed the Eastern Orthodox God, who will now refuse to save me.* I apologized and told everyone standing around in my heavily accented English, "I vill never steal gum again." And I didn't.

I graduated from stealing gum to scraping up old gum from the sidewalk, putting it in my mouth and chewing it. I remember enjoying the vestiges of mintiness and sweetness that remained in it. Some of the pieces would have a little gravel or dust stuck to them. No matter. It was gum and I loved it. Chewing sidewalk gum went on for a while, until finally I got an abscess on my lip. The abscess was like a large pimple that grew and grew. No one had a clue where this pimple had come from, but I had my suspicions. My punishment had begun.

I was sitting in the reading group in first grade in Liberty Street Elementary School and trying my best to read English. Without warning, the pimple started to bleed, because now I was always touching it or biting it. Again, I was ashamed. I was bleeding from the mouth and I had disappointed my lovely teacher. There was blood everywhere. My classmates were yelling and were disgusted. My teacher took care of me and wiped the blood off my face. She must have told my parents something, because very soon after that incident, I ended up in the hospital to have the abscess lanced and removed.

The hospital was quite cold and not friendly. I was petrified of what needed to be done with my lip. I remember the green and white walls of the corridors and other children in hospital gowns sitting in beds in a large room. They looked innocent and sweet, the hospital smocks too large around their thin, tender necks. Their faces were beautiful and unmarked. Only I had a pimple on my lip.

Chapter Eleven

Rockland Lake

IT WASN'T LONG AFTER THE fighting incident on our porch on Brookside Avenue that we moved again. We moved to the outskirts of a tiny village called Rockland Lake, about five miles north of Nyack, on Lake Road off of Route 9W. The house we rented was the largest of a colony of bungalows situated on top of a hill overlooking Rockland Lake, a natural spring lake that was largely untouched. Only the locals swam and fished there. A driveway from Lake Road came straight up to our house, which was surrounded by woods with a meadow on one side and a stream on the other side. When the absentee landlords came up from the city, they stayed in the big white house on Lake Road.

Our house was a two story with a large kitchen downstairs facing the woods. There was a good-sized dining room that became my father's studio, and a large living room with a full porch attached that faced the driveway. The old upright piano that we bought was in a prominent place at the foot of the staircase that led up to the three bedrooms upstairs. (Piano lessons started up again.) From the landing at the top of the stairs, another staircase led back down to the kitchen. I had my own lovely bedroom at the top of those unique double stairs. My parents had their own bedroom (always with separate beds) and there was another small bedroom for renters or guests. Unlike the apartments that we had been living in, this house was large, spacious, and quiet.

Wildlife was abundant and kept us busy and amused. Not long after we moved in, two large raccoons climbed onto the roof on the second floor, climbed through the open bathroom window and found their way to my father's bedside table, where he kept large amounts of medication and crackers and jam in case he got hungry in the night. Because of his many stomach operations, he had to eat small meals often, even if this meant eating crackers and jam in the middle of the night.

The raccoons had a feast before my mother and father discovered them and shooed them back through the bathroom window. Not long after that incident, the two raccoons brought their three little babies and the feeding frenzy began. We started to throw all our food scraps out on the roof and soon the whole family of raccoons was eating out of our hands. I have photographs of me standing in my pajamas feeding a baby raccoon. I was eight years old.

The silver-haired fox that came out of the woods one day amazed us with its gorgeous long silver hair and huge silver tail. We started leaving food scraps for him and soon the fox was a regular on the meadow. Then there were the numerous birds, possums, skunks, rabbits, and deer. It was a virtual animal paradise.

Then one day Vaska appeared. Vaska, short for Vassiliy in Russian, was the name we gave the long-haired grey and white angora cat who meowed in the night and was invisible during the day. Little by little he got closer to the house during daylight hours and became accustomed to our movements. Very patiently, I sat for long periods of time near him, barely moving, letting him get used to my voice. And then the big day came when he took food from my hand and I could touch him. Vaska was mine! He did eventually come into the house, but never at night. At night, he always slept in the woods.

Except for the Rodzianko family, my cousins, who bought a house about one mile away, there were no other kids who lived near me. Papa was busy painting his canvasses, so most days I busied myself with all sorts of outside activities. I would sail stick boats for hours down the stream, through the culvert under the road, then out to the lake. I walked in the woods by myself and created secret maps of meadows and clearings that I found. I learned to ride a bike and rode all day on the driveway. I fed the animals. I picked berries and worked in our little garden. And of course, there were all the Walter Farley horse novels I read on rainy days. I was happy in our little paradise.

Even the Rockland Lake School was great. It was a small brick building with two large rooms–third and fourth grades in one room, and kindergarten, first, and second grades in the other. I was in the third and fourth grade room with the same teacher for two years. There were about thirty students total. The school was about a mile from my house and when the weather was good, I biked to school. There was one little girl in my grade with whom I became friends and who lived up the street in the little village. Sometimes after school I went home with her.

Now that we had a little more room in our house, friends and relatives came to visit. There were parties. I had my first real birthday party with a long table set outside. Lots of kids came, mostly relatives, and we ate cake and drank soda. We chased each other playing the good guys/bad guys game in the woods. We played "Pounce." I got one of my favorite birthday gifts from my parents: a pair of red saddle shoes I had seen in a window of a shoe store in Nyack.

We hosted a White Russian Cavalry Cadet party–a biannual gathering of my father's cadet schoolmates from the military school in St. Petersburg, Russia. Every two years, the cadets gathered with their wives and children to celebrate. Just like in Czarist times when Czar Nicholas' children would dress up in military dress, my friend Tatiana Bogdanovich and I dressed up in White Russian cadet uniforms: white high colored shirts with epaulets and embroidery.

There was always a lot of delicious Russian food– tons of *zakuski*–pickles and caviar, meat and fish hors d'oeuvres to accompany the vodka. There was *borscht*, *pirogis* with meat and cabbage, *vinaigret* (beet salad), fish and tomato salad, *pelmeni* (Russian ravioli stuffed with meat or cheese), *kotleti* (Russian hamburgers), *golubtsi* (stuffed cabbage), fish and meat platters, and roasted potatoes, of course–oh so good and plentiful! And of course, there is no Russian party without Russian music. My parents sang Russian romances, harmonizing with each other. Sometimes I sang with them. George Seversky, a singer who became famous in Paris before emigrating to the United States in 1951, accompanied himself on the guitar as he sang Russian romances and gypsy songs. Vladimir Derwies, an opera singer, played the piano and sang his own compositions and opera arias in his wonderful tenor voice: Tchaikovsky's *Eugene Onegin* and *The Queen of Spades* stay vivid in my mind.

We had our own swimming hole at the lake, where I learned to swim. What a joy it was when, on hot days, a visitor or relative suggested a swim. The path there took us through the woods and along the lake with carpets of green ferns and delicate goldenrod on either side. Finally we got to a clearing where there was a kind of sandy beach and a natural entrance into the water. I threw my towel down and ran into the water. And what a special joy to spend time with Mama at the swimming hole. It only happened once or twice, but I remember her relaxing and enjoying herself as she swam in the lake. I didn't want to leave her side.

My mother still worked in the sewing machine sweatshops. My father would bring her to the train in Congers, New York, about five miles from our home. There she would board the train for New York City to work every day. It was a long commute and she was tired when she came home. But she seemed happier, more rested at the Rockland Lake house. She worked in the garden and enjoyed the many visitors who came. We were all so happy at our little Rockland Lake paradise.

The letter from the State of New York came unexpectedly. The state had bought the lake and all the property around it, and was making the entire area around the lake a state park adjoining the already existing Palisades Interstate Park. Like other landowners, our landlords did not put up a fight and sold the property quickly. We had to go. We lost our paradise–our little Russian *dacha*.

I didn't even finish fourth grade at my favorite school before we packed up our bags and ended up back in Nyack, in a cramped three-story walk up apartment right smack in the middle of town, next to the movie theatre on Broadway. I brought my cat Vaska with me because I couldn't bear to be without him, and I walked him on the sidewalk on a leash. He stopped eating and drinking. He wouldn't use the litterbox. He hated the sidewalk. He hated the noise. He hated Nyack. We had to bring him back to the forest. One day, my father and I put him in the car and we drove back to Rockland Lake. I opened the door of the car and I let him go. He ran into the woods, stopped, looked back once, and vanished. I was devastated.

Several years later, I went back to Rockland Lake to see what had become of our enchanted forest, lake, and cottage. I drove into the beautiful new manicured state park, with its huge asphalt parking lots, hoping against hope that our house had somehow remained. I drove up and parked in the newly paved road that had once been our driveway. I stood by a padlocked chain link fence where a sign read "Authorized Vehicles Only–No Parking." I looked through the chain links to where our house had once stood; where my parents and I were briefly so happy. The house was gone, demolished long ago. I let the memories rush in and tears streamed down my face. In that moment, I couldn't help thinking that if my family had been allowed to stay in Rockland Lake a bit longer, it would have given Mama and Papa a time to catch their breath to set their lives in motion for a better life in America.

Chapter Twelve

38 Gesner Avenue

MY PARENTS CLUNG TO OUR "little dacha" in Rockland Lake until the last moment, hoping that something would change and our house would be saved from demolition. Nothing changed. The state bought the property, and we had to find something fast. The cramped three story walk-up apartment on Broadway in Nyack near the movie theatre may have been all that was available at that time, and we stayed there only long enough to find something better. We all felt like my cat Vaska, who stopped eating and drinking until we took him back to his beloved forest, but we could not return as the cat did, to vanish in the shelter of the trees.

The return to Nyack was a shock and it happened too fast. Within three months, we rented an apartment on the second floor of a white Victorian house on 38 Gesner Avenue in South Nyack. On the exterior, the street and the house were nice. Gesner is still lined with elegant pastel-colored Victorian homes; the houses become ever larger and fancier as the avenue descends downhill to the shore of the Hudson River. At that point, the Hudson River is very wide, and still in touch with the Atlantic Ocean; the salty water flows north and south with the tides. At the end of the street is a stone wall, and beyond is a pebbled beach with a view of the newly built Tappan Zee Bridge crossing the river like a snake.

The Victorian house where we lived stood on the top of the hill and was owned by the Shakmatovi, a well-to-do Russian aristocratic family who also owned a home in Switzerland. They were a nice family. The father worked for the UN, the mother was home and they had two daughters approximately my age.

The Shakmatovi renovated the second floor of the house and created an income-producing living space. There was a kitchen at the top of the stairs, and a bathroom at the end of a small hallway. The two main rooms were separated from the kitchen and the bathroom by doors that made the apartment seem divided. This division cut the rooms off from the natural light source–the large windows facing the street–and allowed the shadow of my parents' gloom to infiltrate the two rooms where we actually lived. There was a dining room/studio where we ate and where my father painted his canvasses, and there was a large bedroom where we all slept. My father's single bed was in one corner separated by a large dark mahogany bureau, and in the opposite corner was a double bed where my mother and I slept together. Both the dining room area and the bedroom were in perpetual darkness and crowded with furniture. In the center of the bedroom sat a round table where I remember doing my homework.

Even though my mother and I slept together, I don't remember her ever reading to me or holding or caressing me. Instead our proximity made me increasingly aware that my mother was unhappy. All the moves and her work at the sweatshops were taking their toll.

I heard arguments between my parents. Mama complained that she was exhausted by her work at the sewing machine sweatshops. Papa's health was not improving with age. By the time my father was sixty-five years old and my mother was fifty-two, they felt the thirteen-year age difference between them, and I also felt the disparity in their age as opposed to my friends' younger parents. At age ten, I was teased by my peers in school who said my parents looked "like my grandparents."

Once, during one of my father's frequent stays at the hospital for surgery, my mother was home from work and hanging clothes outside on the laundry line. I went to her to complain that the Shakmatovi girls wouldn't let me borrow one of their bicycles; I was bored and wanted to spend the whole day with her. Her response was that I must be independent; that I must be different from others; that "different was good" and that realistically, spending the whole day with her would be a burden to both of us. Now, I reflect on my mother's answer and wonder if she was correct on both counts. Was she sanctioning my childhood friendship and sparing me her drudgery? Then, I drew no value from her answer, only hurt. In my mind, I offered her daughterly companionship and she rejected me. I was left lonesome and ill-fitting in the "nice" neighborhood and "lovely" house.

There were attempts at socializing with the Shakmatovi, but the family was busy with their work and traveling abroad to Switzerland. Although the daughters were close to my age, we had opposite dispositions: they were content to stay at home with their parents. I wanted to run free outside.

My early independence and my time alone in Rockland Lake had bred an independent spirit. I was already wild and wanted to roam. This desire propelled me onto the broken pavement of Gesner Avenue. I was frustrated–the Shakmatovi girls had bikes and I was forbidden to use them. At last, liberation! On my tenth birthday, I received the present of all presents: a brand-new blue bicycle with thin tires, sleek and fast. At last, I had my own steed and the race was on.

In fifth grade, I made friends with Julie Caceres, who, to my delight, was in the same class and lived across the street. Her house, a brown, unpainted wooden hovel amidst the decorative Victorians on the block, looked as if it could fall down at any moment.

Julie and I were very different. She was beautiful; I was skinny and wore glasses. Julie was very good at all the sports; I kept up. Julie was cool, steady; I was hotheaded, impulsive. She was a follower; I was a doer. There was a positive aspect to our disparities. Julie felt herself to be weak and perceived me as strong. I felt self-conscious and was viewed as confident. She loved my zest, my energy. I thrived in her companionship. I even enjoyed going to her shanty house–it felt more like home. Julie loved to come to my house to eat homemade Russian food and to warm up when it was cold in her house.

Julie's father, John Caceres, a short, stooped, rough Italian, reminded me of one of the gnarled dwarf trees that had died in their overgrown backyard. He worked for the local electric company. Every day after work, he went to a bar in Nyack and drank beer with whisky chasers. He came home drunk, sat in silence at the large table in the dining room and ate the food that Carolina, his wife, prepared for him. He watched the TV, which was always on, tuned to random stations. Carolina, Julie's mother, was an angel, and worked everyday from four p.m. to midnight as a waitress and kept the family together. She helped make ends meet for their four daughters: Marlene, Florence, Julie, and Janet, the youngest. All the sisters had dark complexions and were beautiful. Julie, a year older than me, was the most attractive, tall and graceful with the body of an athlete, a smooth olive complexion, high cheekbones, and almond-shaped brown eyes. The two older sisters didn't want anything to do with us and Janet was too young. Julie and I became inseparable.

The Caceres family did not want anyone to know how they lived inside that hovel of a house, and for a long time, I was not allowed to see their indoors, but met up with Julie only on the sidewalk or on their crooked front porch. When I finally did enter, I was astounded at what I saw.

John Caceres did nothing to maintain the house. The roof leaked, the ceiling boards were exposed where the plaster had fallen, and large pots stood ready on the kitchen floor to catch the rain. There was no hot water. The kitchen at the rear of the house was large, but with only a refrigerator and a hot plate in lieu of a stove. The pantry shelves appeared almost bare. The kitchen back door opened onto a sagging, splintered porch, looking out at a backyard overrun with weeds and bamboo plants. No one ever went out there. The steps were rotted and felt dangerously soft underfoot. Vines twined up the cracked banister.

Upstairs, there was a small bathroom with only a tub–no shower–and it amazed me that four girls could function without running hot water. Julie had to boil water on the hotplate for an hour before taking a bath and washing her hair. In the girls' bedroom, there were two bunk beds: one bunk bed for the older sisters, Marlene and Florence, and the other for Julie and Janet. At age eleven and eight, the two younger sisters still had bedwetting problems and the sheets didn't get changed. There was an ammonia sting of urine in the room. On several occasions, I slept with Julie in the lower bunk bed; the bedwetting episodes had eroded the springs and we were forced into the damp hollow in the center of the sagging mattress. We shivered together–the bedroom was ice-cold as the heat didn't reach the upstairs.

Far below, in the basement, there was the grunting heat source: a black coal stove which sat like an ugly troll. The stove spread heat but also spewed coal dust, which settled throughout the house, on every level and object. The girls took turns cleaning (or trying to clean) the house. John Caceres taught Julie how to shovel the coal into the furnace and how to tamp it down. Once, something went wrong with the stove and Julie and Janet, who happened to be home alone, almost died from the carbon monoxide fumes. They had headaches for days.

Yet I preferred to be in Julie's disordered house with the hustle-bustle of the pretty sisters and the constant chatter of the TV, than in my parents' dark (and TV-less) apartment. I became a fixture at the Caceres', a fifth wheel to turn.

On school mornings, I crossed the street and Carolina drove all of us to school. After school, Julie and I walked home together. This went on from fifth grade at Liberty Street Elementary School, through the Junior High, and into the Nyack High School years. In spite of Julie having to repeat fifth grade so we were no longer in the same grade, Julie and I remained close friends for seven years, until a sexual catastrophe occurred and changed our lives. The "snobby" Shakmatovi girls were left in the dust of our fast-flying chrome flashing English racer bikes.

In the sixth grade, my A+ plummeted to a C- and my education took a nasty turn. Mrs. Horn, my teacher (who later was fired for being an alcoholic), hated Russians and made my school days miserable. (These were the 50s Cold War years in the states and even Russian names were looked upon askance). She hated another Russian boy in my class, Vanya Habalov, who turned into a hopeless alcoholic in his later life. Mrs. Horn often made me and Vanya cry by picking on us. When I was chosen to substitute at a dance recital for the constantly absent or tardy Susan, one of the popular wealthy girls (she used to arrive in school in a limousine), it led to disaster. Susan decided to return to dance on the night of the show, but the director told me that I could dance.

After that incident, my new name, "Margie," was on the loudspeaker every day for a week when Mrs. Horn and the principal, Mr. Crane (with whom she was having an affair) attempted to force an apology from me. I would not apologize and Mrs. Horn proceeded to take me out of chorus and banned me from class trips. During class trips, I sat with second graders in my former second grade teacher's room. My parents' interceding on my behalf was out of the question. They did not speak English well enough. With my new identity as "Margie" and armed with my imaginative skills, I survived my school days by becoming the class clown from sixth grade through twelfth grade, until I graduated high school in 1965.

When we weren't in school, Julie and I were always outdoors. We rode the bikes together from morning to nightfall. We rode for miles to the stables on South Mountain Road in Nanuet, a neighboring village, where we became expert trail guides and generally assisted at the stables. We didn't get paid. We worked in the stables for the sheer love of it. Sometimes in the evening when the owners left, we saddled up our favorite horses, hiked up our stirrups, and keeping our heads low and our hands intertwined in the horses' manes, we raced the horses on a quarter mile track; the track blurred by the tears welling up in our eyes from the speed. Exhilarated at the end of the ride, we walked the horses, put them to rest, got on our bikes and pedaled five miles over the mountain to home.

We belonged to an ill-regarded neighborhood gang of kids who played Truth, Dare, Consequences, or Repeat and delighted in mischief. I still have a scar on my elbow from falling over a garden wire (I was nearsighted and refused to wear my glasses) in somebody's yard after being dared to throw gravel at a passing car. The furious driver stopped the car and chased me into the night. I got away, but I thought I had broken my arm. Back at Julie's house, the arm was bandaged up and eventually healed, with only the scar to recall the incident. My parents never had a clue.

We also made grown-up friends in the neighborhood. Mrs. Williams, a soft-spoken, elderly lady, lived in a stunning glass and bright stucco modern house at the bottom of Gesner Avenue, right on the river. She befriended us and gave us cookies, let us play with clay in her studio, and gave Julie and Janet lessons on the piano. Not having a piano in the Gesner apartment, I enjoyed sitting down and playing for Mrs. Williams. Unlike my father, she had no expectations and didn't stand over me with a ruler. We spent hours at her house. Mrs. Williams also had a canoe, which was off limits to kids. One evening, a few of us snuck the canoe off its moorings and, without any lights, paddled it on the Hudson about a mile, all the way down and under the Tappan Zee Bridge. Going down was easy.

Coming back up against the tide was another matter. We barely made it back up to return the canoe to its proper place. Mrs. Williams either never discovered our transgression or chose not to reprimand us.

Door Bell Night, the night before Halloween, was a major event during which we followed a prescribed routine: press door bells, knock, and flee. One night, we detected a trap set by one neighbor's door and sent Janet, Julie's younger sister to ring the bell. Sure enough, Janet got a pail full of water dumped on her head. She never forgave us for setting her up, but the laughs were all worth it. Halloween was a serious competition for best costume and who collected the most candy. We trick-or-treated as far as Upper Nyack (at least four miles from home) to Helen Hayes' house, a white mansion on the river. We had no idea who Helen Hayes was, or how famous an actress–she played the Dowager Empress in the Ingrid Bergman/Yul Brynner film version of *Anastasia*. We knew only that dollar bills were given out. I do remember a very well-spoken, graceful lady coming to the door and yes, handing out the little green precious bills. I couldn't be sure it was Helen Hayes, but we certainly told everyone that she was. Little did I know that, years later, I would be working at the Helen Hayes Theatre in Nyack as the wardrobe mistress for the touring production of *Oh! Calcutta!* Or that the actual Anastasia's history as the slain Romanov grand duchess would mean so much to me as a Russian émigré.

One Halloween we were caught by the Nyack police for being out after the ten o'clock curfew. The police scared us by putting us behind bars. This was very effective. After sitting in a cell, I had never been so thankful to see my father when he arrived to secure our release.

Nyack pleasures abounded in all seasons. In the winter, there was ice skating on the man-made ice ring at the Nyack Park on Piermont Avenue. Julie was a tremendous ice skater, graceful and fast, executing dazzling spins and backward turns on the ice. She tried to teach me to skate as gracefully as she did, but I could barely keep up with the others on my used boys' hockey skates, which lacked support at the ankles–skates my father had dug up in a thrift shop. The Whip, a game in which all the skaters held hands and whipped the last ones in line across the ice, terrified me. Too often I was on the tail end and skidded out of control. My feet numbed, felt lifeless, and I fell so often that the next day, I was covered with black-and-blue marks. There were other, more pleasurably exciting improvised sports. We would lug our wooden sleds to the steep sledding hill on Gesner Avenue. The sleds would go so fast that we would jump the wall and glide out onto the frozen Hudson River.

When I asked for roller skates, my father dug up a pair of what he said were "French roller skates." Everyone else wore the other kind of skates, metal platforms with clamps that locked in their shoes. They used keys to lock their shoes in fast. I had the French skates with the boots attached and two rubber wheels in the front and one in the back. They looked funny, made the other kids laugh, and I wouldn't use them. I began to suspect that being different was not for me. I wanted to belong.

In the summer, we children had passes to the Onteora Country Club on Route 303 in Nanuet, a full summer babysitting program to satisfy the parents' need to keep us busy. The Cacereses had belonged to the club for years. I begged my parents for membership, and I succeeded. Every morning we were dropped off at the club and picked up at closing. If we couldn't get a ride, we biked. We swam and dove and played in the man-made pool all day. Julie, as always the perfect athlete, was an excellent swimmer and diver, and as usual, I could barely keep up. With so much outdoor exercise, we were always starving, and I remember Carolina giving me a little extra money for the snack bar. Once a Frito truck stopped at the club to deliver Fritos and Julie and I wouldn't stop singing "Munch, munch, munch a bunch of Fritos, corn chips" to the driver. He got so tired of us that, to our delight, he threw us several bags of the yellow chips.

One sunny day, Julie and I returned from school and parted company on Gesner Avenue to drop off our schoolbooks in our respective homes. We planned to meet up later.

I walked up the stairs of our apartment and heard screaming. I ran into the kitchen and found my mother thrashing her hands in the sink. She had broken all the glasses and dishes in it. The sink ran pink with blood. She turned to me, her arms in the air, blood running down between her fingers, spilling onto the floor, and she was screaming "Куда моя жизнь пропала? Куда моя жизнь пропала?" ("Where did my life go? Where did my life go?")

I dropped my books on the stairs and ran back out into the street. In that moment, an unexplained fear gripped my heart. I was afraid to scream and I was too stunned to cry. I fled. I fled the violence, my bleeding mother, the darkness in our apartment, and ran to Julie's dilapidated house, hoping to catch a cartoon on TV.

Chapter Thirteen

47 Washington Avenue

IF WE WISHED TO ESCAPE from clutter, we were not successful when we moved around the corner from Gesner Avenue to 47 Washington Avenue. My mother's nesting instincts and her inability to throw anything out were out of control, and our new small one-bedroom apartment rental resembled an overstocked, neglected antique store.

While on the outside the new house looked enormous–a towering white Victorian with green shutters–inside it was broken up into four separate apartments. Our apartment was at the top of the stairs on the second floor. Immediately, my mother set about breaking even that space into smaller sections by means of large furniture dividers.

When we opened the front door, the Art Deco bureau that divided the living room from the dining room (the same bureau divided my father's bed from our bed on Gesner Avenue) stood to our left. The bureau created a narrow makeshift entrance with the coat closet and mirror on the opposite side. This entrance led to the dining table in the center of the apartment where we ate all our meals. The table pressed up against the wall and had space for only three chairs around it. Next to the table sat another smaller table set on a diagonal, a place for teapots with cozies, coffeepots and food pots during meals. On the dining table, which was always covered by a tablecloth, were antique salt and pepper shakers, the sugar bowl, and an antique toaster that opened up on both sides. During mealtimes, plates and silverware competed for space.

The living room was behind the large mahogany Art Deco bureau. There were small tables in every nook on which rested dozens of small, framed photographs of dead ancestors, family, and friends. Large armchairs, dining room chairs, bookcases and desks stood against the walls or were aimed at us on diagonals. A large couch doubled as my mother's bed and also as a seat for the fourth bridge player when my parents played bridge, which was often. There were many pillows on the couch and when my parents went out, the pillows were used as warmers for the potatoes that were boiled earlier.

The walls were covered with large framed photographs and beautiful paintings by friends and family. Each painting and photograph had a story. The Russian Orthodox Icons were hung in the corner of the room facing the entrance with candles and pussy willow branches sticking out from behind the icons. As palm trees are mostly nonexistent in Russia, pussy willows are given to Russian Orthodox churchgoers on Palm Sunday. Underneath the icons, our piano stood, loaded with framed photographs stacked behind piles of sheet music. *Chachkas* were everywhere. There was no television. Underneath the bookcases, tables and armchairs were stacks of books and paperwork and *chachkas* and photographs that didn't quite make it to the tabletops.

Every space was forced into multiple functions: the kitchen was not just a kitchen. Hidden behind the dining area on the right, it served as a studio, and a bedroom for my father. The Russian Orthodox icon of Jesus Christ with the red candle votive was in the corner and the walls were covered with photographs. On the left were the stove, the sink, and the refrigerator in a row. On the right was my father's bed, and snuggled in amongst the many cushions was his little stuffed bear with little beady crooked eyes, a pudgy nose, and a huge red ribbon around its neck. Didn't every father have a teddy bear on his bed?

Next to his bed was the nightstand with bottles of pills and more photographs. Behind the bed was my father's workspace, a small studio area that included two tables. The larger table was his worktable with canvas hanging from the wall to dry, or on the table if he was painting. The second table was where the oil paints and brushes and all the painting paraphernalia were kept. The kitchen smelled of oil paint and turpentine. The air was close and musty- the windows were kept closed to keep in heat in winter, and the rooms always smelled of sickness and medicine. Mixed into this stale air was the indefinable odor of home.

There was a single improvement to the new arrangements: At last, I had my own bed and could leave my mother's. We had separate beds in the one small bedroom on the left side of the eating area. The room was eventually given to me, and my mother moved to the couch in the living room; the extra bed was left for guests. Each bed had a small side table and there were two large bureaus lining the remaining wall space. The bureaus were filled with fabrics, ribbons, bows, doll parts, Christmas wrap, doilies–anything that my mother could use to create her assorted projects: little miniature stuffed animals, dolls, more *chachkas,* or homemade clothes. My bedroom also served as my mother's storage space, her fantasy world made up of odd bits of the past and present. The one closet in the room was stuffed with my mother's clothes, while my clothes were hung on a makeshift pole suspended between walls in the corner.

Walking space was limited in the apartment. This was especially true during the weekly bridge game nights, a large part of my parents' social life. My mother, my father, and two other players sat around the card table in the middle of the living room, in a haze of cigarette smoke, surrounded by wine and vodka bottles, and various *zakuski* (a Russian word for snacks to eat while drinking). The bridge games were serious, but between the games, there was much laughter, discussions of the game, arguments about the cards played, drinking, eating. For my parents, the bridge games were a temporary escape from their daily drudgery. For me, it was a time when I could escape too. I could come and go unnoticed.

Chapter Fourteen

Pushing The Walls Out

THE FACT THAT OUR APARTMENT was cluttered with stuff and my parents didn't speak English very well, was a source of embarrassment for me. I brought no one home except for Julie. As a teenager, I just wanted to belong. My displaced parents were even displaced in Nyack. My father was sick and my mother's mental health fragile. Except for the last year, we moved so often, I couldn't put down neighborhood roots. I didn't know what to do with my father's never-ending pain and suffering. My mother's increased exhaustion from working in the sewing factory and her endless responsibility to cook and take care of my father was depressing her. She was drinking more alcohol and the apartment was filling up with my mother's crumpled up poems, vodka bottles-empty and full, drugs and guilt. I had long given up the idea that my parents were there to help me. They had few resources to help themselves. The guilt I felt for not wanting to stay home to take care of my parents forced me away from the apartment, into the street. I repeated my mantra: "I'm on my own, I must take care of myself; I'm on my own, I must take care of myself; I must take care of myself."

In the late 50s, at age ten, I became obsessed with the popular musical *West Side Story*, a huge Broadway show that hit the New York scene in 1957. I learned all the music from the LP record I borrowed from a friend. I sang the songs, acted out the speeches, and choreographed the dances, all in the confines of my bedroom: jumping from bed to bed, from chair to chair, making faces in the mirror, using my makeshift closet as a dressing room, creating my own theatrical and musical fantasy. My older brother, who became an ordained Lutheran minister in the right-wing Missouri Synod, told me as he glanced into my room one day, that I was blasphemous when I sang "Maria, I just met a girl named Maria. . . ," a holy name. My parents were always yelling for me to keep the noise down, but I continued belting out the songs in my tiny room. During one of my renditions of the Jets and the Sharks, I began to understand that theatre and music were my ticket away from the foreign clutter and depression. I knew then that I had to sing and dance and perform. I had to.

For ten years, I was forced to play the piano and listen to my father scream at me until I quit at age sixteen. Papa wanted me to become a classical pianist and always insisted, "Aristocrats don't dance, they play the piano." Like the forbidden chewing gum, this was another aristocratic tradition for which I couldn't care less. The rift between my parents and I grew wider.

Svetlana Umrichin, "my second mother," as I called her, worked at the St. Sergius Russian school in New York City, teaching Russian; she commuted to New York from Nyack. Mika, her daughter, a year younger than I, was taking ballet lessons from Larissa, the Russian ballet diva from Moscow. I wanted to dance, to take classical ballet lessons like my friend Mika. I begged my parents to let me take lessons from Larissa, but my father would not let go of the piano dream.

In 1961, when I was thirteen and he was twenty-three, Rudolf Nureyev, a peasant from Siberia who had leapt to fame in Russia, defected at Le Bourget Airport in Paris while on a European tour with the Kirov Ballet. The Soviet world was scandalized. The free world was thrilled, especially the many Russian émigrés in Nyack with their Anti-communist sentiments. I knew about Nureyev because Mika had a huge poster of him tacked to her wall. With his high cheekbones, full lips, and arching muscled thighs, Rudolph Nureyev was the most handsome, desirable man I had ever seen; I fell in love. I was entering puberty and my fantasies about Nureyev spun out of control. Yes, he had chosen to become an immigrant–he too was "displaced," but not in a camp–he flew onto the most famous stages in the Western World. I imagined dancing a *pas de deux* with Nureyev, our warm bodies gleaming with the perspiration of our impassioned exertions, bodies entwined, pausing for an instant to look deep into each others' eyes as we finished each movement...

When Mika's parents learned that Nureyev would be performing at the Metropolitan Opera House in New York City, they immediately bought tickets for themselves and Mika. I begged my parents, "Let me go see Nureyev with Mika's family." I tied myself to the piano and promised years of practice and concert recitals to let me go, and by some God-given miracle, my father acquiesced. Of course others were paying for my ticket and, as usual, I was the tag-along.

I didn't care. I would go see Nureyev in any guise. The date arrived. I don't remember the car ride from Nyack to New York City. I was floating on air. I was going to see Nureyev dance in *The Nutcracker* by Tchaikovsky.

We arrived. We took our seats and along with the thousand people in the audience that night, we were mesmerized by Nureyev's stage presence: his leaps, his cat-like dance movements, his sensual *pas de deux* surpassed even my highest-flying expectations. I had never seen anything like him, his grace, his leaps, his effortless landings. He was beyond human. I was struck by the electric response of the audience–so much love and attention going out to one human being on stage. The stage: a place to be to receive unconditional love. Love. This meant anything was possible.

Nureyev. It was the curtain call and the audience was on its feet. Mika grabbed my arm, and without a word to anyone, we ran for the stage. We hurled ourselves toward the downstage front, right at his feet. We were looking up at him; he appeared larger than life, as he took one curtain call after another. We saw his sculpted face up close, the Tatar cheekbones, his cat's eyes. We screamed at the top of our lungs, "Bravo!"

At last, after hundreds of bouquets of flowers were thrown onto the stage, Nureyev disappeared for the last time, and we ducked behind some curtains on the right of the stage. Unspoken, unpremeditated, we somehow followed a daring plan. Clasping our hands together so as not to lose one another, we battled the crowd to get a closer glimpse of our hero, our idol, Nureyev. We were caught up in the moment and there was no stopping us. We spoke only Russian as we realized that somehow we had managed to infiltrate the bowels of the Met. Backstage, we were in the midst of a *Nutcracker* fantasyland: snowflake ballerinas in white tutus, multicolored soldiers, sugar plum fairies, harlequins, owls, mice, gnomes, Russian, Chinese, Arab, and Spanish dancers ran to and fro, screaming orders.

We pretended that we belonged. To our shock, a dancer in harlequin tights led us to Nureyev's dressing room. But after all, we were innocents. We too were Russian. We too were immigrants—we were family. Nureyev opened the door to his dressing room. Mika held my hand as Nureyev greeted us in Russian.

He gave us each a glass of champagne and bid us to sit and wait for him, which we did. We both lost our minds and all sense of time and space. Her parents did not know where we were, but we didn't care. We were waiting for Nureyev to change into his street clothes. We were ready to go home with him. We didn't care what country.

After what seemed to be an eternity–we had not touched the champagne for fear of being beaten to death–Nureyev emerged, as beautiful as ever, from behind his dressing room drapery. We exchanged some breathless words in Russian. "Какие вы прекрасные девочки!" ("What magnificent girls you are!") He seemed thrilled that he was meeting children who spoke his language. He asked us to accompany him to his limousine. He opened the back door of the Met and the three of us were greeted by hundreds of people waiting for him to get into his limousine. Mika and I were the lucky ones. I had him by the right arm and Mika had him by the left arm. He kissed us both on the cheek. We saw him into the limousine and bade him farewell.

The car drove off. Nureyev departed to his new life and Mika and I returned to our previous existence, but forever altered. The *Nutcracker* fantasy tale was over, as translucent as snow falling behind a scrim on stage, and never to be forgotten.

The next week, I instituted a drastic change. By now, my Russian braid hung below my waist and pulled my hair back so severely that I got headaches, and my mother's combing sessions after shampooing my hair left me in tears from her painful yanking. I had had enough. Walking home from school, Julie and I passed a hair salon. We walked in and I asked the hairdresser, "Please can you cut off my braid?" At first she said no, but after several more entreaties, she reluctantly scissored off the braid. My hair sprung out in all directions, a metaphor of what was to come.

Attending the Russian Orthodox Church at the Tolstoy Farm every Sunday and singing in the choir became tedious. Listening to the priest remind me what a sinner I was made me want to sin more, and the dogma filled with me with guilt and damnation. Instead of going to church, I visited my Aunt Sandra's cherry tomato garden, picked vegetables from Alexandra Lvovna Tolstoy's garden, and got caught jumping in the haystack in the barn with a boy from the farm.

I was a skinny kid, with skinny legs–in high school they called me Olive Oyl, from the Popeye cartoon. My hair was a mess because I wouldn't curl it with pink hair rollers every night, and my clothes were obviously from a thrift store or homemade. A good school day was when I could borrow a piece of clothing from Julie, who in spite of her poverty was always dressed impeccably. I started smoking my mother's Raleigh cigarettes, blowing smoke out of the bathroom window. It wasn't long before I was buying my own packs. Despite my desire to blend in, as a typical American kid, a very Russian addiction took hold.

There was never enough money. My mother barely earned enough at the factory sweatshops, and my father could only paint the canvasses when he was well enough, which was becoming less frequent. At fifteen, I started cleaning the Upper Nyack mansions with my mother on weekends. I hated it.

My mind was on boys, and the Russian high school where Svetlana Umrichen taught and gained us entrée was full of them. Now as teenagers, Mika and I were out-of-control boy crazy. A lively written communication sprang up between Svetlana's male students at St. Sergius and us girls in the Nyack Russian community. This communication was enhanced with parties in New York City and in Nyack, chaperoned by parents and teachers. I was in love with a guy named Sergei (Serge), Mika was in love with Yaroslav (Roman), and several boys were running after Julie, whom I had brought along with the group to join the fun. This evolved into an innocent and joyful time, during which we received letters, wrote love letters, and existed in a bubble of teenage infatuation. It was a time of close body contact "slow dancing " to R&B music and hot and heavy make-out sessions on the couch: grinding and groping and pelvis-to-pelvis movement without a final release. (I had gotten lessons on how to French kiss from my good buddy, Cousin Andrei). I didn't feel a need to tell my parents how much fun I was having. By this time our communication had slowed down to a drip.

The St. Sergius adventure came to an abrupt end when my father found out that I was meeting boys at the Umrichens. A searing scandal ensued. My father refused to speak to Svetlana and all ties with the Umrichens were broken. My mother lost her good friend Svetlana, and was left even more isolated. I was forbidden to go to Mika's house ever again, and it was fifteen years before I saw Svetlana again. Years later when we were reunited, Svetlana confessed to me that she wanted to adopt me and take me away from my parents but that would have been too scandalous for Nyack.

My parents and I were trapped together in the cramped apartment with our anger, frustration, and confusion, and I was desperate to find a way to push the walls out and escape.

A chance for independence arrived in the form of my junior driver's license, which I obtained on my sixteenth birthday, having passed the drivers test very easily. A new challenge arose: how to get my father to let me have the car.

Chapter Fifteen

Driving With The Baron

MY FATHER, THE BARON, NEVER drove an automobile until he came to America at age fifty-five in December of 1949. Soon after our family settled into the renovated elephant stalls at the Clarkstown Country Club in Nyack, the necessity of driving and owning a car in the American suburbs became apparent to him. Depending on our Displaced Person relatives for rides was unthinkable. With Aunt Alina's help, Papa learned how to drive on her 1943 black Packard, tooling around the property's dirt roads and maneuvering the stick shift transmission.

Eventually, my father got a New York State driver's license. I don't know how he managed this with his heavy Russian accent and lack of fluency in English, but they did grant him the license. He could not read much else in English in those days, but he could read the big colorful STOP and YIELD signs. For Papa, driving an automobile was the first step towards independence and self-reliance in this new country. Not only was driving a necessity, but the sense of being in command fed into my father's memories of his dashing former life as a Russian Baron and an officer in the White Russian army in Estonia, when he rode fine steeds in steeplechase races, trained horses to jump, and English setters to hunt; a life which had vanished from his reality. The car seat was his saddle, and the automobile would now take the place of his steed and carry him forward to fresh adventures in a new world.

For Mama, who tried unsuccessfully to learn to drive from my father–big mistake–and whose life was filled with laborious duties which she hated, driving was the one thing that she didn't have to do, and it was the one thing that my father could do for her. In America, she would be driven or she would not go.

For me, the car was an escape.

Our first car was a used 1939 yellow Chevrolet and my father called it "Kanareyka," Russian for canary. I was still very young during Kanareyka's time, but I do remember that at Christmastime, Papa, a small, thin man, would get dressed up in his grey Fedora hat, his huge immigrant long coat and outsized trousers and drive to the car maintenance garage to give the mechanic a bottle of wine. Anyone from the clan of relatives who knew anything about cars was revered by Papa and considered "on call" if he needed something fixed right away. It was not a good day for anybody if there was something wrong with my father's automobile.

Our next car was a used 1952 green and white two-tone Chevy (my father swore by Chevrolet). Papa taught me to cry on cue in case he was stopped by the police, which happened often. I was six years old when Papa and I were tooling along a highway at a clip and he noticed that a policeman wanted to pull us over to the side of the road. He turned to me in the passenger seat and told me that when the policeman came to talk to him, I should start crying right away, which I did. The policeman leaned his head down to get a closer look at me and Papa said in a heavy accent, "My daughter is sick and must be to home." The policeman looked around, made sure we had nothing suspicious in the back seat, and let us go. I had saved Papa a lot of trouble and money and he was relieved and amused. It was my first lesson in Konstantin Stanislavsky's approach to method acting, strategies that I perfected and applied often in my life.

Going to New York City with Papa to deliver his canvasses was a special treat for me. He took me with him because he needed a decoy in case he ran into any problems. For starters, we went to the city during the business day, which meant I missed school. Going to the big city, to Madison Avenue with all the shops and inviting restaurants and the crowds and the noise was the icing on the cake.

Papa parked the car and headed to Rosetta Larson Needlepoint Design on 68th and Madison Avenue. There, my father showed his canvasses to Rosetta

Larson, the proprietress, and they discussed the paintings: the colors, the designs, and the amount of money that she would pay him. Later, her staff ladies in the main store needlepointed the designs into rugs and chair seats and sold them for a great deal more money in Madison Avenue retail stores. During these discussions, I was allowed to go outside and walk only on that block and not cross any streets. I took my time and I took in everything, pressing my fingers and face against the windowpanes to get a closer look at the wares. There were so many exquisite things in the shops. There were antique stores with bright and colorful jewelry, magazines, lamps, and furniture. There were the restaurants with their goodies in the windows; the delis with the meats and the cheeses. Everything was colorful, exciting, and plentiful, a stark contrast to what was at home. After the needlepoint negotiations, my father collected me and usually bought me something to eat, another big treat. I always got the same thing: a lettuce and tomato sandwich on white toast with potato chips.

On one of our special trips to New York City, as we approached the toll booth to the George Washington Bridge, my father noticed that there was no actual person in the toll booth to take his money. I believe the toll was twenty-five cents at that time. Instead there was a dish-like receptacle into which one had to throw in a quarter.

In Russian, he said, "Что это такое? Где человек? Да чёрт с ними!" ("What is this? No person? The hell with them!")

And he drove through. In an instant all hell broke loose. Bells and sirens went off. I looked back and the toll takers from the manned booths were running after us. My father stopped the car. I slid down under the dashboard because I was petrified that we would be taken to jail.

My father yelled to me, "Начинай реветь!" ("Start crying!")

And I did. A policeman came to the car window. He asked my father why he didn't throw in the quarter and my father answered in his best English, "I don't see vere."

The policeman looked under the dashboard at me crying, asked for the twenty-five cents, and let us go. Nothing more was said about the tollbooth experience, and my father became very adept at throwing the coin into the dish, but he did it with anger. For him, it was like throwing money away–money that he didn't have.

The last car Papa owned was a used 1963 grey, nondescript Chevy. It was ugly, but I didn't care. I learned how to drive simply by watching my father through the years. Driving came naturally to me. Long before it was legal for me to drive, the family went to Toronto, Canada to visit relatives, and during our visit, my father got sick. I only remember that Papa was in pain and couldn't move his leg to push down on the clutch. It was decided that I would drive home from the Canadian/U.S. border. Pillows were stuffed under my seat to make me look taller and older, and I drove all the way to Nyack without incident, Papa supervising all the way. I was fourteen years old.

Days after my sixteenth birthday, I got my junior permit, which meant I could only drive during the day. It didn't matter. I had a license, which allowed me some freedom and a great deal of independence. Almost. What stood between me and my freedom was the begging. Papa enjoyed this last vestige of control he had over me. He knew how much the use of the vehicle meant to me.

" Категорически Нет!" ("Categorically No") – his favorite phrase.

Begging to use the car became a game that I learned to play, and often it was based upon fictitious ploys–elaborate stories with false destinations, companions, and events. The events were not as important to me as my need to escape our gloomy apartment, which rested in an inversion of guilt and despair. Often I had no destination at all. I just drove. Sometimes I got in the car, closed all the windows, eased out of the driveway, and then screamed at the top of my lungs. Only away from "them," my father and mother and that place, the stuffy apartment, could I breathe again.

One tactic that consistently worked with my father was to instruct my best friend Julie to ask for the car–in perfect Russian.

"Можно нам пожалуиста машину сегодня вечером?" ("May we please have the car this evening?")

We practiced for days until she got it right. (Even now, fifty years later, she can still say this phrase perfectly). Papa found this so amusing that he softened and handed over the car keys.

Of course, there were the never-ending chores that I promised to do in exchange for the car: play the piano, translate for him at the doctor's office, translate all his official correspondence to doctors, insurance companies, landlords, the motor vehicle department, even to Oral Roberts, the spiritual healer from Tulsa, Oklahoma, who, Papa was convinced, would heal him. And I would take sacred oaths regarding the cleaning: clean my room, clean the apartment, wash the dishes, clean the car, dust, mop. . . It was endless.

As soon as I had my license, I didn't like driving with my father. In my opinion, he was a terrible driver. My father avoided using the brakes because he thought he would wear them out. He didn't like to engage the clutch because it would exhaust the gears.

The last time I drove with Papa was en route to my brother's house in New Jersey for American Christmas. (Because my mother and my two brothers were Lutheran, we celebrated both Russian and American Christmas.) My mother, as usual, sat in the back seat satisfied by being driven. Meanwhile, I saw that my father was driving too slowly in the passing lane of the Garden State Parkway, and I suggested that he move into the right lane. He ignored me, and when I told him he was a terrible driver, he slapped my face. In a rage and at full speed, I opened the passenger door to jump out onto the pavement. My mother screamed. My father grabbed my jacket and prevented me from falling out of the car. The car swerved, but luckily there were no cars near us. He stopped the car on the side of the road. I begged him please to let me drive, but he refused. The dark cloud had settled once again upon us all. I was blamed for the dissension and told that I was good for nothing. I closed my eyes to hold back the angry tears, and as we continued to my brother's house for the festivities, I vowed that I would never drive with my father again.

Papa was still driving until he was well into his eighties. One day my parents were driving into town, went through a red light, and plowed into a semi-trailer truck. The car was totaled, but miraculously, my parents survived, unharmed. The Baron's steed was dead. His independence was clipped forever, and he never drove again. It would be difficult for my father to rely on relatives and friends for transportation, but this was the reality now. There was no money to buy a used vehicle and my mother was secretly relieved that her husband would no longer be driving. There had been too many previous close calls.

Chapter Sixteen

Drugs

IN 1965, MY BROTHER GEORGE worked in New York City for a company called Barber Greene and settled down in Paramus, New Jersey with his new family; he had a wife and three children. My older brother Kurt, the Lutheran minister, was sent by the Missouri Synod to Toowoomba, Australia to start his own parish. Could he have gone any further than that? Did George have time to deal with Mama's depression? Mama's hopes of her sons "saving" her dwindled, and her moods worsened. One early evening, I became terrified when I saw Mama hysterical on the floor, flailing her arms and screaming at the top of her lungs,

"Я не могу больше, я не могу!" "I can't any more, I can't!"

I stood by helpless while my father bent over her and held her shoulders and tried to calm her down. She writhed on the floor for a few more minutes, then got up and ran to the door, opened it, and screamed, " Я бегу топиться в Гудзон." ("I'm running to the Hudson River to drown myself.")

My father ran after her. I waited in the apartment, in the dark. I was too frightened to follow. After what seemed to be an eternity, my father returned. I cried out, " Где Мама?" ("Where's Mama?")

" Она идёт." ("She's coming.")

A few minutes later, Mama came inside, exhausted and pale, sat down on the couch, and asked for a vodka.

Sometimes I would call my brother George to tell him what was going on, but he was busy with his own family responsibilities and couldn't help. We rarely saw him.

Papa's mysterious ailments were worsening with time and his myriad doctors were puzzled. My father was so desperate that he made me write letters and send the little money that we had to Oral Roberts, a charismatic Methodist-Pentecostal televangelist faith healer. "Maybe. . .a cure," my father would say in Russian.

Dr. Altschuler, a Russian doctor in New York City, knew exactly what to do. He prescribed Dexamyl, "Elixir" as we called it, to my father. Dexamyl was an "upper," an anti-depressant, anti-anxiety, amphetamine-based narcotic that was highly addictive. On the street, the blue little triangles were called "purple hearts," or "Christmas Trees" if they were white with little green beads in them. *Quadrophenia*, a film made by the popular band The Who, has a scene with the main character taking "purple hearts." Jerry Lee Lewis was known to be addicted to Dexamyl, and the 1966 Kinks song "Big Black Smoke" makes reference to the drug with the lyric, "And every penny she had was spent on purple hearts and cigarettes." The drug was banned in 1973.

Dr. Altschuler, the hero of the moment, was going to ensure that Papa would be out of pain, but he did not foresee the consequences. My father's Dexamyl was in a liquid form and he would take a couple of teaspoons as needed. He was able to control his doses. One day, he gave Mama a couple of teaspoons, thinking it would elevate her mood. For her, it was an immediate and dangerous addiction.

The runs to the pharmacies began. I would drive from one drug store to another to try to get the Dexamyl prescription filled. Some pharmacies wouldn't accept the prescription. Often, the "Elixir" would run out before the prescription did, and I would come home empty-handed, only to be sent to another drug store.

I'm not sure when or where Mama went to "dry out" from the drug addiction because my parents kept this information from me. It was a big secret. I think it was a source of embarrassment for them. I do remember a period of time when Mama was not home, and I remember Papa going to the wealthy Russian aristocracy in New York, friends of the family, to ask for money to help defray the cost. Mama had to go to an institution to "dry out" twice. She came home the first time only to start the "Elixir" again because it was still in the house.

I felt better in the streets.

Chapter Seventeen

Outsiders

I DIDN'T BELONG. I WAS not American. I wore strange homemade, thrift-shop clothes and spoke with an accent. The white boys and their blonde good-looking, well-dressed white girlfriends who listened to WABC AM radio and blasted bubblegum music and went to all the dances and proms were the popular "in" crowd in high school. I was an outsider, and as an outsider, I sought out other outsiders to fill my needs.

It was 1963 and the U.S. was in the throes of the Civil Rights movement and the escalation of the Vietnam War. JFK's shooting in November, which Julie and I witnessed on her TV, race riots in major cities, the march on Washington, and Martin Luther King's "I Have A Dream" speech—all were obvious signs of unrest between the whites and the blacks. In Nyack, many streets like Franklin and Depew Avenue were considered "black" and were off limits to the white population. Our Nyack high school was called "grey" because one-third of the student population was black, the result of a large influx of Haitian families at that time. Rather than staying clear of the potential race problems, I was not going to stand by and watch the racial injustices. I was still reeling from the drugs and the injustices at home and the drama created by my father with Svetlana. Thus inflamed, I plunged headfirst into the black world.

This decision was profoundly influenced by Mitchell Gates, "Mitch" as he was called, a young black man who was still a senior in high school although he should have graduated several years before... Mitch was cool. He was handsome, popular among the white in-crowd and the blacks, wiry, strong, played basketball like a God, and I was in love. In my life, at sixteen, a junior in high school, what counted was that a young man was paying attention to me. The color of his skin was of no consequence. Mitch was accepting, even admiring, of my Russian face with high cheekbones and my grey-green eyes, skinny legs, and homemade clothes. My chestnut hair was short and curly; I made a conscious effort to curl it in the pink curlers every night. In gratitude for his admiration, I was ready to hand him my life. And I did.

His mother's basement apartment across the street from Liberty Street Elementary School, where I spent six of my elementary school years, was small and cluttered and smelled of fried chicken. No one was at home when Mitch brought me here after school one day. He laid me down on the small couch and, masking his intention with kisses on my face and sweet love words, lifted up my homemade skirt, pulled down my tattered underwear and took my virginity. He made his conquest and it was all over before I knew it. He kissed me on the mouth, told me he loved me, got up, and zipped his pants.

I put on my coat, opened the front door, and slowly walked the mile home. What did I just do? Was this all there was? Why this emptiness? There must be something more… something? Mitch does love me. He must… He must!

My secret brought me to the steps of my apartment. No one at home. Good. I didn't have to lie to anyone. I walked into my bedroom, sat down and wrote a letter to my new friend "Frenchie," Lidia Shikhova.

Prince Grigori Shikhov, a prominent Russian aristocrat, arrived in Nyack in 1964 with his wife Ksenia and two children, twins my age, Vasili and Lidia. The family had emigrated from exotic Morocco, where they lived in a refugee camp. The Shikhovs had escaped World War II through France, eventually winding up in northern Africa. Uncle Grisha, as I called the Prince, was best friends with my cousin Father Serafim, the Russian Orthodox priest in the Nyack Russian church. They had met in a German prison camp, along with two other Russians, and managed to stay together until their escape in the chaos of the war. All four friends eventually arrived in the States.

I became very good friends with Lidia and her twin brother Vasya, as he was called. They couldn't have been more different from each other. Vasya was levelheaded, relaxed; Lidia was wild. She was sexy, smoked cigarettes, loved boys and spoke French. I loved her for her freedom and her gutsiness. She was afraid of nothing. Julie hated Lidia for taking me away from her and because Lidia and I did crazy things together. I often stayed at Lidia's house and we went out into the streets late at night, smoked cigarettes, and drank vodka with dubious characters–vodka we stole from her alcoholic parents, the Prince and the Princess Shikhov. Lidia and I had a lot in common. We were both running away from serious problems at home; fleeing from unhappiness. We were outsiders.

The Russian conservative and religiously moral community was alarmed by Lidia. She was perceived as a "bad girl" who would turn too many innocent heads; she had a terrible reputation and I wasn't too far behind. It wasn't long before her family was on the move again, this time to Minneapolis, Minnesota. I was told that Uncle Grisha got a job in Minneapolis, but I knew the move was instigated by the Russian community protecting itself from Lidia's "sinful" behavior. I lost Vasya with his good humor and his ability to make light of difficult situations, and I lost Lidia, my free-spirited, wild friend who taught me how to live on the edge. When Lidia left, I felt devastated and alone.

Dear Lidia,

How are you? What are you doing? There is no one to hang out with; no one to talk to. . . You remember Mitch, the guy who I really liked? Well, guess what. We did it. We went "all the way" today after school. He took me to his mother's apartment and we did it on the couch! I'm no longer a virgin! I really love Mitch and he told me that he loves me. I believe him. We're happy together. Please write soon. I miss you so much. Hi to Vasya. Love,

Mourka

I put this letter inside a book, which was stacked under other books on my bureau. The plan was to take the letter to school and mail it on the way home. In the morning rush, I forgot to take the letter.

That afternoon I came home from school and walked through the makeshift entrance of our Washington Avenue apartment. Mama was standing there in front of the ironing board, the hot iron upright, steaming; a pair of scissors on the board on top of some ironed fabric. She looked up at me with an odd expression and said in Russian, "Что это?" ("What's this?"), holding up my letter to Lidia.

"Что?" I said, my face turning hot.

"This letter you wrote to Lidia. Is it true?"

"Yes," I said, "It's true. How did you find the letter? Why did you look into my books?"

Her answer was a swift throw of the scissors aimed at my chest. I felt the blow close to my heart; my clothes shielding me from the blade penetrating my skin.

"*Prostitutka, Prostitutka,*"she screamed.

"С ума сошла?" ("Have you gone crazy?") I yelled back in Russian. "You are crazy," I screamed again as I turned and ran down the stairs, out the front door and into the street. In tears, I walked the mile to Mitch's house, where I knew at least for the moment I would be comforted from the shock of my mother's discovery and her response.

Later, when I came home, it was quiet. There were no apologies; there were never any apologies. My mother never told my father about the loss of my virginity–she protected him from the "bad girl" I had become; an image of myself which I carried with me for a long time.

Dr. Krutz, a German Jew and our family doctor, resembled a frog and spoke with a nasal whine. With my mother sitting in his examining room, judging and waiting, he gave me an internal examination. After the procedure, Krutz assured my mother that I was all right and that I was not pregnant. I was relieved, but the humiliation I felt that day was never forgotten.

The humiliation didn't end there. I was told by my mother that I had to confess my sin to Father Serafim, my cousin, the priest at the Nyack Russian church. I did as I was told.

"Yes, Holy Father, I have sinned."

"And what was your sin?" the priest asked.

"I had sexual relations with a boy," I said.

"Really? Marry Mitch?"

I nearly choked. I could just see it. Me in a white lace mini and Mitch, in his gas station blue jumpsuit, his cigarette dangling on his lower lip, hip-hopping into the Russian Orthodox church. The bells tolling in rhythm of our dance. . .

It was after that confession that I stopped going to church altogether.

Every day on our walk home from school, Julie and I passed the Mobil gas station on the corner of Broadway and Cedar Hill Avenue in South Nyack. The station was a hang out for handsome, well-built black guys with their fast, hot drag racing cars. The black boys would be there everyday polishing and tinkering with their cars, making passes at the white girls. After school, Mitch worked here pumping gas, and it was a place to meet. Lidia was gone and Julie and I resumed our friendship. It wasn't long before I introduced her to the black crowd and she got sucked in. As beautiful as she was, her shyness did not attract any of the in-crowd in school. The Russian boys from New York City had been attentive, but that chapter was slammed shut for both of us when my father put an end to that adventure. Why not try the black boys?

One day Julie and I were in the gas station, passing time with the guys after school when suddenly Mitch announced, "Oh shit! Here comes the Baron." Julie and I hid behind the cars, peeking from behind, as my father drove up to the pumps. Mitch went out to pump gas for him. My father rolled down the window and in his thick Russian accent said to Mitch, "Check zee tires, check zee oil, check engine, clean front vindow, clean back vindow, von dollar gas, plees."

Tall, handsome Royce with his 1964 lizard-green Pontiac GTO pursued Julie for a while before she acquiesced to be his girl. Soon, Julie, Royce, Mitch, and I were the happy foursome tooling around in Ronny's hot car. We went to basketball games and watched Mitch play. I was so proud to be his girl. We went to parties. We danced to soulful Motown records: the Temptations, Martha and the Vandellas, Marvin Gaye, Sam Cooke, to name just a few. None of this "bubblegum" music for us! I loved to dance. And I danced sexy to rhythm and blues. I remember being escorted out of a school dance because I was dancing too provocatively to Booker T & the MGs' popular song "Green Onions."

Being with Mitch had its downside at school: In my senior year, a large and very jealous black girl attacked me in the hallway. She pushed me against the lockers and I swung back with all my might and punched her in the nose and made her bleed. At that point all hell broke loose and we tipped over an entire table full of dishes and food in the cafeteria before faculty members peeled her off me. I was badly bruised. The girl was suspended from school and I was suspended from using the cafeteria for the rest of the year. I walked to the nearby deli for lunch.

One day when I stayed late after school, Mr. Martin, the only black teacher in school and my study hall teacher, pulled me under the steps at a back entrance of the school and pressed me up against the wall and kissed me hard on the lips. I struggled to get away from him, but he wouldn't let go. He pinned me to the wall. I felt him hard against me. It was a noise from the steps that finally made him release me. Why did he try and force me? What was his thinking–that if I was seeing one black man, I was fair game for every black man? Did he even know about Mitch? I could have had Mr. Martin and his job hung up on the nearest lamppost, but I told no one except Julie. Yet another secret to keep.

I was Mitch's girl, his "Margie," the little Russian immigrant. It was his birthday party and Mitch was handing out the coats at the end of the evening. He picked mine up and said, "Well look, what we have here?" Mitch was holding up the shapeless black coat that my mother had made with the big plastic buttons down the front, the furry collar looking like someone cut off a mangy squirrel's tail and glued it on top of an existing collar. I was humiliated.

Julie, thinking she was helping me out, retorted, "So what if it's a homemade coat!" Another blow.

One of our foursome's favorite places to go on weekends was the drive-in theatre in Nanuet. As money was scarce, Julie and I would take turns hiding in the trunk of the car to get in free, avoiding the head count at the admittance booth, which would charge two dollars per person. We didn't go to the drive-in to see movies. We went for long make-out, petting and kissing sessions that would last as long as the movie did. Oddly enough, Julie did not lose her virginity to Royce at the drive-in. She lost it to Mitch.

My naïveté and the bliss of having a boyfriend, especially "the first" boyfriend, kept my blinders on until one day, Mitch told me he no longer loved me. I watched as Mitch became obsessed with Julie. He stalked her in school and on the street. He begged her to "go" with him. She was interested, but resisted Mitch in deference to me. He blamed me for standing in his way, for turning Julie against him. Once, when Julie and I were driving around in my father's car in Nyack, Mitch appeared out of nowhere, threw himself onto the hood of the car, pulled me out of the driver's seat, grabbed me around my neck, and proceeded to choke me. I heard Julie screaming to let me go as my head started to spin out into darkness. Only when Julie promised that she would go out with him did he finally let me go. Later, Mitch beat Julie on her head for an hour in his sister's apartment and threatened to kill her if she ever left him. She was petrified. Nevertheless, Mitch's persistence and charm wore Julie down and he finally made his conquest. This time there were consequences that changed all of our lives.

Julie became pregnant the first time she slept with Mitch. When I found out that Mitch had impregnated Julie, I went into the bathroom, took the razor, and made sharp lines on the left side of my face until my cheek bled. The next day I went to school, holding my hand to my face, and when people noticed, I told them the cat scratched me. My parents never noticed the scratches. Other than a few sad looks in my direction at school, I didn't receive the kind of attention I was hoping to get.

When she started to show, Julie told her mother everything, quit school, and went to live in a Catholic home in New York City for pregnant girls. Abortion was out of the question because of her Catholic upbringing. I went to visit Julie in New York several times. I drove my 1954 red and white two-tone Ford, my first car. Once the car stopped in the middle of the FDR Drive because the "float stuck." The motor died and I had traffic backed up to the George Washington Bridge. It was hours before a crew came to "unstick" the carburetor in my car and I could continue on my way.

Julie gave birth to a little girl in January of 1965. She saw her for about two minutes before the nuns took her away and gave her to a couple already lined up to adopt the child. Julie never saw her daughter again. Julie had broken all ties with Mitch and she swore me to secrecy. Mitch knew nothing of Julie's whereabouts, the Catholic home. He knew that he had a daughter, but he never saw her. Julie didn't even name her daughter.

Thirty-three years later, while I was working as a public school teacher in Newburgh, New York, I was walking out of a restaurant with some of my colleagues and I heard someone say behind me, "Margie?" I turned around and looked into Mitch's eyes. In one instant, his small, wiry stature brought back a rush of adolescent memories. He had recognized my voice as I was chatting with my friends. I was shocked to see him and even more shocked to be called by a name that I thought I had buried forever. We talked a little bit about the friends we had in common back then, and then he asked me if I knew where Julie lived. He wanted to get information to help him find his daughter. I told him I knew nothing about Julie, which was a lie. He gave me his card, and asked me to get in touch, but I never did.

Julie had done everything possible to prevent her daughter from finding her. She cut that segment out of her life by forever sealing the adoption record. Julie graduated from Nyack High School in 1966 and met Russ Brown, a white man who ran a service station in West Nyack. He fell in love with Julie despite her past transgressions, and married her with a promise that she would never see me again. She kept that promise for twenty years.

Jason Williams or "Jace," as everyone called him, was one of those tall, handsome black men I met at the infamous Mobil gas station on the corner of Broadway and Cedar Hill Avenue in Nyack. He had the fastest and sleekest car of the group–a 1963 white Chevy Impala 427 with tinted windows, no grill in the front–and I was impressed. I loved cars. He was a bit older, more mature than the rest, probably in his late twenties. Jace was very aware of the raw deal that I had received from Mitch and was quite happy to pick up the pieces. It didn't take me long to succumb to his soft-spoken and gentle manner. I craved the security and warmth that his lanky body offered, and unlike Mitch, Jace was sincerely committed to being my man; Jace loved me, and we became an item for nearly two years.

Jace would pick me up on weekends always in the dark, always two blocks away from my house in his awesome car. I would hear his engine roar blocks away from where I stood waiting for him. My parents knew that I had a boyfriend named Jason, but that was all. "I'm going out," I would say, and off I went. I loved it when my parents played bridge and I wasn't asked where I was going. I didn't have to lie.

One late evening when Jace dropped me off in front of my house, I kissed him goodnight and climbed out of the car only to be surprised by my mother, who was hiding behind a tree. She asked me in Russian if that was "Jason." I said yes.

"Он чёрный!" she cried out. ("He's black.")

"Well, he's not black exactly, Mama," I replied in Russian. "He's a nice sort of chocolate brown, don't you think?"

We both climbed up the long stairs to the apartment in silence, chalking up my guilt another notch. Again, I was a dirty, bad girl. If my mother had embraced me at that moment and shared her youthful transgressions, her love affairs, her abortions, her fears, my life could have taken a different turn. Instead, the deafening silence between us shut down communication and propelled me away from my home and onto my own path. Alone.

Jace and I had fun. He would take me to Harlem, to the Apollo Theatre. I saw Ray Charles and Otis Redding perform. In the mid-sixties, I was one of the few white girls dancing in the aisles to the fast tunes and wailing at the top of my lungs during the Blues numbers. We went to Smalls Paradise on 125th Street to dance, and to Count Basie's bar, where I saw Miles Davis sitting dazed in a chair. We went to parties. We went to black bars where I drank my favorite: straight Russian vodka on the rocks. Jace drank Bourbon. We danced. We made love in his car or in motel rooms.

Jace taught me how to race cars. Because I was a natural at the wheel, racing came easily to me. First we raced illegally on the Garden State Parkway, specifically the extension from the New York State Thruway where there was an exact quarter-mile straight stretch where the drag racing cars could roar out into the night. There were regular drag racers, Royce with his GTO, Sonny with his bright red Catalina, Cliff with his blue Malibu, and maybe four other guys. And of course, there was Jace and me with our beautiful white Chevy Impala, the front of the car looking like a hungry mouth, cruising down the Garden

State Parkway. The racing gang would meet around two in the morning, when there was less traffic and less chance of being seen by the police. The guys would choose the cars and the drivers and they would bet on the race.

I raced only one time on the Garden State Parkway. Jace and I split the wad of prize money after I nosed our Impala at breakneck speed, with tires smoking, ahead of a white guy with a less impressive machine. Jace and the others were so impressed with me that we all went down to Chick'n'Charlie's, a black bar in Nyack that was still open, and the bartender popped a bottle of champagne. They put me up on the bar and I danced and danced and danced. I was seventeen years old.

Once, Jace took me to the Flemington Raceway, a professional quarter mile drag racing track in New Jersey, to race in the women's Powder Puff races. I remember sitting in the driver's seat, at the start line, listening to last minute instructions from Jace, gunning the engine, preparing to pop the clutch at the exact time. I sat on pillows to see better and was given a three-car length lead because I was racing a guy. I took off! I thrilled to the squeal of the tires as I slammed through the gears, the back end of the car zigzagging as I accelerated, watching the track lights going by so fast and, seconds later, the finish line flags above me.

It must have been around five a.m. when Jace dropped me in front of my house. I walked up the stairs, only to discover that the door to my apartment was locked. I walked around the house to the fire escape stairs, climbed up, opened the window screen, and found myself looking down the barrel of my father's old shotgun.

"Это я, Папа, это я," I said in Russian. ("It's me, Papa, it's me.")

"Я знаю." ("I know,") he answered.

"Ты что. . . с ружьём?" ("What are you doing. . . a rifle?") I screamed as I lunged through the open window, climbed on the desk that stood by the window, knocking the telephone and papers off, and landed on the floor. I saw my mother lying on the couch in her depressive stupor as my father returned to his kitchen bed. Again, we all retreated into our corners, the silence louder than all the screaming and accusations.

I graduated from Nyack High School in 1965. Because I refused to wear regular glasses, I wore my prescription sunglasses when I walked across the platform to receive my diploma. Without them, I was blind as a bat. Any dreams that I had to go to the Sorbonne in Paris to study languages or go to Stony Brook University on Long Island to become a Russian/English translator were dashed due to financial constraints, poor grades, and a lack of parental and counselor support in school. I don't remember once, in four years of high school, speaking to a school counselor to discuss my future possibilities.

In 1965, some of my friends went off to Vietnam to fight in a war we knew little about. I never understood the farewell parties that resembled the festive occasions in the film *Gone with the Wind,* when the young Southern men were enthusiastically going off to their annihilation. Our parties, too, were full of innocence and ignorance of what was to come. I lost at least three friends to the Vietnam War. I stopped speaking Russian altogether in fear of being called a Communist. This fear only added to my confusion and isolation from my parents and culture.

Then came a personal catastrophe. Jace's brother told me that Jace was married, and that he and his wife were expecting a child. I was so desperate for the relationship that even this did not stop me from seeing Jace, even though our weekends together happened less often. Before cell phones, there was little communication and Jace simply would not show up to our meetings. He never called my house. I would find myself walking the streets alone, waiting for him. All night long, I made repeated trips to "our" corner, listening for the roar of the car engine. After a long while, I would walk alone into town to the black street, look in the black bars asking if anyone had seen Jace.

If this would not bring results, I would walk home and beg my father for the car and drive nine miles up 9W from Nyack to Haverstraw, where Jace lived. There was a bar near his house where I would sit and drink and hope that he would show up. Others would try to pick me up, but I was steadfast, waiting for Jace. Sometimes he would show up and we would go off together. I would be so happy. Later, I found myself driving home drunk from Haverstraw, and by some miracle making it home, walking past my mother, drinking vodka and writing poetry on the couch, into my bedroom where I would pass out onto my bed.

In 1966, my college choices were slim, and I took out a school loan to enter Rockland Community College in Suffern, New York, a two-year state college. I hated it. It felt like an extension of my high school, and instead of attending classes, I chose to play cards in the student lounge and promptly failed the first semester. For a short time, my mother worked part-time as a seamstress at Ronni J. Cleaners in New City, halfway between Nyack and Suffern (she had finally quit the sewing machine sweatshops). That summer, I also worked there as a counter girl; the job paid my expenses. I bought my second car, a two-tone 1956 Chevy that took me to work and to school. My world was opening up. I was meeting new people at school and my relationship with Jace began to wane.

Joe Chase was the presser at Ronni J. Cleaners. He was black, tall, strong, and had a scar by his left eye that made him look rough. But he had a body to die for. Besides pressing and steaming clothes at the cleaners, Joe ran the very popular pool hall in Spring Valley, another town in Rockland County about six miles from Nyack. Joe knew everybody and everybody knew Joe. The moment I stepped foot into Ronni J., he knew who I was. He knew I was Jace's girl, and carefully and quietly, we got to know each other, speaking between clients and avoiding stares at work. Perhaps because it was so clandestine, our attraction for each other became electric. The sexual energy between us while we did our jobs at the cleaners was exciting and frightening. My body trembled when he would brush up against me when no one was looking. One day, he gave me his phone number at the pool hall and told me to call him after hours. I did.

The first time we made love was in the billiard hall after hours, on top of the pool table with just the table light swinging above us. Hot, sexy Joe Chase. I was captivated by his sexual passion and couldn't stay away from him. We met again several times. He would take me across the Hudson River to Westchester County, to black bars and later to motel rooms where our lovemaking reached new levels of intensity. Once he took a photograph of me naked on the bed. At least I had the presence of mind to make him cut off my head in the photo so as not be recognized later.

I was not in love with Joe, but I was excited by my ability to arouse such desire and fervor. I was pulling on emotional strings and playing a dangerous game; thinking that I was in control. Although he never hurt me physically, I felt that he was capable of hurting me; that if he knew that I was playing him, he could become dangerous.

One night, Joe picked me up several blocks from home and we were on our way to a black resort eight miles from Nyack. He walked into the bar to pay and get the key to the room while I sat and waited in the car. Suddenly, a cold fear crept over me and an inner voice told me to run–now, immediately. I opened the door and jumped out of the car and ran as fast as I could into the woods surrounding the resort. Scared, I hid in the bushes for over an hour while I heard him calling me, yelling and driving his car back and forth along the road. If he had found me, Joe Chase might have killed me.

When at last, hours later, the night became silent, save for the sounds of distant cars and nearby crickets, and I was sure that Joe had given up looking for me, I crept from my hiding place and walked towards Nyack. Realizing eight miles was too far to walk at night, I saw a house with lights and walked toward it. I knocked on the door. A very kind middle-aged black man answered the door. I told him a semi-truth: that I was at the resort down the road and the person I was with wouldn't take me home. I asked the gentleman to drive me home, and he did. I was never so relieved to be home, in our little cluttered Washington Avenue apartment. I was safe.

Although I was petrified to face Joe at the cleaners the next day after school, I was able to tell him that I no longer wanted to see him; that I was tired of sneaking around, that it was over. Joe was angry, but he got over it. I was relieved. My attraction to him disappeared as quickly as it appeared.

I also broke off my waning relationship with Jace. In spite of his new family, he was less than pleased about losing his toy. He stalked me when I was in Nyack and often I would see his car in the parking lot in front of the cleaners in New City. It seemed that everywhere I turned, he was there, but I avoided any kind of interaction.

Then one night, it was dark when I pulled into my driveway behind our house and got out of the car. I was laden with books and bags from school and didn't notice the shadow coming out of the shadows toward me. It was Jace. There was no time to run. Jace pushed me down across the hood of my car, sending my books and bags flying. I struggled, but he pinned me down, murmuring over and over under his bourbon-smelling breath, "How dare you leave me, girl!" I was too frightened to scream. He ripped off my skirt and raped me on the hood of my car, banged my head against the metal, and walked away. I fell to the ground in a daze and heard him drive off. I never saw Jace again.

Slowly, I picked myself up, gathered my belongings and trudged up the stairs. I opened the door to the apartment; my father was already in his bed. My mother was not home. She was in the rehab institution at that time. I looked into the mirror of our makeshift hallway and saw leaves sticking out my hair and my face smudged. My father asked me in Russian how I was, to which I replied. . . I was fine. I walked into the bathroom, combed the leaves out my hair, took off my ripped skirt, washed Jace's bourbon and semen off my body, went to my room and closed the door. My father never had a clue.

Chapter Eighteen

Baltimore, Maryland

THERE WAS AN AFTERMATH TO THE RAPE.

Two months later, I was driving my 1956 two-tone Chevrolet on the New York State Thruway with Brooke, a new friend I'd met in college. Distracted by our conversation and chatter, I missed my turn onto the Garden State Parkway South. I drove onto the side of the road, stopped, put the car into reverse and headed backwards on the Thruway towards the missed exit. Brooke and I were both looking back and were unaware of the cop car in front of us, which was backing up with us. The cop was waving his hand, flashing all lights. When Brooke and I finally turned around, we realized that we had been caught making the illegal reverse. I looked at the cop innocently–I had learned this from my father ages ago–and admitted the mistake. He waved us off, helped us back onto the exit of the parkway, and our adventure resumed.

That was autumn of 1966 and I was nineteen years old. Brooke and I were heading for Baltimore, Maryland, where I was to have an illegal abortion. I got pregnant when Jace raped me. After swallowing many glasses of quinine water and drinking huge amounts of alcohol in failed attempts to abort, I managed to obtain five hundred dollars from a friend of a friend for the abortion. Brooke and I scraped together the rest of the money for a hotel room and gas–there was not much left for food, a minor consideration.

Somewhere deep in my pocketbook were the memorized directions that I had to follow. I was to go to a certain Howard Johnson Motor Lodge in Baltimore.

I was to check in, get a room, and wait for a taxi that would pick me up, alone, at a certain time. I was not frightened. Perhaps it was naïveté, perhaps ignorance, but I know I was in deep denial of the danger that awaited me. My angels were working overtime.

When hunger overwhelmed us, we stopped at a food store and crammed some bread, ham, and cheese into our pocketbooks. A few smaller items also found their way directly into my purse, delicious things like a can of crabmeat and a tin of sardines. Just as we were about to walk out of the store, a fire alarm sounded. Brooke and I jumped out of our skins, ran past the cashier, and out the door, the food still safe in our bags. We giggled about the siren all through lunch.

It was dark when we got to the Howard Johnson. We checked in. I looked out the window and noticed a taxi waiting at the entrance. It was time to go. Brooke and I hugged and I walked alone, down the hall, into the lobby, out the door and climbed into the taxi. I felt like I was moving in slow motion. My thoughts were not on the danger of what was to come but the necessity of going through it, to get it done and move on. The blinders were on.

The cab driver told me to lie face down on the back seat of the car and not to get up. I did as I was told. I felt the taxi winding around curves and going uphill. About twenty minutes later, we stopped at a dark house. He told me to go in. I was greeted by a woman who asked me for the money, which I had in an envelope. She took the money and told me to go into an adjacent room, take off my clothes, and put on a paper dress. I went into the room and there was a woman lying on the bed in one corner. She was lying on her side, groaning. We didn't speak. I didn't want to know. Soon I walked into a very bright room and I was told to lie down on the cold metal flat bed and to put my feet into the stirrups. My legs began to tremble. The doctor and nurse were wearing sunglasses. The operation began. The doctor told me that there would be cramping. Soon the cramping started and intensified; tears of pain rolling down my cheeks. The procedure lasted fifteen minutes, an eternity.

And then it was over. The doctor asked me if I wanted to see the fetus. I said no. I was led into the original room. The other woman was gone. I was told to lie down for a while; that they would come for me. It was in this quiet moment that

I realized what had just happened. I could bleed to death. I could get an infection. Would I see Brooke again?

After about twenty minutes, I was given some pills for the bleeding and some menstrual pads. I got dressed and slowly and painfully walked out of the house and into the waiting taxi. Again, I was told to lie face down on the back seat. I was never so happy to see the Howard Johnson and Brooke rushing towards me. It was really over.

The next morning, I wasn't bleeding too badly. I was going to make it. I was lucky. We packed up, dumped the leftover tin of sardines into the swimming pool a few floors below us and watched as the dead sardines and the oil spread over the turquoise-colored water.

Chapter Nineteen

Leaving Home

AT NINETEEN YEARS OLD, WHEN I left home in a fury with potato soup on my shoes, I did not know where I belonged. Home on Washington Avenue in Nyack was not the place to hang my hat. The dark apartment with the camphor-scented mustiness and the claustrophobia of the sick rooms was oppressive. And there was too much furniture. I had too many secrets to feel comfortable with the Russian relatives cloaked in their religious righteousness and Imperial Czarist ideas. The Russians were good; I was bad. I was the black sheep who wouldn't buy into the guilt-ridden Russian Orthodoxy; I had enough guilt of my own. Even the name "Margie" I was branded with all through school enabled me to hide behind a caricature of myself and further isolated me from my Russian roots.

The abortion marked an end to my adventures with black men, and I left them gaping at the crumpled photo of me naked with my head cut off. I walked away from the black culture. I was now well versed in the black street language and humor, and richer in my appreciation of the blues and soul music, but I didn't belong there either. The late 1960s were not conducive for a white woman to be accepted by blacks, and I was tired of the secrecy and the dark nights. I needed a new deck of cards, but where and how to get them? I had no visions or dreams, no hopes and no motivation to do much of anything.

I made a few friends in college, and with them I turned to alcohol to drown out the emptiness. On a dare, I once drank a full tumbler of straight gin on the rocks–I had a reputation for knowing how to hold my liquor. Before I drank the gin, I told my friends that I had to pick up my mother later that afternoon at the Tolstoy Farm in Valley Cottage, where she had gotten a job taking care of the elderly at the new Russian retirement home.

It wasn't long before I passed out. Somehow my friends carried me to my car, laid me down on the back seat and kept driving me around for hours with the windows open, hoping that I would become conscious enough to pick up my mother. The thought that I could have died from alcohol poisoning never entered anyone's mind. At the entrance of the Tolstoy Farm, my friends woke me up and propped me up in the driver's seat. I gunned the engine in first gear and promptly drove into the wall of bushes in the driveway. The farm staff had to get a tractor to pull out my car. I crawled back into the back seat and one of my friends, Dan, ended up driving my mother and me home. I have never again been able to drink gin in any form.

After that incident, my friend Harry decided that he would sacrifice one of his therapy sessions with his psychologist and give his hour to me.

Psychological help? Me? I told the psychologist that I was fine, that I was taking care of myself, that I would sort myself out, and that I had no money or time to waste on head-shrinking conversations. In fact, I avoided any kind of mental health discussions and pooh-poohed the entire psychological profession, considering therapy a luxury for bored people to find themselves. For me it was all about doing instead of being, and so I plodded on.

During one of my card games in the student lounge at college, someone mentioned that the college theatre department was looking for students to audition for a play called *Spoon River Anthology* by Edgar Lee Masters. My curiosity got the best of me, and having nothing to lose, I went.

When it was my turn to audition, I walked onto the stage and slowly turned to the dark theatre to read for Jim Naismith, the director. I took a deep breath, and to my surprise, the timbre of confidence strengthened my voice. I straightened up, getting taller as I read on, with a slight defiant smile on my face. I read the script as if it was the most natural thing I had ever done. In that moment, I remembered the little girl who stood on stage at age seven in an extraordinary rooster costume and looked down at the scary, black-clad Russian Orthodox priests in the front row, and yet hit the high C note at the end of the Russian version of Cock-a-Doodle-Do.

Jim Naismith didn't know it at the time, but when he gave me the parts of Rosie Roberts, Mrs. Williams, and of course, Russian Sonia in the production of *Spoon River Anthology*, he threw me a lifeline. I found myself thrust into the hustle-bustle of the theatre world: rehearsals, lights, sets, music, costumes, makeup. I soon felt the electric charge of performance and above all, I was meeting interesting people—my kind of people. I was relearning a language that was familiar to me as a young girl, and at nineteen, I couldn't get enough. I loved it all. According to Jim, I "nailed" my parts in the performances, and feeling the success, I went back for more. I called myself "Mourka," my Russian name.

The next production at the college was *I Am A Camera*, a 1951 Broadway play by John Van Druten and the precursor to the very popular musical *Cabaret*. I landed the part of Fraulein Schneider, the landlady, a character role for which my knowledge of Russian helped me to achieve the required German accent. I "nailed" that part too, and after the performances, Jim Naismith told me that I had a natural talent. That was all I needed: someone to believe in me and give me direction. After *I Am A Camera*, I made a decision to go to New York City to become a professional stage actress. At last, I had a dream to pursue. The fact that I had no money did not deter me.

In between working at the cleaners, classes, and rehearsals at the Rockland Community College theatre, I was seeing a nice white boy by the name of Virgil. He was a student and built sets for the productions in the theatre department. We became friends. One evening, Virgil needed to type a paper for one of his classes and didn't have access to a typewriter, and I invited him to work in the apartment in Nyack. I had a typewriter and I knew that my mother was staying at the Tolstoy Farm retirement home overnight; Virgil could sleep on the couch. It was an innocent gesture and it felt good not to sneak and to finally bring someone to our apartment. My father was home when I introduced Virgil to him and I explained the dilemma. Virgil worked through the night. I had gone to sleep in my room and my father slept in his usual place in the kitchen.

In the middle of the night, I got up, woke Virgil, who was by this time sleeping on the couch and brought him back to my bedroom. It wasn't for sex. I craved his warmth; for his body to be close to mine in the safety and comfort of my own bed, my own room.

It was early in the morning when my father found us. We had our arms around each other and we were fully clothed. We had not made love. My father screamed at us, told Virgil to get out and I quickly prepared to leave for school as well. My father and I said very little to each other and I left feeling embarrassed at the incident–stupid for getting caught by my father, but innocent in the act. As usual, I went to work after school.

I got the call at the cleaners from my mother around five p.m. She said in Russian, "What did you do to your father?"

"Why? What happened?" I asked.

"He tried to commit suicide. He overdosed on sleeping pills," she said. "You better come home right away."

When I got home, I found my father lying in his bed, very weak. My mother was seething. "How dare you do this to your father!" I tried to convey my innocence, but to no avail. In their view, I had almost killed my father and there was nothing I could say except to beg for forgiveness, which I did–over and over.

The suicide incident propelled me to make my move to New York City as soon as possible. I had enough guilt to last me a lifetime. It was time to move on. I made plans with my dear cousin Andrei, who lived on West 88th Street and Broadway in Manhattan. He generously invited me to stay with him and his roommate until I got on my feet. I quit college, quit my job at Ronni J. Cleaners, and said good-bye to my friends.

The dreaded afternoon arrived when I was to tell my parents of my plans. I left this conversation for last. My father was not home, but I had to spit my words out anyway. I was standing next to the radiator by the bathroom door when I said in Russian, "Mama, I know what I want to do with my life. I want to go to New York to become an actress, a dancer, a singer–a performer." Mama was en route to the dining room table with a large pot of hot potato soup she had just made. She looked at me incredulously, threw the hot soup at me, and yelled in Russian, "What is this going to do to your father?"

My father walked in. I repeated my plans to him, and quietly and calmly he said in Russian, "Mourka, aristocrats don't dance."

I shouted back, "I'm going to push out the walls of this house. I can't breathe in here from all the *chachkas* and furniture. There's wrapping paper in boxes and bags in the drawers and under the beds. There's fabrics and furs and ribbons and threads and brooches and photos of dead men on horses long dead in the war, and sheets that smell like camphor and crying and crumpled-up poems crammed under pillows and bottles and bottles of pills and Elixir and vodka and pain and sickness and sadness and NO! NO MORE! No more!"

I changed clothes, packed a suitcase and walked out the door.

Chapter Twenty

Manhattan

WHEN OUR FAMILY FIRST ARRIVED in America in December, 1949, we were met by my Aunt Alina and her little boy, my cousin Andrei. I was two years old. I took one look at Andrei's beautiful red hair and fell in love. Seventeen years later, it was Andrei who, in one blissful evening, introduced me to marijuana and the Beatles album *Sergeant Peppers Lonely Hearts Club Band*. As I sat on the couch in his living room, the combination sent me off into amplified marijuana bliss and I stared at the round bottoms of hundreds of Budweiser bottles, stuck into Andrei's large windows, that created the perfect kaleidoscope effect for *Lucy in the Sky With Diamonds*.

Andrei was a composition major, and his roommate Keith Eagan majored in conducting at the Juilliard School. Keith often stood on a makeshift podium in front of the sink in the tiny kitchen and conducted an imaginary full-size orchestra with a bottle of Budweiser in one hand and his conducting baton in the other, a Wagner score in front of him as Wagner symphonies blasted on the stereo set. Every day, Keith would drink three large bottles of Budweiser, all of which ended up in the kaleidoscope windows in the living room.

It was a free and easy time in Andrei's two-bedroom apartment on the third, floor at 211 West 88th Street, where I paid no rent but washed many dishes to keep the cockroach population down to a minimum. The apartment was warm and cozy, and there were always people visiting with whom I chatted and philosophized. I entered a new world of discussion and debate, and I took in information like a sponge.

In the late sixties there was a lot to talk about in New York City–the escalating Vietnam War, the resurgence of rock and roll. The Beatles, The Rolling Stones, and The Who were all having concerts in New York. On Broadway, the musical *Hair* depicted the sign of the times: blue jeans, nudity, and all manifestations of nonconformity. I could finally hide my skinny legs in tattered blue jeans and my thrift shop clothes were right in style. I slept on the couch when Andrei's girlfriend, Carrie stayed overnight; otherwise I slept with Andrei in his bed. Carrie was suspicious. "Why is your cousin staying at the apartment? Is she really your cousin? Is she sleeping with you?"

There was never any sex between Andrei and me. When we were teenagers, he taught me how to French kiss in my bedroom on Washington Avenue in Nyack, but that was the extent of it. Years later, after a tumultuous marriage with Carrie and a more devastating divorce, Andrei wished that I had stayed in his bed and Carrie had been relegated to the couch.

At that time, it was relatively cheap to get high from the garbage bags full of marijuana that we used to get from the half-Cherokee, half-black pot pusher, who worked our block. Stoned, we would listen to everything from James Brown to Nina Simone, Miles Davis, and Thelonius Monk to Wagner, Mahler, and Schoenberg. I got a free Juilliard music appreciation course. Sometimes the salsa music from the fourth floor would compete with the listening appreciation, and I would be compelled to go upstairs and get private salsa dance lessons from the handsome Dominican guy who lived there.

Despite an anxious and nervous energy that hid a myriad of fears, I was forming my own character: a personality based on individuality and a strong sense of survival. It felt good to be on my own. I was a "free spirit" and often complimented that I looked "exotic" with my Russian high cheekbones. I wore my hair loose and long, to my shoulders. I was told that there was still a trace of my European accent and everyone seemed to like it. With my different looks and manner, what had been odd in the past seemed an asset. I began to feel less displaced.

This sense of fitting in and enjoying a restful, indulgent time didn't last too long.

Like everyone else, I had to earn a living. Because I was still a floating, unmoored person, I naturally went to an agency for "Temps" (a term which certainly suited my entire lifestyle). The temporary employment agency landed me a job as a receptionist and switchboard operator at ANTA (American National Theatre and Academy) on West 53rd Street. Besides being a legitimate Broadway theatre, ANTA was an organization that provided services to the theatre profession and had its offices above the theater itself. When I worked there in 1968, ANTA had established the ANTA Washington Square Theatre as the temporary home of the Vivian Beaumont Theater, which would later be part of Lincoln Center. ANTA had many successful productions, including the hit musical *Man of La Mancha* and Arthur Miller's plays *After the Fall* and *Incident at Vichy*.

Walter Abel, a famous stage, film, radio, and television actor whose theatrical career spanned sixty years, became ANTA's president in 1966. I was always happy to see the sixty-nine-year-old Walter come through the door. He was always dressed impeccably in a black suit and sported a walking stick. He was jovial and flirtatious and once invited me backstage to watch from the wings as he performed–for luck. I heard him say, "Here we go" as he stepped onto the stage for his entrance.

The receptionist/switchboard operator job at ANTA was not as exciting as I had first envisioned. To make the days pass, I listened in on conversations on the switchboard and offered advice to speakers when appropriate. By listening in one day, I discovered that ANTA had its own employment agency that offered theatrical jobs to out-of-work actors. I made friends with the person in charge, and although I was not yet a professional actor, I was given the opportunity to interview for the secretary position for Peter Feller, a Tony Award-winning set designer whose company, Feller Scenery Studios, built over a thousand sets for Broadway shows as well as for out of town shows. Feller had a full construction department, a costume department run by his wife Kate, and a lighting department, all located in a huge building next to Yankee Stadium in the Bronx. I wasn't too enamored of the idea of traveling to the Bronx every day, but I did notice that the building was teeming with good-looking carpenters building sets, working on stage lights, and making costumes. I landed the job.

And I saw stars–sort of. One Saturday morning before a matinee, I walked into Angela Lansbury's dressing room with Peer Thame, my first boyfriend in New York, a good-looking Englishman who worked for Pete Feller as a stagehand and knew his way around backstage. The room was a mess: open makeup cases, powder, lipstick, and eyeliner were strewn all over the dressing counter, and costumes were lying on couches, chairs, and on the floor. Lansbury was playing the leading role in *Mame*, for which she won a Tony Award for Best Actress in a Musical in 1966. After setting aside a few filmy pieces of lingerie, Peer and I made love on Angela Lansbury's comfortable puffy couch. For a short time I could fantasize that the makeup and the mess were all mine.

Then there was Roy Stevens, another friend I met at Feller's. He worked as a stagehand on Tom Stoppard's comedy *Rosencrantz and Guildenstern Are Dead* at the Neil Simon Theatre on West 52nd street. I would meet him at Charley's Bar next to the theatre and we would have a drink together in between his cues. He had our drinks and kisses timed to the second.

And I saw star athletes, most notably Cassius Clay, or Muhammad Ali, as he was known when he became the heavyweight champion in 1969. Cassius Clay was trying his hand at acting in a Broadway show called *Buck White* (which closed after seven performances) and I saw him leaving the theatre after a rehearsal. I joined a crowd of people following him and to my surprise, Clay/Ali picked me out of the crowd, lifted me onto his shoulders, and in this way, walked with me for several blocks downtown with the huge crowd around us, screaming and yelling in broad daylight. I took Clay's gesture as an omen of lifting me to stardom, and so inspired, I began to prepare myself for the theatre world.

Every penny I made working at Feller's went to classes and for the subway to get to dance classes at Luigi's Jazz Studio on 62nd and Broadway four times a week. The lessons left my muscles aching, screaming. It didn't matter. I was finally free to dance. Luigi, whose motto was "Never stop moving" and "Dance from the inside out," became my hero and mentor for many years and his technique lives in me still. Luigi used his technique, which consisted of a series of ballet-based exercises, for his own rehabilitation after suffering paralyzing injuries in a car accident at the age of twenty-one. His efforts paid off because he went on to have a successful dance career, and became a world-renowned jazz teacher.

I started voice lessons with Rose Allen on Seventh Avenue and 55th Street. Her sister Sue Seton was a vocal coach for stars like Bette Midler; Carol Lawrence, who was in the original production of *West Side Story*; Shirley MacLaine, who was starring in *Sweet Charity*; and Katharine Hepburn, who was struggling as a singer in *Coco*. I often rode the elevator with Bette Midler and Katharine Hepburn as we ascended to our respective voice teachers. I'd hide my feelings of awe and make believe I was just one of the gang.

My heritage resurfaced in an exciting way. Katharine Sergava, a Russian acting teacher at the famous Herbert Bergdorf Acting Studio, had high hopes for me to become an excellent actress. We worked on Chekhov, Gogol. . . I was in my element, and she loved me because I was Russian. I also took classes from Uta Hagen, famous for her Blanche DuBois opposite Marlon Brando's Stanley Kowalski in *Streetcar Named Desire* in the 1950s and Martha in Edward Albee's *Who's Afraid of Virginia Woolf* in 1963 on Broadway. I didn't know about Uta's accomplishments when I was crawling on the floor and doing method acting "be an animal" exercises in her classes at HB. As silly as I felt, I was determined to learn the acting craft and to shine.

Eating was not a priority. There were days when I ate only two hot dogs with sauerkraut for fifty cents from a stand by the Yankee stadium, in the vain hope that someone would cook something at the apartment. When I was downtown and very hungry, I would go to the Automat and ask for boiling water into which I would squeeze Hunt's tomato ketchup to make tomato soup.

The day when Pete Feller announced that he had to let me go, I didn't believe him. "You're joking," I remember saying.

"I'm not joking," he said, and quickly added, "It's not anything you did wrong."

"What's the problem, then?"

I remember my legs felt like they were going to buckle under me when Pete told me that his son had just gotten married to a girl from Ohio, a newbie to New York City, and she needed a job. It was, after all, a family business–jobs were handed down to family members.

The incessant wind that blew around Yankee Stadium every day couldn't blow away my tears of rage, couldn't stifle the sobbing that shook my body that day as I walked to the subway on my last walk from Feller Scenery Studios.

Two weeks later, John, Pete's right hand man and my good friend (or so I thought) invited me to dinner at his apartment in Fort Lee, New Jersey. Considering that he was old enough to be my father, I took his invitation as a benevolent act of wanting to feed me. I also harbored a hope that the son's wife didn't work out and that I would be restored to my job. I was wrong on both accounts. After serving me a delicious dinner and plying me with champagne, he tried to lure me into his bed. I refused and walked out of the apartment feeling betrayed, angry, and very much alone. Another injustice, another slap on the face, more potato soup on my shoes.

Chapter Twenty One

Mourka A Go-Go

WITH GREAT TREPIDATION, I WALKED up three flights of stairs of a towering midtown Manhattan building, and opened the door into a dingy and cluttered office space. I was responding to an ad I had seen in the *Backstage* newspaper: "Go-Go Agent Looking for Girls." I stepped into the room and was surrounded by hundreds of black and white photos of dancing girls revealing their beautiful bodies in a multitude of poses and costumes.

"Oh my God, I could never look like that," I thought. I nearly turned back when Phil, the dance agent, glanced up at me from his desk, which was also piled up with black and white photos. He took his feet off the desk and introduced himself. It was too late to run. After a brief introduction, Phil very kindly asked me to put on my costume and do some dance moves for him. My heart sank. I told him I didn't have a costume yet.

"No problem, just strip down to your underwear," he said. In spite of the initial embarrassment of having to dance in underwear that had seen better days, I closed my eyes, and slinked into a blues number I conjured up in my head. I danced for about a minute when Phil thanked me, hired me on the spot, and gave me the address of my first gig. He even lent me money to buy an outfit. I was in. To hell with Pete Feller and all "nine to five" secretarial jobs!

My outfit: black bra, black panties, black fringe hanging just below my waist, black fishnet stockings with the line down the back of my legs, and black high heels. Sexy black. I was going to dance up a storm, using everything I learned in the black bars in Nyack and in my jazz dancing classes. No bumping and grinding for me. It had to be a class act or I wasn't going to do it.

On the next Friday night, my first gig was this little after-hours club on the Lower West Side. I rang the bell and, after a minute, I could hear the machinery of an elevator.

A face appeared in the porthole. "Yeah?"

"It's Mourka. Mourka, the dancer?"

A guy by the name of Jerry, wearing a suit made out of some slippery silvery stuff, opened the door with a key. A few floors up – God knows how many – he opened up another door with a key. The whole place was wrapped in aluminum foil. Every single thing was glittery silver metal and mirrors. From the middle of the ceiling hung a silver cage.

Oh shit. Jerry led me into a small dressing room. The walls in here were black, not silver. He handed me a large round hatbox. "Take that off and wrap yourself in this."

"Aluminum foil? I can't dance in aluminum foil."

"So? Dance different."

"Listen, I don't just bump and grind. I'm a jazz dancer. I… dance. I can't dance in aluminum foil."

"Hey. This is what you gotta wear. We got a concept here. . ."

"Get somebody else."

"What do you mean get somebody else? You're killing me. I got no time for this shit. Okay. Okay. Wear what you brought, put this on over. . . No? We'll add fifty bucks to what we're paying you. . . NO? We'll add a hundred to what we're paying you. . . Dese fuckin' artist types."

And so I danced in this cage wrapped in aluminum foil. The cage was suspended several feet off the ground. It turned when I turned and swung when I moved. I slid in my high heels. I had to hold onto the bars to stay vertical. Yards of foil were shivering and crackling around me. The music blared; the large crowd drank, smoked weed, ogled, and jeered.

At six a.m., I took the subway home with two hundred and fifty dollars I hid in my shoes. Jerry asked me back the next night. I made more money in two days than I made working a full week at Fellers. I felt rich.

I should have taken a cab home my last night at the after hours club. Instead, Jerry, the manager with the slippery silvery suit, who wooed and flattered me for two nights, invited me to spend the night with him at a hotel. I accepted. We smoked some pot in the room. It was laced with God knows what, and I went into a paranoid hallucinatory state never to be forgotten. In my hallucination, I saw a newspaper with the headline "After-Hours Club Manager Seduces Go-Go Girl and Murders Her." I froze. The more he beckoned me to his bed, the more vivid the headline.

Very slowly, not to upset "the murderer," I put on my clothes and, never taking my eyes off of him, backed out of the room, opened the door and ran into the hallway, down the elevator and into a taxi. I barely uttered my address to the cabbie standing in front of the hotel as we raced uptown. Manhattan streets: a kaleidoscope of neon red, green, yellow colors weaving in and out, colliding, bursting, my eyes straining to focus. At home in my apartment on W. 99th street between Riverside Avenue and West End Avenue, I got into my bed, pulled the covers over my head and shook for hours before I finally succumbed to sleep.

Why didn't I quit dancing after that first experience? I needed the money to pursue my dream of becoming a stage actress. The classes were expensive. The truth was that most club dates went smoothly, but then there were others. . .

Coming home late was an issue. Not having a car, I had to rely on rides home from bar patrons.

A gig ended somewhere far out on Long Island. The man who took me home was drunk and drove through a barricaded construction site on the freeway, fencing and metal flying through the air. By some miracle, we got through to the other side of the construction site, unhurt. I was so frightened that I asked him to drop me off at the next exit, Flushing, Long Island. I slept through the night under the boardwalk in Flushing, freezing. I woke up to footsteps on the boardwalk and the sun shining on my face through the cracks.

I danced several times at a club near Yonkers Raceway. Customers would ask the go-go girl what horses to bet on and I would tell them. I got a reputation for picking winners and the dollar bills hanging out of my bra proved it. Perhaps I gave out an unlucky number, I don't know, but after one gig, I fell asleep on the subway and didn't wake up until the middle of the next day. Someone had laced my club soda with something and I rode the subway all night and all day from Mount Vernon to Coney Island and back. I couldn't wake up. The last thing I remembered before I nodded out was the wad of money the club paid me safe inside my shoes.

A handsome, rugged looking Native American from Texas waited all night in a bar in New Jersey to take me home. The club owner said he was okay and I agreed to ride home with him. There was a mysteriousness about him and a sexual energy I could not resist. I invited him to my apartment. When he undressed, I saw he had these blue dots tattooed all over his body.

"Interesting."

"Yep. One for every year I spent in the pen, back in Texas."

"Interesting," I said as I carefully ushered him out.

He tried to come back several times and almost broke the apartment door down before I threatened to call the police. Much later I found out that he had broken parole by crossing the state line from New Jersey to New York, got caught and was sent back to Texas.

On the subway returning from a club date about four a.m., I was sitting reading a book and trying desperately to concentrate on the words in front of me. A very large, rough-looking black man, the only other person in the car, was sitting directly in front of me with his feet stretched out in front of him, staring straight at me. He never took his eyes off of me. I was afraid to move, petrified that if I moved, he would pounce on me like a cat on a mouse. I froze. Should I move to the next car? Should I get off at my stop and walk home? Would he follow me? What should I do? My mind was racing.

West 96th Street. My stop. I closed my book, picked myself up and walked onto the platform. He followed. I walked up the steps onto the street, desperate to find a policeman, anyone to yell to for help… No one. Everything was closed.

My stalker was a few steps behind me. Sweat poured down my back. I had three blocks to go. He was still behind me. I made a left onto my street. *Do I run? Do I scream?*

I did nothing. I was too afraid. I got to my door, went up the steps of the brownstone, gathered all my strength, turned to him and screamed, "What do you want?" He looked at me from the bottom of the steps and quietly said, "I just wanted to make sure you got home all right."

When I told my parents I was dancing in clubs, my mother said in Russian, "Wear a mask and no one will know it is you."

During the day, acting, dancing, and singing lessons resumed, and I go-go danced at night. I started pounding the pavement auditioning for plays and musicals, often ending up in frustrating cattle calls and lineups. I remember when Busby Berkeley was auditioning for the musical *No No Nanette* and the audition call was for "5'3" blondes. No singing or dancing required, just show up." There must have been hundreds of us. We all looked alike. About fifteen girls would line up on stage and one by one, he would wave the girls off. Infuriating!

I did end up landing an Equity Showcase acting job, but the play was so bad that after a week of rehearsal, I quit. What was I thinking? An Equity union card would have opened doors for me. Was the excellence of the Russian theatre and culture lurking in the background? Did Sergava, my Russian acting teacher at HB, instill a desire for a quality performance? Was it my rebellious nature standing up against mediocrity?

I was now sharing my apartment on 99th Street with Brooke, my friend from college who a year earlier had accompanied me to Baltimore for the abortion. Brooke was a tall, beautiful redhead who was holding down a secretarial job in Manhattan. In her spare time, she became an Ayn Rand groupie and made good money posing nude for fine artists at the Ayn Rand Institute in downtown Manhattan. Brooke introduced me to *The Fountainhead* and *Atlas Shrugged,* and although I enjoyed reading the literature, I didn't understand the elitism and the secrecy of the group that Brooke had joined. I asked her if I could pose for the artists too. She told me that I wasn't good-looking enough.

I started taking birth control pills, which were prescribed to me by a general practitioner, but they were making me gain weight. I went back to the doctor explaining the problem (I couldn't possibly gain weight and not fit into my go-go costume). Instead of prescribing another kind of birth control pill, the doctor, in all his wisdom, gave me a prescription for what in essence was amphetamine, or "speed" as we called it on the street. The theory was that the medication would speed up my metabolism, I would lose my appetite, and hence lose weight. The theory worked, but added an addiction to the mix. My days felt like I was on fast-forward laced with feelings of ecstasy. The sensation was so euphoric that I shared the pills with Brooke. It wasn't long before the two of us would not leave the apartment without them.

Was it not that long ago that my father gave my mother the Elixir, the "purple heart" amphetamine? The connection never entered my mind then. I was too busy surviving and keeping my personal dreams and hopes alive to think of my parents at home. It was too painful to know that I could not help them and that they could not help me. For me, this period of time in New York City was a tableau of shadowy clubs, alleys, people gathered in dimly lit rooms, others shooting up drugs in bathrooms, crowds in apartments running like cockroaches when the lights came up and the sirens sounded. I was dancing on tabletops and bars to the sound of Motown, jazz, rhythm and blues, my soundtrack to this precarious time. What was that white light in the darkness that kept me from falling into the abyss?

The owners of the all-Italian bar in Paterson, New Jersey, the armpit of the East Coast, kept requesting me to return and dance in their club. They were nice people and made sure I had safe rides home. I agreed. I danced at the club three weekends in a row when I met Vittorio, a thin, dark Italian young man with eyes and a mouth like a Botticelli god. He spoke English with a strong Italian accent, which added to his charm, and when he asked me to go to Atlantic City with him for the weekend after my dancing gig, I went.

I woke up to a beautiful light-colored room, the white curtains billowing in the ocean breeze and sunlight streaming in the windows. Outside the window, I could hear the ocean waves lapping onto the warm sandy beach. I lay on the bed in the light of the moment. Vittorio, my handsome, dark Italian, picked me up off the bed and carried me onto the veranda and there I stood and stared into another world. I was exhausted.

My mother was in her late teens and twenties when she pursued men to fill the emptiness in her heart after her mother's untimely death. The boyfriends, the first husband, the Baron, and later her sons all played the roles of hopeful saviors, men who would save her from her realities: a divorcee, a single parent, and an overworked and stressed-out mother. I, too searched for love and for someone who would whisk me off into another world and take care of me.

With Vittorio, I felt secure and safe and so I wrapped his life around mine and in a flash, I let my own visions, dreams and hopes disappear. I moved from my apartment in the city to a tiny pink colored room with pink curtains in a suburban house in East Paterson. Pam, the owner, shared the house with Mary, a beautiful tall blond in the other upstairs room across the hall; Mary and I shared the bathroom. Every morning, it took Mary an hour in the bathroom to put on her makeup and to tease and spray her hair. I tried to fit into this suburban scene in the room with the pink curtains, but the curtains only masked the grey, dull life around me. I had no job, no aspirations, no dreams. I stopped taking birth control pills and lost my appetite–my body signaling depression. I stopped eating except for mussels marinara with Italian bread in a Clinton, New Jersey bar where Vittorio would take me to try and fatten me up. It was not enough. My body became dangerously thin and wasted. Vittorio would bring me to his Italian home on Sundays where I picked at the homemade pasta with meatballs that his mother made. She would scream, *"Che cosa! Mangia, Mangia!"* But I just couldn't. I was not hungry.

Determined to conform to a more stable life in Paterson, I quit go-go dancing, stopped all my lessons in New York, bought a light blue Fiat Spider convertible and looked for a straight job. The job as New Jersey Bell telephone operator lasted until lunchtime, when I clocked out for lunch and never went back. I finally landed a job as a teller in the Paterson National Bank in the middle of the city. I remember the client files would say "Negro" if the client was black. I hated the job. One day, I was so bored that I "accidentally" pushed the burglar alarm with my knee. In minutes, there were twenty handsome policemen investigating where my knee accidentally touched the alarm. "Happens all the time," they said. I was off the hook.

I got seriously ill with the flu and when Pam called my parents, they came to visit me in my pink room. It was the first time that I had seen them since I left home. I was overjoyed to see them. They brought homemade Russian *borscht* and a hot plate so that I could at least boil some water for tea in the morning. They didn't stay too long and when they left, I was overcome with unbearable loneliness and cried uncontrollably for what seemed like hours. The hot *borscht* brought me back to life and I slowly regained my health.

My bank career ended as quickly as it began. Women were tellers and men sat behind huge mahogany desks and felt important attending to their banking responsibilities. Fridays were the long days when we worked all day, took a break for dinner and came back to work until nine p.m. Sixty-year-old Charlie Vreeland, the bank manager with the biggest desk, was known to put away a few drinks during dinner and to come to work in the evening wigged out on booze. Every Friday night, Charlie would walk behind all the tellers and pinch their behinds as they sat and did business with the clientele. One Friday night when Charlie touched my behind, I screamed for all to hear, "Take your hands off me, Charlie, and go to hell!"

I lost my job instantly. On Monday morning, I marched into the bank's main offices and told the personnel office that if they did not give me a good job recommendation, I would go to the newspapers and expose Charlie Vreeland's "pinching nonsense" to the rest of the world. Within days, I received an excellent recommendation in the mail for a job I would never perform again.

I tried very hard to fit into Vittorio's Italian family, where everyone had high hopes that he would marry the skinny little Russian girl. I had another illegal abortion, this time paid by Vittorio, and under different circumstances. A kind of vacuum cleaner sucked out my insides and after some excruciating pain, I miscarried into the toilet. It wasn't long after the abortion that Vittorio, my handsome god, hit me in the face for something that I had said. I packed up my little pink room, threw my belongings into the Fiat and fled East Paterson, back to 99th street, Manhattan, and Brooke.

For weeks, Vittorio begged me to return. Early Christmas morning, in a moment of weakness and excruciating loneliness, I found myself sitting with the bums at the 42nd street Port Authority Bus Station, waiting for a bus bound for New Jersey. (My beautiful light blue Fiat died when it was broken into in Manhattan, and the thieves slashed the convertible roof to bits.) Vittorio picked me up at the bus station in Paterson in a brand new red convertible XKE Jaguar, gave me the keys and told me it was mine if I stayed. I stayed with him the weekend and on an uncharacteristic balmy Sunday night in December, we drove through the muggy night in the red XKE Jag to Manhattan to bring my suitcase back to Paterson. The top was down and I stared straight up to where I knew there once were stars. When we got to my door on 99th Street, I thanked Vittorio for the car, returned the car keys, kissed him on his Botticelli mouth, and never looked back.

Mourka's great-grandfather, Baron Egor Federovich Meyendorff (1794-1879),
Adjutant General to Czar Alexander II

Mourka's grandfather, Baron Bogdan Meyendorff,
Adjutant General to Czar Nicholas II

Baron Bogdan Meyendorff, Mourka's grandfather (third from left) walking with the German Kaiser, (center) and Czar Nicholas II (far right)

*Czar Nicholas II (right) sending Mourka's grandfather, Baron Bogdan
Meyendorff to the Russo-Japanese War*

Mourka's grandfather, Baron Bogdan Meyendorff and grandmother, Baroness Elena Meyendorff (nee Countess Shuvalova) having breakfast in Kumna, the Meyendorff summer estate in Estonia.

*The Ulk grandparents, Jaan and Margarethe with Mourka's mother,
Rita and her brother, Eugene in Russia*

*Mourka's father, George and his twin sister, Alexandra (Aunt Sandra)
as children in St. Petersburg, Russia*

*Kurt Ulk, first husband of Mourka's mother and their two sons, Kurt and George,
Mourka's half-brothers in Tallinn, Estonia*

Mourka's father as a young man in Estonia

Mourka's mother as a student in Estonia

*The masquerade ball in Tallinn, Estonia where Mourka's mother
and father met in 1939*

Baron George Meyendorff's passport to pass through Nazi Germany in Dec. 1942

Front cover of the Nazi passport

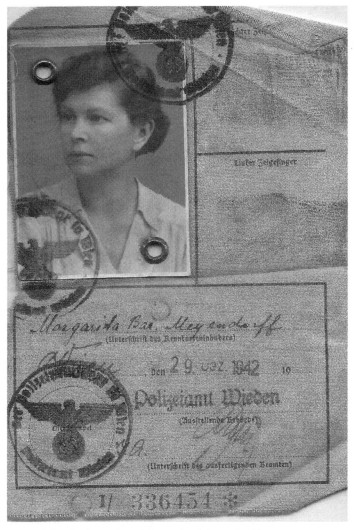

*Mourka's mother, Margarita Meyendorff's passport
to enter Nazi Germany in Dec. 1942*

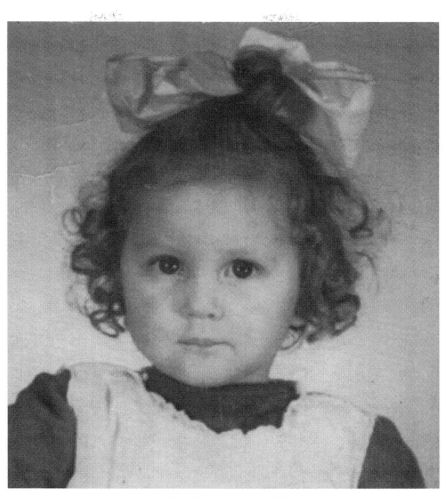

Mourka at 3-years-old

Mourka in the Displaced Persons camp in Germany, 1948

Mourka, her mother and two brothers leaving Germany in Dec. 1949
with Displaced Persons tags fastened to their lapels.

En route to the Clarkstown Country Club Nyack, NY, December 1949, a look-out on Route 9W (from left to right) Mourka, Aunt Sandra, George, Aunt Alina holding her son Andrei, Kurt and Rita

Mourka's father and mother in front of the renovated elephant stall apartments at the Clarkstown Country Club, Nyack, NY

Mourka's debut in "The Three Sisters", Nyack, NY

Mourka (tallest) as a "snowflake" in Nyack, NY in the play "Snegurechka"

Mourka as the "tsarevich" (left) in the play "Baba Yaga"

Mourka and her two brothers, George (left) and Kurt (right),
Brookside Ave in Nyack, NY

Mourka and her friends, Brookside Ave, Nyack, NY

Mourka at 8 years old in Nyack, NY　　*Mourka's mother in Nyack, NY*

Mourka wins first prize at the Russian aristocratic masquerade ball
at the Plaza Hotel, NYC

Mourka's father, the Baron and Jessie,
Mourka's daughter in New Paltz in 1981

Mourka's two children, Jessie, age 7 and Jarett, age 3, Samsonville, NY

Miklos and Mourka vacationing in the Dominican Republic in 2005

Chapter Twenty Two

Out of Town

DECEMBER, 1969. SITTING IN THE back of the plane en route to Wilmingtom, North Carolina, smoking Marlboros and watching city lights twinkle on the ground below, I wasn't sure who was flying higher, me or the plane. I was flying "out of town" and being paid as a professional actress on a four-month dinner theatre tour in the South: Wilmington and Charlotte, North Carolina; Greenville, South Carolina; and Atlanta, Georgia.

When I received the phone call that I'd landed a part in a play, my legs buckled. My mind had raced as I said *yes* to opportunities that until then were only fantasies.

Yes, the weekly salary would be fine. *Yes*, I could rehearse eight hours a day. *Yes*, I could be fitted for costumes. *Yes*, I could be away from New York City for four months. *Yes*, I could get on a plane for the first time in my life. *Yes*, I could come in to sign the contract. I could do anything, I thought.

I was twenty-two years old.

My contract was for the character role of Estelle Novick in the romantic comedy play *Tunnel of Love,* a 1950s Broadway hit. In 1958, the play was made into a film directed by Gene Kelly and starring Doris Day, who received a nomination for a Golden Globe Award. The play follows a married suburban couple who are unable to conceive a child and who turn to an adoption agency. The plot thickens when the adoption agency representative (Estelle) becomes pregnant and the husband of the couple is suspected of sleeping with her. After a few minor shifts and curves in the plot, the play ends on a happy note.

It didn't matter to me how silly the play was–I was going out of town and getting paid as an actress. With only Mondays off, performing *Tunnel of Love* six days a week for four months was a challenge, but having the character role allowed me to keep the energy and the laughs going. Every night I had the audience in stitches as I made my entrance looking very pregnant in the second act, channeling Barbra Streisand's pregnant entrance in *Funny Girl*.

I had one major setback in the four months of touring when I fell off a horse in Greenville, South Carolina (our third stop on the tour) when I was pretending to be a jockey in a steeplechase race. The horse successfully jumped a five-foot fence, but I did not, and I fell backward on my back. I could hardly walk, but with adrenalin and heavy painkillers, I was still able to perform. This time the pregnant lady had a cane.

I met Caleb Jolly at the Pineville Dinner Theatre in Charlotte, North Carolina, our second city on the tour. Jolly, as he was called, was the director and was involved in all aspects of the dinner theatre, from supervising the food in the kitchen and managing the restaurant to nightly introducing every show. Pineville was his theatre and he was proud of it. Jolly was very good-looking. He had slicked-back blond hair, a handsome chiseled tan face, a taut abdomen, and he spoke with a breathy cigarette-laced Southern twang. He was always impeccably dressed in a light-colored suit, complete with shiny cowboy boots. Jolly was married and was twenty-seven years older than me. Within a week at Pineville, I felt Jolly's interest and attention directed towards me. He flirted and flattered me with gifts and flowers; told me that I had a special charisma on stage and that he loved how I made the audience laugh. He whipped up special desserts for me, which I shared with my actor colleagues. They were thrilled with the attention I was getting from Jolly and were enjoying the trickle-down benefits.

It wasn't until my last week at the Pineville Dinner Theatre that I succumbed to his invitation to take me out on a dinner date. The flattery was beginning to be difficult to resist. I don't remember the fancy restaurant, but I do remember Jolly asking me to wear something nice. I ended up wearing my costume from the show–the only dress I had which still made me feel lovely. We were seated outside on a deck illuminated by blinking fairy lights. The maitre d' poured the expensive red wine meticulously into large goblets as I ordered the shrimp cocktail appetizer. (For me, the appetizer section on a menu had always been something to gloss over, but Jolly insisted.) The appetizer came with the largest shrimps I had ever seen, draped over a beautiful crystal glass with cocktail sauce in the center. I could have been happy just eating that. Steak was not something that my family could ever afford, and I never heard of Chateaubriand until Jolly ordered it for me to accompany the large lobster tails served with lemon butter. Chocolate mousse, also a new revelation, topped off the evening dinner date. Giddy with fine wine and rich food, I walked out of the restaurant knowing that I was going to open a door to a new adventure.

There were many more shrimp cocktails and Chateaubriands that followed as Jolly continued to court me, taking time out when he could from his beloved Pineville Dinner Theatre and driving to Greenville, South Carolina and then to Atlanta, Georgia to visit me. I would wait for him to appear in his 1969 canary yellow Thunderbird. He would let me drive and we would race through the southern countryside and throw our cares to the wind. More than once, Jolly would take me to a fashionable clothing store and say, "Pick out anything you want." And I did. I landed my "Sugar Daddy" and Jolly landed me. The shoe fit and I became his princess.

I wrote letters home to my parents to let them know I was well. Once, I wrote only to my mother–I had a longing to connect with her and her alone. I told her in the letter how happy I was working as an actress; that I was fulfilling my dream; that I was being take care of. I wanted her to be happy for me. She wrote back in Russian, "Don't write only to me. You know how jealous your father gets." I wrote home less often.

The call from Arkady came unexpectedly while I was still at the Tally-Ho Theatre in Atlanta. He was in town on business, saw my name in the newspaper and decided to call me. There are not too many "Mourka" names, especially not in Atlanta. I put the phone down and my mind raced backwards to when I was twelve years old and madly in love with Arkady, who was nineteen. Arkady was the son of Uncle Vladimir and Aunt Irina Derwies, friends of my parents and avid bridge players. As young men, Uncle Vladimir and my father had served the Czar's army as White Russian army cadets and attended the Academy of the White Russian Cadet Corps, across the street from my father's house in St. Petersburg, Russia.

The Derwieses made their escape from Russia to the west by way of Poland, then France, and finally immigrated to the United States in the 1950s. As a child, I heard many escape stories, but Aunt Irina's story stayed with me for years. During the chaos of World War II, the Derwieses were on a speeding train headed for the Polish border with a raging forest fire on both sides, most likely started by air raid bombs. The heat, the smoke, and the noise of the fire was terrifying as they lay on the floor trying to breathe, praying that they would not be bombed or swallowed up by the fire. They made it to Poland, on their last gasp.

Arkady was born in Paris and when the Derwies immigrated to the United States, Uncle Vladimir, who was a well-known opera singer in Paris, wrote a beloved Russian song for Arkady, called "Oranges." I remember the first line: "Fly, fly, toy airplane and bring my little son to a land where there are no wars, and where oranges grow freely in groves."

Arkady had grown up in Astoria, Queens. He was charming, intelligent and extremely attractive, and at twelve, I was hungry for attention–any kind of attention. We saw each other when our parents would get together for bridge games or family gatherings. He would tease me, pester me, physically bat me around for fun, and always beat me in Canasta. I was like his pesky little sister. Once, at one of our infamous White Russian cadet parties in Carmel, New York, he even hung me from a rock during a walk in the forest. In between the playful cruelties, there were some casual hugs and kisses and I hung onto every one of them. I was smitten.

Arkady enlisted into the U.S. Army and I wrote letters. Occasionally he wrote back, but most often he didn't. I listened to the Shirelles' great Motown hit "Soldier Boy" over and over and over again. I kept a photograph of Arkady in my wallet. I considered him to be my first love and fantasized that someday we would be together.

Arkady got married and he and his wife had two little girls. I was heartbroken. For years, whenever Arkady's name came up, I felt a twinge in the pit of my stomach. Eventually, the dreams faded and I more or less forgot him.

And then, ten years later, the phone call from Arkady. In Atlanta, Georgia? I invited him to the show and agreed to have dinner afterwards. I could hardly concentrate on what I was doing on stage. I didn't know what to expect.

A balding middle-aged man with a slight bulge at his waist was walking towards me, arms outstretched in the lobby of the theatre. In a flash, my adolescent dreams vanished and I was sitting across a table in a hotel restaurant with a man I didn't recognize. Arkady plied me with champagne and I listened as he told me how unhappy he was in his marriage and how generally disappointed he was with his life. He was bitter and angry and I couldn't help think that he should have waited for me. Perhaps, we could have made a better go of it together.

The evening became stranger as he drank more alcohol and after the meal, he asked me to accompany him upstairs to his hotel room. He said he had something to show me. I realized quickly that he had lured me upstairs to have sex. I asked him please to call me a taxi or to take me home. I wasn't going to stay. He became angry and didn't understand why I was leaving. Under the circumstances, I didn't feel like explaining. Arkady took me back to the theatre, but before I got out of the car, I saw a strange look on his face. He took my hand and twisted my thumb backwards. I cried out in pain and he said, "This is so you never forget." And I never did. The mean young man who occasionally hurt me and who I was in love with had reappeared.

One early morning in April of 1970, I finished my final *Tunnel of Love* performance in Atlanta and was planning to return to New York City to regroup when I received a frantic call from Jolly in Charlotte, North Carolina. The two-character comedy play *The Owl and the Pussycat* was opening up that night at the Pineville Dinner Theatre and the female lead in the show was sick with the flu. Would I please get a script from someone in Atlanta, board a plane for Charlotte immediately and do the show that night? Of course I would.

Jolly was waiting for me at the airport and took me to the theatre where I had barely enough time to go through the blocking of the show with my lead, Reid Kasper, an actor I had never met. I was fitted for costumes, complete with a blond wig that was too big; someone did my makeup and it was time to step onstage and deliver the performance. Jolly announced the show as usual and explained the cast change in the program. I didn't have time to be nervous. There was nothing to lose, so I let it rip!

The performance was brimming with spontaneity and improvisation. Thanks to Reid's professionalism and his ability to stay in his Felix "owl" character, I was able to sail in the part of Doris, the "pussycat." Several times the script flew out of my hands or I lost my place and without breaking character we were able to pick up where we left off. Reid and I had a blast. The audience loved every minute of it and gave us a standing ovation. The review that came out the next morning read, "Script In Hand, She Saved and Stole the Show."

The Owl and the Pussycat was first staged on Broadway in 1964 and starred Alan Alda as the owl and the black actress/singer Diana Sands as the pussycat. The film, which came out in 1970, starred George Segal and Barbra Streisand, added several other characters and omitted the interracial quality of the play. The delightful comedy about two unlikely people coming together was a huge box office hit both on Broadway and in movie theatres. When I told my parents that I was in the stage production of the *Owl and the Pussycat*, they promptly went to see the movie. Later, my father wrote a letter to me and was curious about how I did the nude bathtub scene on stage.

As far as Jolly was concerned, I could do no wrong after I took the Pineville Dinner Theatre by storm. I ended up doing the entire month run of *The Owl and the Pussycat*. When the run was over, Jolly told me that he would produce any play of my choosing and I picked the part of Gittel in *Two for the Seesaw*, a sensitive two-character Broadway play which opened in 1962 and starred Henry Fonda and Anne Bancroft. A very successful film followed, starring Shirley MacLaine and Robert Mitchum. Reid Kasper and I were already in rehearsal for *Two for the Seesaw* when contractual obligations intervened, and the administration reminded Jolly that his theatre was under contract to receive plays produced only in New York. There was only one thing to be done: to start our own theatre.

The Showboat Dinner Theatre in Greensboro, North Carolina was looking for a manager, and overnight Jolly and I packed up and left Charlotte for new horizons. Reid Kasper had another theatre commitment in New York and our production of *Two for the Seesaw* had to be scrapped. Unfortunately, I never had another opportunity to perform Gittel. Instead, I became a producer, director, set and lighting designer, casting agent, office manager, and assisted Jolly in whatever else it took to run a theatre, from sweeping the stage to working the box office.

Every month, we cranked out a new play, and my theatrical skills soared above and beyond my own expectations. I flew to Jacksonville, Florida to the Alhambra Theatre to watch John Carradine as Jeeter Lester in a production of *Tobacco Road,* which I wanted to produce and direct at the Showboat. Carradine and I sat in a pub after his show and he was very happy to share his expertise into the wee hours of the morning.

I flew back to Greensboro, and within a month we had a fine production of *Tobacco Road.* I performed in several more plays, including Ellen in *LUV* and Miss Paddy in *The Curious Savage.* The newspapers and television got wind of my Russian aristocratic background and there was a series of newspaper articles about my history; Eyewitness News filmed an interview with me in my dressing room at the Showboat. I loved all the attention. I put my "Baroness" card to good use and became a "star" in North Carolina.

Jolly and I had a strange and wonderful relationship. He was my lover, my father, someone with whom I felt safe. I was probably the most exciting person to come into his life in a long while, and he was going to ride this adventure as long as possible. We needed each other. He needed my help and talent to set up theatres and I needed him to continue my theatrical work. It worked, sort of. . . He would get jealous when I made friends with fellow actors who were my age, and would try to isolate me by threatening to leave and take everything with him. This would send me spiraling into a depression and I would cry inconsolably for hours. I couldn't focus on the tasks at hand.

Jolly and I lived together in a trailer next to the theatre and I noticed that he was medicating himself daily. One day he gave me a tiny little pill and said, "Here, this will make you feel better." And it did–that lovely ecstatic feeling of amphetamine again. I was hooked. I plunged deeper into Jolly's isolated theatre world, fortified with pills and my acting and directing abilities. I asked him no questions. I was too afraid the bubble would burst.

Brooke, my roommate in New York City, who could no longer hold onto our apartment alone, came to visit me in Greensboro, on the pretext of wanting to take some time to travel. She stayed about three days and we caught up with each other's lives. One evening when Jolly and I were both working in the theatre, Brooke found our stash of "black beauties" (amphetamines) in the bathroom cabinet, took out all the powder from the capsules, put the plastic capsules together and split without even a good-bye. I never saw her again.

I don't really know why we left the Showboat Dinner Theatre in Greensboro in January of 1971, having operated it successfully for about six months, but one brisk morning, Jolly and I were heading for the VIP Dinner Theatre in Huntsville, Alabama in his beautiful yellow Ford Thunderbird. I had my suspicions. Jolly's wife Agnes was probably putting pressure on him to come home, accusing him of having a mid-life crisis. I also sensed that Jolly's finances were not what he presented them to be, and that bank creditors were breathing down his neck to pay back debts. I didn't ask questions and he offered little information. Jolly went and I followed.

Huntsville, Alabama was the home of the National Aeronautics Space Administration (NASA). Marshall Space Flight Center (MSFC) was NASA's leading facility for developing rocket propulsion systems and technologies. During the 1960s and 70s, its primary focus was the Apollo program: man's first visit to the Moon. MSFC also had a major role in developing Skylab, the United States' first space station. Another NASA facility, Huntsville Operations Support Center (HOSC), monitored rocket launches from Cape Canaveral.

The VIP Dinner Theatre in Huntsville was up for sale when Jolly heard about it. I don't think he wanted to buy it; he didn't have the money, but somehow he managed a deal to operate the theatre until a buyer came along. Jolly knew he had a captive audience with NASA's employees–there was no other theatre in town–and in fact, we packed the house nightly with one show after another. Reid Kasper flew down to Huntsville from New York in February and he and I again wowed the audience with the *Owl and the Pussycat*, VIP's first show and a shoe-in to attract an audience to our new theatre. The two-character musical *I Do, I Do*, written by Tom Jones, followed. The show spans fifty years, from 1895 to 1945, and focuses on the ups and downs experienced by Agnes and Michael

Snow throughout their marriage. The audience loved seeing both actors applying makeup on stage and aging fifty years in front of them. I got married every night for a month in a beautiful white wedding dress, and even found a Russian voice coach in Huntsville to help me belt out the famous *I Do, I Do* show stopper, "Flaming Agnes." (Good thing we didn't do this in North Carolina. Jolly's wife Agnes would have killed me).

I directed *Tobacco Road* successfully again with a new cast. We couldn't find an actress to play the role of eighty-year-old Ada, Jeeter's wife, so I took the role. It was a stretch, but the reviewers liked it.

By May, we were on the road again, heading for Kansas City, Kansas to stay with Jolly's sister. This time I knew we were on the run. There were too many strange phone calls and knocks on our door from men asking questions. Jolly tried to shield me from his wife's wrath and his financial mess, but it was getting harder and harder. The bubble was still intact with our endless supply of tiny little pills and his Ford Thunderbird escape-mobile, but in reality, Jolly was broke.

"I know you," my customer at the Kansas City airport restaurant announced as I brought him his lunch.

"I doubt it," I said. "I don't know anyone in Kansas City." I was worried he was with the police. I looked over to the kitchen counter where Jolly was working as the airport restaurant chef.

"Yes, I know you," the man repeated. "I saw you in a show in Charlotte, North Carolina. The one called *The Owl and the Pussycat*."

"Oh, yes! That was me, Mourka, playing the pussycat. Pineville Dinner Theatre."

"Great show," the man said as he placed a large tip on the table. I watched him leave and promised myself that I would be out of Kansas City within the week. Straight to the north was a great theatre town, Minneapolis, Minnesota, and that was where I wanted to go.

Years later, I read this handwritten, European-style cursive entry in Mama's journal:

<u>May 9, 1971</u> - Liulik[1] has a fever. His temperature is going up. It is three in the morning. He woke up because he clearly heard Mourka's voice in a dream. And we don't even know where she is. Lord, please return our child to us. Save her, protect her and have mercy on her.

So many years later I realized. . . they both loved me.

....

1   My father's nickname

Chapter Twenty Three

Minneapolis

JOLLY AND I LEFT KANSAS City, Kansas together and headed north on Interstate 35 to Minneapolis, Minnesota. This time the move was on my terms, and it was my friends that we were going to stay with until we got settled. Lidia and her brother Vasya lived in Minneapolis along with their parents, the Prince and Princess Shikhov, the same family that got ousted from Nyack for Lidia's scandalous behavior. Jolly and I had very little money and no theatre contacts in Minneapolis, but I didn't care. I was out of Kansas City, out of his sister's house and out of the waitress job at the airport.

We arrived late at Lidia's disheveled one-bedroom apartment, which she shared with her six- year-old son, Little William. I noticed right away that Lidia was high on some sort of drug and that she wasn't very enthusiastic about our arrival. She spoke rapidly, and within minutes we learned that all was not well with her relationship with her husband Big William; that he was physically and emotionally abusive to her and that she was thinking of leaving Minneapolis with her son. It wasn't long before things got from bad to worse for Lidia. Hooked on painkillers and alcohol, she lost custody of Little William and had to move back in with her parents. One day, she just disappeared. Vasya was faring a lot better with a wife, a child, and an excellent architectural job, having gotten an engineering degree at the University of Minnesota. It was not easy for Vasya to keep his sense of humor with Lidia's troubles and his parents, the Prince and the Princess Shikhov, getting drunk on vodka every night.

Within days of our arrival, Jolly and I found jobs and an apartment. Our small one-bedroom apartment was on the west side of Minneapolis and the restaurant where Jolly worked as a chef and I as a waitress was just down the street. We had the breakfast shift.

It was January 1972, three months after our arrival, when I saw the ad in the *Minneapolis Star and Tribune*: The innovative Cricket Theatre in northeast Minneapolis was looking for torch singers for a play called *The Pornographic Sampler*. Paid position. I didn't even know what a torch singer was, but I hadn't been inside a theatre for nearly six months and I was feeling the withdrawal pains. A crowd of performers showed up and everyone sang and danced for the director. After the audition, I still didn't know what a torch singer was.

The next day, I got the callback and was surprised to find myself alone with the director and the playwright at the theatre. There was a change. The torch singers were scrapped and the director wanted me, just me, to play the part of a stripper. Was this all premeditated?

Would I mind stripping in front of an audience? "Not all the way, but down to skimpy bra and panties?" the director asked.

Within a week, I got a professional stripping lesson from a well-known black New York City stripper who gave me a beautiful sequined, layered outfit, complete with long black silk gloves that came up to my elbow, which I would slowly take off to sexy, jazzy music. She prepared me well.

The Pornographic Sampler was an original play within a play by Fred Gaines that took on tones of Pirandello's *Six Characters in Search of an Author*, and was set in a garish burlesque house, with the stripper (with a strong Russian accent) setting up the audience for impending titillation. The play unfolded into a seedy "This is Your Life" theme when an elderly man comes to see the performers act out his past. In the end, the man finds himself in the burlesque house watching the striptease finale.

Two weeks before the opening of the show, I awoke with enormous pain on the lower left side of my abdomen. Jolly rushed me to the General Hospital in the middle of the city where, within hours, I had an emergency operation for a removal of an ovarian cyst as big as an orange. When I regained consciousness from the operation, my entire abdomen was bandaged. When I was able to sit up, I lifted the bandage and cried out in astonishment. I had a raw, stitched scar from my navel straight down to my pubic bone. The surgeons took out the ovarian cyst on my left side and "while they were in the area" with my insides exposed, they took out my appendix on my right side. They cut my stomach muscles in half to get to a healthy appendix, and by the way, how was I going to dance and strip at the Cricket in a week and a half?

I gave my name as Mrs. Caleb Jolly, a person who did not exist in Minneapolis, and never paid a penny for that operation, half of which I didn't need. With great trepidation, soreness, gobs of makeup for the scar and lots of painkillers, I managed to dance and strip in front of full houses on the opening weekend of the show. After one show, I did overhear an audience member say, "Did you see that huge scar on the stripper lady?"

One week into the run of *The Pornographic Sampler* on a frigid January Minnesota night, when I had gotten a ride home, I opened the door to the apartment and felt a strange emptiness. I ran through the apartment, screaming, opening empty closet doors and pulling out empty drawers. I ran outside. The car's parking space–empty.

"You S.O.B.! No money, no car, not even a goddamn note!"

For several days I waited for Jolly to come home. I slept by the telephone and would wake at every sound, hoping for a familiar footstep. Jolly never returned and I never heard from him again. I had no contact information for him–an era before cell phones. A frightening but familiar feeling formed at the pit of my stomach, gnawing at my insides: alone again. A stranger in a strange place. *Where do I go? What do I do?*

I quit the restaurant job and had Vasya take me and my meager possessions to his parents' large Victorian house in South Minneapolis, a place I could stay for free until I could get my bearings. I loved the Prince and the Princess Shikhov, Uncle Grigori and Aunt Ksenia, who, when steeped in their alcoholic haze, could poke fun at their misfortunes. We would sit around the table, eat, drink vodka and reminisce about the people we knew in Nyack. We shared a lot of laughs. They were friends of my parents and were feeding me delicious *borscht* and beet salad, my favorites. I wished they were my parents–somehow they didn't seem as depressing as my parents. I wanted to stay there forever and be taken care of. I ended up staying with them for almost two weeks while I looked for work, more acting jobs, and another place to stay. At night, I was still performing in *The Pornographic Sampler*.

One night, I was asleep in Lidia's old room, in her little twin bed, when I heard the door squeak open. I saw a figure in a bathrobe coming towards my bed. The figure crossed the room, climbed on top of me, and opened his bathrobe, his erect penis next to my face. The Prince, drunk, reeking of alcohol and cigarette smoke, held me down with one hand and with the other was trying to put his penis into my mouth. I screamed and pushed him as hard as I could away from me. He fell on the floor, babbling and shushing me from screaming. I screamed even louder, "Убирайся от сюда, свинья какая!" ("Get out of here, you pig!")

I didn't stop screaming until he picked himself up from the floor and left, murmuring something about me not telling anyone about this incident. I got up, dressed–poised for another possible attack–packed my suitcase, and sobbed as I waited for dawn. How could Uncle Grigori do this to me? My childhood naïveté didn't believe that Russians did such things. The ultimate betrayal.

As soon as it began to get light outside, I quietly walked down the steps, wanting to escape unnoticed. To my surprise, the Princess Ksenia was up, sitting at the table in the kitchen and holding a gun in her hand. She aimed it at me and said in Russian, "I don't know who to shoot first, you or him."

Scared out of my mind, I turned and ran out the door and didn't stop running until the house was so far behind me that I no longer could see it if I turned around.

The cool fresh air outside was a relief as I found myself wandering in Minneapolis, homeless and near penniless, not knowing where I would lay my head that night. I put one foot in front of the other, my survival instinct not allowing me to succumb to the fear and anxiety of being alone. I shuddered at the thought that Lidia, when she was younger, must also have been sexually abused by her father. I shoved the incident with the Prince deep into the far corners of my mind, not to be revisited for another forty years.

I headed for Dinkytown, USA, a district of Minneapolis occupied by various small businesses, restaurants, bars, and apartment buildings that mostly housed

University of Minnesota students. Al's Breakfast, the smallest restaurant in the city with six stools at the counter, was located here, and I remembered going there for breakfast with Jolly. Perhaps I could find work and a place to stay among the many poor, transient students.

I got lucky. After perusing several public offices for rental notices, I found a note announcing availability of rooms at a local sorority. My guardian angels were working overtime again and I was able to move into a small furnished room at the sorority, with a promise to pay for the room within the month. To this day, I don't know if the sorority elders knew or cared to know if I was a student or not. Nobody checked. I knew I had a temporary place to stay and was no longer homeless. I remember falling asleep in my bed that night feeling safe, surrounded by girls younger than myself and protected by my new sorority family.

Within days, I found a job as a breakfast-lunch counter girl at the very popular Gray's Drugstore in the center of Dinkytown. Rumor had it that several years before, Bob Dylan had lived in the apartment upstairs from Gray's while attending the university. I fit right into Dinkytown's student scene and with the locals who became my customers at Gray's. I enjoyed pouring coffee and serving breakfast and lunch and got a reputation as the little Russian girl who always smiled. I was also well liked by my sorority girls at my university digs because they thought I was a "cool" artist type. I would find reviews and notices about *The Pornographic Sampler* taped to my door when I returned from the nightly performances. Things were going well but I couldn't help feeling that I was somehow floating on air; that there was no sound foundation to my life; that at any moment the flimsy arrangement I had made, could be whisked out from underneath me.

It was during the last week of the *Sampler's* run that I got to know Mari Rovang. Mari was the female lead and exposed one of her breasts–a first for Minneapolis. In spite of mixed reviews because of the partial nudity, the play attracted large audiences. The cast all knew one another and were friends, but because I had entered very late in the rehearsal process, I was not readily accepted, nor did I make any huge advances to make friends. Mari noticed me laying out solitaire and reading fortunes to cast members with playing cards that I always carried.

"Who is that blonde stripping onstage and telling fortunes backstage?" Mari mistrusted me and we spoke only in passing.

One evening as the cast gathered for the performance, I noticed that Mari was upset and was searching for something.

"What's wrong?" I asked.

"I forgot to wear underwear and I'm wearing this flimsy see-through dress. The audience is going to see everything!" Mari explained.

"No problem, I have an extra pair," I told her.

"What are you doing with an extra pair of underwear?" she asked suspiciously.

"What are you doing without any?" I asked.

We laughed hysterically at our inside joke, and after the show, went out for drinks. We couldn't get enough of each other that night, sharing stories and past experiences, ending the evening with a tearful, soulful rendition of "The First Time Ever I Saw Your Face," lip-syncing with Roberta Flack and wishing we had men deserving of the lyrics.

Mari, of Norwegian heritage, was beautiful: thin with long silky reddish-brown hair down to her waist, a sensual mouth that opened wide when she laughed, and a personality which pulled me into her world. Mari asked me where I lived and I told her of my temporary situation at the sorority. Without skipping a beat, she invited me to stay with her in a house she shared with two other women. This began our forty-year-old friendship, which continues today.

It wasn't long before I moved into the house in South Minneapolis with Mari, Lois, and Lona, the two other women. Lois was an attractive blonde gay woman who always wore jeans and cowboy boots, and Lona, also beautiful with long curly hair, was almost entirely bedridden in her large, sunny room, battling lymphoma combined with Hodgkin's disease. She died a year later in 1973. Mari and Lois had their own rooms and I was given a corner in the living room by the fireplace. No matter. I felt so fortunate to be in this home and in the company of three wonderful women who took me in.

Mari played the guitar and sang. She wrote poetry and painted and drew beautiful sketches in her journals. I was in awe of her talents and glad for our friendship. Mari introduced me to the music of Joni Mitchell, Cat Stevens, and Bob Dylan, to name a few of the folk artists who were rocking the world in the early 1970s. I was experiencing a personal renaissance of music, art, poetry, and theatre, soaking up this new world like a sponge. There were always friends stopping by at the house, looking in on Lona, to share a bit of conversation and a drink or two. None of us had much money but we ate well, drank cheap wine, and often stayed up philosophizing through candlelit nights. If we had a little extra money we would treat ourselves to *spaetzle* and a beer at the Black Forest German restaurant, or have a beer or two at Caesar's Bar, the 400 Bar, or the Viking on the West Bank, the hippie/artsy section of Minneapolis.

Mari and I both auditioned for a production of Brendan Behan's play *Borstal Boy*, adapted from his autobiographical novel. Its title comes from the Borstal, a British juvenile prison on England's eastern coast where Behan was imprisoned from 1939-1942 for carrying explosives into the United Kingdom on a mission for the I.R.A. Behan's prison dialogue was studded with four-letter words, and the novel was originally banned as obscene in Ireland.

Borstal Boy, the adapted play, was being produced by the Irish Cultural Institute at the Arts and Science Center of St. Paul, the twin city to Minneapolis. Tomas Mac Anna, at that time the artistic director of the Abbey Theatre in Dublin, Ireland and a 1970 nominee for the Tony Award for directing *Borstal Boy* on Broadway, was invited to be the guest director. It was a major production and rumor had it that Princess Grace Kelly would be in the audience opening night.

I was determined to be in this play, and when neither Mari nor I got a callback from the assistant director who was in charge of casting, I went to the second audition anyway.

"Of course I got a callback. Don't you have my name on the list? It should be there! There must be some mistake." I told the people guarding the audition space.

They let me in. I auditioned for the second time and Tomas Mac Anna cast me in the part of Sheila, young Behan's girlfriend, one of the few female roles in an a cast of thirty men. What fun.

I loved working with Tomas Mac Anna. An extraordinary director, he drew the best out of his actors and I was thrilled to be in the cast. I learned much from Mac Anna and gained another level of love and appreciation for the theatre world. My most cherished memory came at the end of the production when I received a beautiful written note from Tomas: "You were the best Sheila. Thank you." I saved this note for years.

After rehearsals, Mac Anna introduced me, Mari (with whom I shared all the entertaining events) and the cast to the many Irish pubs in St. Paul, where we would drink Guinness and listen, hypnotized, to him spinning tales, singing Irish ballads, and reciting hundreds of sorrowful (and humorous) Gaelic poems from memory late into the night:

> *"Thunder and lightnin' it's no lark*
> *When Dublin city is in the dark.*
> *If you have any money go up to the park*
> *And view the zoological gardens."*

The adapted play was no exception to the rough, bawdy, and humorous language used by the prisoners. I remember a short song from the play that the prisoners sang:

> *"Hitler has only got one ball*
> *Goering has two but very small*
> *Himmler has something sim'lar*
> *And poor ole Goebbels has no balls at all."*

The closing night cast party was held at a very fancy country club with Guinness flowing out of barrels, Irish music playing and people dancing jigs through the night. The grand finale was when the cast of thirty men, Mari and I jumped into the swimming pool half naked with only underwear and tee shirts on. It took days to recover.

"Eight Days in May," as the period of anti-Vietnam War protest from May 9-16, 1972 came to be called, witnessed the largest, most violent University of Minnesota demonstrations of the Vietnam War era. On May 10, a crowd of protesters marched through the campus and Dinkytown, following a published schedule of antiwar activities. There were about eight hundred demonstrators in Dinkytown when, in a final effort to break up the crowds, a police helicopter flew overhead spraying tear gas on the assembled protesters. While this was moderately effective in dispersing the crowds, the windy day caused the gas to permeate the University and Dinkytown residences and businesses. The gas was so thick that residents and the University Hospital had to close their windows to keep the wind from blowing tear gas inside the buildings. The University experienced the most turbulent and controversial day of its history.

On the morning of May 10, I was doing my usual waitressing at Gray's. I knew there were anti-Vietnam demonstrations on the University campus, but I had no idea that the unrest would spread to Dinkytown. Soon police and civilians alike were coming into Gray's in droves, asking for food and water. I could hardly keep up with the crowds–old people, young people, students with armbands, police. I didn't discriminate. I gave everyone water.

When my shift was over, I felt more exhausted than ever in my life and I hurried to go home to get away from the chaos. The minute I stepped outside, I heard the helicopter overhead and within seconds I was covered in a cloud of tear gas. I could hardly breathe from the smell and my eyes started to burn and tear. I fell down on the sidewalk and someone picked me up and dragged me away from Gray's corner onto a patch of grass where I sat with dozens of others, nauseous, with my face in my hands, waiting for the wind to take away the awful smell and burning. When I finally reached Mari's house, it was all I could do to rinse my eyes with water to stop the burning. What an injustice after all I'd done for the police that day!

Chapter Twenty Four

The Children's Musical Theatre Wagon

SUMMER, 1973. THE POP-UP CAMPER could sleep six, and so it did–in various couplings. Mari leaped into a berth next to Matthew, the handsome macho guy in our group. She was not going to miss this chance of sleeping with Matthew and marking her territory with him. The rest of us grabbed our sleeping positions. Rob and Laurie, the young male and female ingénues, whose sexual orientation none of us could figure out, climbed into the double bed on the opposite side of Mari and Matthew. Gay, sensitive Fred took the single on the bottom and I grabbed the other single opposite him. All was well. Most of us were just beginning to fall asleep when the camper started moving back and forth. Matthew and Mari were trying very hard to be discreet in their lovemaking, but the camper was small and responded to the slightest thrust. The rest of us were now wide awake but silent, hoping that the rocking would soon subside, along with the muffled moans and whispers. It took about fifteen excruciating minutes but finally the movement came to an end and out of the silence, Fred remarked with perfect timing, "I feel like a knick-knack on a shelf."

The six of us burst into laughter, marking our first night in the camper together and the beginning of our six-week tour with The Children's Musical Theatre Wagon.

Dan Swensen, Mari's theatre instructor from Waldorf College in Forest City, Iowa, was the director, producer, and the mastermind behind The Children's Musical Theatre Wagon. He imported Matthew, Fred, Rob, and Laurie from the Julliard School in New York and hired Mari and me out of Minneapolis to comprise the six-person cast. He then set us up for two weeks in an isolated rustic cabin on Lake Sylvia, just north of Minneapolis, to compose music, write lyrics, write original dialogue and choreograph movement for the well-known children stories *Cinderella* and *Pinocchio* and then take the plays on the road to remote villages in northern Minnesota, South and North Dakota, Iowa, and Wisconsin, where live theatre was rarely seen. Eight weeks for ten dollars a day.

The six of us were busy. With Mari playing the flute, we sang, danced, played music, and wrote. In the cabin, scripts, sheet music, pencils, pens, and various musical instruments were strewn about, but within two weeks as scheduled, we produced original dialogue, sophisticated lyrics and well-composed music for the two plays. Always with my Russian culture lurking somewhere in my consciousness, I used a Russian gypsy tune for the Fairy Godmother song in *Cinderella*.

We had one distracting moment at the cabin when we heard someone screaming for help from the middle of the lake. A rather large woman had fallen off a pontoon, and Mari and Matthew rowed out in our little boat, zigzagging due to their vastly divergent muscular strength, over to the raft to attempt to help her. They struggled to get the drowning woman back up on the raft. She had so many layers of clothing on–skirts, girdles, stockings–that she was unwieldy. Her slightly built, older husband looked on, helpless. Finally after many pulls and shoves, Mari and Matthew heaved the woman's body onto the deck of the raft. The woman lay there like a beached whale, sputtering complaints as Matthew and Mari quietly rowed back to shore, wondering if the husband wasn't a little disappointed at the outcome.

David cast us in the two plays. Rob and Laurie played the prince and princess in *Cinderella,* Fred played the wicked stepmother, Matthew and Mari played the stepsisters, and I played the Fairy Godmother. Rob played the main role in Pinocchio, Fred played Gepetto, Laurie played the good little boy, Matthew and Mari played the wicked boys (Sandwich Man and Candlewick), and I played the

Blue Fairy. Having the part of the fairy in both plays had its perks. Wide-eyed little children would come up to me after the performances and ask me to grant them their wishes. I would say something in Russian and wave my magic wand and the children would run off squealing with delight.

The set and the costumes were made by David's friends Edie and Joseph Gazzulo, artists extraordinaire, who lived in St. Cloud, an hour west of Minneapolis. Edie made the brightly colored and exquisite costumes, which underlined the humor and the absurdity of the characters. Joey built the set, which consisted of three beautifully painted backdrops for each play that folded onto a stage constructed on wheels and designed to be erected within a half an hour for the performances. The name of our touring company, The Children's Musical Theatre Wagon, was painted brightly on the side of the stage, advertising our theatre on wheels.

We were quite the entourage of vehicles. Our pop-up camper was hitched to a Westphalia VW camper where David slept, and the stage was hitched to a yellow Ford LTD. We were a gypsy caravan, exuding a colorful theatrical vision on the highways of the north-central states. We would pull into a little town and see our names on the movie marquee, announcing the time and place of our performance. Children and adults would wave as we drove on the main street. We were celebrities.

Although the itinerary was well planned by David, there were a few unforeseen circumstances. When we pulled into International Falls, Minnesota, a town on the border of the United States and Canada, we discovered that the Veterans of Foreign Wars were holding their national convention here. They had taken every campsite, and we had no place to park our vehicles overnight. There was only one place we could go–the drive-in movie theatre. We squeezed our vehicles in between a multitude of parked cars filled with love-making teenagers and watched the movie several times before the cars dispersed and it was quiet enough to fall asleep.

Sleep was crucial to us, as it soon became evident how physically challenging it was to drive to a destination, set up the stage, get into our costumes, put on makeup, perform, change, break down the stage–sometimes twice a day–drive to a campsite, and set up the camper for sleep. We would fall into our beds exhausted.

It was after a particularly tiring day when the six of us were awakened in the middle of the night near Hinckley, Minnesota. Several police cars were shining their headlights into the camper and a farmer with a rifle in his hands was yelling at the top of his lungs, "Get these fucking hippies off my land!"

We had no idea what was happening and slowly piled out of the camper. I could hardly see without my contact lenses, but it seemed that we were surrounded by police aiming guns at us, and an irate farmer running around with a rifle. Earlier, we had attempted to park the camper behind a gas station rest stop, and in the darkness, we hadn't realized that the back wheels of the camper extended two feet onto the farmer's lawn. The farmer had called the police and now the entire Hinckley police department and the cursing farmer watched as the six of us, barefoot and clad in only our underwear and tee-shirts, pushed the heavy camper two feet off the farmer's property. I'm certain that our semi-nude appearance was the best thing that happened in Hinckley in a long time.

I did not own a pair of glasses out of vanity, and had a habit of storing my contact lenses in paper cups by the sink in the camper at night. While cleaning up, someone in the group would accidentally throw them into the garbage or spill them into the sink. In the morning, blind as a bat, I would find myself crawling on the floor of the camper, digging in the garbage or extracting my lenses from the sink drain. The minor miracle of the entire tour was that, although these contacts were lost on many more than one occasion, they always turned up. Every time.

In Hibbing, in the central iron-mining region of Minnesota, we camped on land that belonged to David's friend. I had to go to the bathroom in the middle of the night and it was quite a walk away. I woke Mari and begged her to come with me. It was pitch black outside. With Mari plagued by night blindness and my lenses already stored in paper cups, neither one of us could see a thing. Holding hands, we had almost reached the bathrooms when we heard a roar coming from the bushes.

We froze. Were we hallucinating, or was that a roar of a lion? In Minnesota? Squinting in the dark, we walked up to a large fence and saw something move in the bushes, and again the roar. This time, a lion's head became distinct, within inches of our heads. We felt the pee running down our legs as we screamed and ran as fast as we could back into the camper. David had failed to tell us that his friend was a keeper of retired circus animals. What we had seen in the dark was indeed a retired circus lion.

Our everyday life between performances included driving through endless flat plains to get to our destinations. To break up the monotony, Mari and I would sing the entire score of *West Side Story* several times or count cattle on the range to estimate a rancher's wealth. We would spot a colorful Kentucky Fried Chicken, Dairy Queen, or Burger King miles away in the dull landscape and would stop for something to eat. Cheap fast food constituted our main diet.

It was after a performance in an armory in scorching hot North Dakota, with a large group of good-looking National Guard soldiers looking on and cheering, that we found ourselves on a back road looking for a place to camp and to take desperately needed showers. Without warning, it began to rain. Without hesitation, we stopped the car and ran into the bushes with our bars of soap. We all got soaped up and successfully rinsed off by the rain, except for Fred who always took longer to do anything. When the rain stopped as suddenly as it began, there was Fred running naked from tree to tree, shaking wet branches to get the soap off his body. We certainly would have been arrested had anyone seen us.

The six of us got along fairly well considering the very close quarters we shared for eight weeks, except for a few R&R stops in Minneapolis to pause the tour for a short time and to sleep in real beds. To our relief, the sexual relationship between Mari and Matthew began to wane towards the end of the tour and we all got more sleep.

It was during the last week of the tour somewhere in Wisconsin when we became mischievous and started taking liberties with some of the dialogue in the plays. I remember a few lines from Gepetto's song in *Pinocchio* when he is carving the little puppet out of wood and dreams about him coming to life:

"He won't eat much, he won't get cold

He'll be my son as I grow old

To me he'll be just like a boy

In this lonely house, he'll be a joy."

At this memorable performance, after singing the song, Gepetto (Fred) stood up, faced the audience and in a loud voice announced, "Today, I'm going to make Pinocchio!"

The six of us burst into laughter and for several minutes the play was suspended because nobody could speak; tears of laughter ran down our cheeks. The adults in the audience who understood the joke were in hysterics, the children laughing because the adults were laughing. We did manage somehow to finish the performance but not without sporadic outbursts of laughter. Fortunately, this was one of our last performances–the innocence of *Pinocchio* destroyed forever.

The Children's Musical Theatre Wagon was the last production I did in Minneapolis, and much to Mari's dismay, it was not long after the tour was over that I gathered all my belongings, piled them into a U-Haul which I hitched to a Trans Am Pontiac drive-away car, and headed for New York. As difficult as it was to leave Mari, I was not prepared to remain in Minneapolis; it was not my home.

I didn't know where my home was. I was still on the move and running away from a closet full of skeletons. I was heading to the Big Apple to try my acting chops and to Nyack to visit my parents whom I hadn't seen and with whom I had little contact for four years. I was twenty-six years old.

Chapter Twenty Five

Topless

I WAS BROKE. IT WAS one thing to live on ten dollars a day in the boonies of Minnesota and quite another to move to New York and try to set up living quarters for myself. New York City was far too expensive, and I had nothing. Into this abyss, I drove the drive-away car from Minneapolis to Nyack to visit my parents.

My mother welcomed me with my favorite Russian dishes–*borscht* and stuffed peppers. I hadn't eaten so well in four years. My father seemed to be in the same position I had last seen him, lying on his bed in the kitchen, the same medicines surrounding him, the same miasma of illnesses and the little pills he used to treat them. He was wan and pallid; he smiled, but that seemed to take all his strength. My mother retreated into her vodka shot glass. I had escaped this gloom, and it was still there, like barometric pressure. Despite the warm welcome, it was clear to me that staying longer than a lunch or dinner would not be healthy for any of us.

Armed with my Joni Mitchell albums and bottles of red wine, I moved into a small apartment in central Nyack, only to find that the landlord's dog would not let me into my place after ten p.m. I moved again, this time into the loft space of an old Victorian home around the corner from my parents' apartment. From here, I could take the bus into New York City and pound the pavements to search for work.

The want ads were filled with low-paying mundane jobs and were depressing to read: "Attendant in bus terminal bathroom," "Night shelver in discount book store." Acting jobs were non-existent, auditions daunting, and my heart was not into the cattle calls. The Pepsi commercial that I landed didn't sell, the crowded asphalt jungle of New York City into which I had put my financial hopes was oppressive, and my bills were mounting. I called Phil, my go-go dance agent.

"You know, Mourka, it's all topless now. In Monticello, they're dancing in the nude," he said.

"At fifty dollars an hour, I'll go topless, but I won't go nude," I said.

Whenever I pass the huge glitzy Palisades Mall on Route 59 in West Nyack, just off the Thruway, I laugh at myself. Somewhere under that massive concrete line of high-end stores once stood a black box night club where I danced topless on the bar in mesh can-can tights, fringe, and spike heels. I slipped my folded ten and five dollar bills into my mesh tights to demonstrate the projected 'tips' that I made, a trick I learned from other dancers. I danced for men who slumped, glazed by alcohol; they seemed to be exhausted as they stared at me. I imagined their wives, home, preparing mac'n'cheese and Campbell's Tomato Soup. . . but perhaps I was wrong. Maybe they were happily married and just wanted to relax. I tried not to think at all. To make the night pass quicker, I concentrated on the music, hoping that the men would drop their quarters into the jukebox and play R&B, Motown and jazz–songs that inspired me and that I could really let go and dance to. I also worked in another bar further upstate, where I danced "topless" but had to wear pasties while onstage. I never understood pasties. Was I not topless still? Stripping them off was like pulling a heavy adhesive Band-Aid off my nipples.

My short stint as a topless go-go dancer went off uneventfully, except for one incident on a remote section of Route 301 near Cold Spring, New York on my way home from a gig. A handsome, polite New York state trooper stopped me for weaving from side to side on the road. I wasn't drunk; I was exhausted. Instead of giving me a ticket, he invited me to his home… to sleep. Was it innocence, stupidity? Without too much hesitation, I followed the state trooper home.

His home was cozy and warm, and I collapsed on his large double bed. He didn't touch me. The next morning, after a delicious breakfast that he prepared, the two of us rode off on his Harley-Davidson and toured the most scenic areas of upstate New York and Massachusetts. We stopped only to eat and make love in small out-of-the-way hotels. I could have ridden forever on his Harley with the wind in my face, my head resting on his muscled back and holding onto to his taut waist. After three days, we returned to his house. I got into my car and waved to my handsome policeman as I drove off. I never saw him again.

In between my go-go gigs, I managed to land a job as the wardrobe mistress for the infamous nude Broadway show *Oh! Calcutta!* at the Tappan Zee Playhouse on Broadway in Nyack, the first stop on the beginning of its U.S. tour.

Working as a wardrobe mistress in *Oh! Calcutta!* was always a great conversation piece. "What wardrobe? Aren't the actors all nude?" The show, a series of revue sketches on sex-related topics, was controversial because of its extended scenes of full-frontal nudity, both male and female. It took its title from a painting by Clovis Trouille, a pun on "O quel cul t'as!" (French for "What an ass you have!") Although the sketches were written by such distinguished playwrights as Sam Shepard, Samuel Beckett, Jules Feiffer, and John Lennon, and there was music composed by Peter Schickele (a.k.a. PDQ Bach) and others, Clive Barnes reviewed the show in 1969 as "likely to disappoint different people in different ways, but disappointment is the order of the night."

I felt that the scenes were tasteless, an excuse for pushing nudity onto a Broadway stage, but I didn't complain. I was happy to be working in a theatre once again. I did what I was told to do: organize the tremendous amount of wardrobe before, during, and after the show and to be poised backstage between skits for fast changes. The actors would often begin a skit fully clothed and remove their clothing as the scene progressed. I did enjoy the nude ballet–no wardrobe, great choreography, and no silly dialogue. Wednesday matinees were especially fun as I watched the "blue-haired ladies" (ladies over seventy who always sat in the front row) giggling and ogling the actors' naked bobbling genitals.

Within two weeks, *Oh! Calcutta!* closed at the Tappan Zee Playhouse and moved on to the Walnut Street Theatre in Philadelphia, and I went with it.

Chapter Twenty Six

Prince Charming

A WEEK BEFORE I LEFT for Philadelphia, a friend and I went to a party in Haverstraw, a town just north of Nyack, where ten years before, I had spent many a night drinking in a bar, pining for my then-married black boyfriend, Jace Williams, a rite of passage not to be revisited.

At the party, a tall, thin good-looking young man, about my age with blond hair and blue eyes and a kind of innocence about him, asked for my phone number. I yelled the numbers out across a crowded noisy room while he was playing chess, never thinking that he would remember them. I was wrong. When it came to numbers, Jeff Anderman had a photographic memory.

A few days later, Jeff Anderman called and the phone call resulted in a foursome dinner date at a German restaurant in Haverstraw. (Jeff's German chess partner and best friend, Klaus, was interested in the girl who had accompanied me to the party.) The dinner moved into an all nighter at Klaus's apartment nearby, where Klaus and my friend had sex and John and I talked through the night on the living room couch. As I remember, we didn't even hug–just talked.

The next day, much to my surprise, Jeff arrived at my new digs. I had found a rustic cabin in the woods in Rockland Lake State Park in Valley Cottage (not far from the "*dacha*" where my family and I lived in the late 50s). He roared up in his orange MG Midget sports car; he carried with him all of his tools, ready to help me fix my new place. Soon, the two of us were laughing, putting up new wallpaper, painting the walls, and continuing our dialogue from the previous night. Jeff did not wince when I told him I was making ends meet go-go dancing and working as the wardrobe mistress for *Oh! Calcutta!* He was accepting of all my activities and I began to notice his good looks, his ease, his intellect, and another strong suit, he played the guitar.

On my way to Philadelphia, I stopped at my parents' to say a quick good-bye and in passing, I said to my mother, "Mama, I met this guy not too long ago. I'm going to marry him."

And I walked out the door.

On opening night at the Walnut Street Theatre, the wardrobe mistress was the only one who received flowers. The flowers were from Jeff. Could a man be this perfect?

The show opened and closed in one night, before the flowers even wilted. Frank Rizzo, the ultra-conservative mayor of Philadelphia, would have none of the nudity and all of us were sent packing. The "last hurrah" for the cast and crew was a party given by Harlow, the first transgendered personality to appear in public. Harlow had grown up as Richard Finocchio, who knew as a child that his birth as a male was a cruel biological error. Now, Harlow was all woman. I was awed by her personality, beauty, and style. At the party, all of us were touching the skin on her arms, astounded at the softness. She was there with her then-boyfriend Hugh O'Brian, the star of the very popular western *Wyatt Earp*. It was another world–strange and exciting, but it was not my world. I packed my bags and drove home to my cabin in the woods and awaited another meeting with the young man who sent me flowers backstage.

I walked in. During the two days I had been away, everything had been painted and cleaned. The cabin was beautiful and spotless. Jeff had finished it all. I had hardly a minute to sit down and appreciate the work that he had done when he drove into the driveway. I realized then that he had made the cabin livable for both of us, and without too much thought and with complete abandon, I welcomed him home. My Prince Charming had arrived.

Jeff was the second oldest child in a well-to-do family of five children, three boys and two girls; he had grown up in Sparta, a town in northeastern New Jersey. His oldest brother Ben was accepted to MIT and became successful in his professional and married life. Jeff, who was brilliant in math and had a great business sense, was expected to follow in his brother's footsteps, but he suffered mental and physical abuse from his father for not succeeding. Jeff had expressed interest in becoming a math teacher and going to Montclair State University to get a teaching degree, to which his father replied, "No son of mine will be a math teacher!"

The relationship between them worsened. To get away, Jeff joined the Air Force and went to Colorado on a soccer scholarship. Sometime during the six months of boot camp, he broke his leg, which ended his career as a soccer player. It took Jeff another six months to bail out of the Air Force.

All that happened in the 60s. Rebellion was in the air. Jeff grew his hair long, bought a Martin guitar, learned how to play it, moved to New York City and made sandals at a leather shop on Bleecker Street. He eloped with his first wife, June, and took his knowledge of making leather goods to New Hope, a touristy hamlet in Pennsylvania where Jeff opened up his own very successful leather shop. All was well for a few years, until June's diabetes and her alcohol consumption overwhelmed her, and she died in a diabetic coma. Jeff packed his small suitcase, gave away his business in New Hope and, with his guitar on his back, arrived at his German friend Klaus's door in Haverstraw.

It was a month later that I yelled my phone number across that crowded room. Little did I know that this flippant, spontaneous act would initiate the beginning of a new journey; Jeff led and I followed, often repeating my mantra, "I'm doing the right thing, I'm doing the right thing, I'm doing the right thing..." Like my mother, who met the Russian Baron at a masquerade ball in Tallinn, Estonia, filled with dreams of another life, I met my blond Prince Charming at a party. I wanted, needed him to take care of me and make my world safe.

The fact that Jeff was out of a job and not pursuing a career did not deter me. The sense of security and safety was paramount, and this was the driving force that pushed me into the relationship. We were both out of work. I stopped go-go dancing. It didn't seem right for me to dance half-naked in a club while Jeff cooked and washed the dishes. The wardrobe mistress job for *Oh! Calcutta!* was over. And so we floated. . . for a while.

By now it was the 70s, a good economic time in the United States when many young people could float for awhile. Jeff relied on his math brilliance and his knowledge of the stock market to play the futures commodity market, a very risky stock market involving future deliveries on material goods. Jeff was very good at these predictions and generally was ahead of the game financially. On a day-to-day basis, Jeff was often glued to newspapers and the telephone in this pre-computer world.

My father wrote a letter to Jeff to the Rockland Lake address and asked, "And what are your intentions?"

We didn't have a clue.

Every night, we curled up for a blissful night's sleep. Not for long, however. Most nights, I was awakened by an animal scream, then a hiss and what sounded like the war of the critter world outside our window. High-pitched shrieks, hisses, crashing branches–the confrontations lasted through the night. In the morning when I stepped outside, instead of the sweet scent of perfumed dew, there was the unmistakable stench of skunk spray. We were Adam and Eve in Eden, all right, but we shared this paradise with some four-footed antagonists. We moved on.

The journey led us to Cragsmoor, New York, an artist colony on a mountaintop overlooking Ellenville. Jeff's friends Phil and Sally Sigunick owned a huge house on top of the mountain, once elegant, now falling down around their ears. Phil was (and still is) an extraordinary artist and a potter, and he and Sally shared their house with a changing cast of friends who came and went and helped with the cooking, cleaning, working in the garden, and the constant house repairs. We were artists, potters, craftspeople, bohemians, philosophers, hippies. We lived like kings and queens in what used to be a four-story hotel with a wraparound porch and a widow's walk on the fourth floor. The house was filled with priceless antiques Phil had saved from his antique business in New York City. Each of us had our own bedroom and the artists in the group had ample studio space. There was even a full printing press studio on the fourth floor.

Putting food on the table was the single challenge. The women got jobs. Sally worked as a waitress at the Terrace Restaurant in Ellenville, and I worked as a cocktail waitress at the Nevele and Fallsview Hotels, the grand old Borscht Belt institutions where Frank Sinatra and Dean Martin and many other pop singers got their start. From time to time, I was asked to be the telephone switchboard operator for the Nevele and would receive calls from the state penitentiary where one of the Slutskys, who owned the hotel at the time, was serving time for evading taxes. He ran the Nevele from his cell.

Sally and I made very little money as waitresses, but the money that we made was spent on lavish meals with great wine and desserts that Sally, a fantastic cook, would create. We would sit around the table, watch the extraordinary sunsets, smoke pot, and philosophize through the night. Occasionally I posed for Phil in his painting studio. Jeff and I played chess in the evenings. I read Alexander Solzhenitsyn's books *The Gulag Archipelago, Cancer Ward, One Day in the Life of Ivan Denisovich,* trying to make sense of what happened to Russia during the Soviet era. What had become of the Russia my parents remembered? Why were some of my favorite musicians Communists? There were more questions than answers.

All seemed well in our mountaintop retreat, but in fact, I began to feel intimidated by the artistry and the talent around me. Twice Jeff picked me up on the main road, running away from Cragsmoor, but without a real destination. My self-confidence was waning. I didn't like not having our own place. Now, feeling homeless in a sense, I often cried. I felt an emptiness, a self-consciousness; a sense that I had nothing to offer to the world. What did I have to talk about? What was that shudder that went through my body from time to time as if I was trying to shake off something?

In March, 1973, fuel prices soared in the United States, and by the end of that year none of us could afford to heat the four-story "white elephant." Almost everyone took off in different directions. Sally left Phil for warm Arizona and died a year later from an aneurysm. She was in her thirties. Phil stayed at the house, and Jeff and I left for Minneapolis en route to California. The journey continued.

In Minneapolis, it was nice to see Mari again, although there was an underlying tension between her and Jeff that was difficult to navigate. They never liked each other. Later, I realized why. But then, it was the first "sign" that he might possibly not be the Prince Charming I imagined. Mari's dislike of him troubled me, as she had always been such a good judge of character. I could not find anything to mistrust in him. But Mari's eyes narrowed whenever she looked at him, and I could see her biting her lip in an effort not to tell me how she really felt. The dislike was palpable.

Jeff and I continued to stay together and we found a beautiful, light apartment on Hennepin Avenue in South Minneapolis, which, without any furniture, seemed huge. Jeff got a job in a leather shop on the West Bank. I waitressed. We continued to float. I auditioned for a community theatre and won the part of Millie in William Inge's *Picnic*, the play that elevated Paul Newman to stardom. Jeff disapproved of my involvement in the play and I ended up not enjoying my participation. He insisted that "theatre could not be a form of high art because it has too many variables–the script, the director, the actors, scenery and music." I didn't believe him, but I didn't argue with him either. *Picnic* would be the last play I performed for fifteen years.

At ten a.m. on March 9, 1974, we were married in a Quaker church in Minneapolis. I wore a plaid skirt and jacket set that I bought for the occasion. Mari and another friend, Bob, were witnesses, and we went to eat pancakes at a pancake house for our wedding meal. I called my parents after the fact. Although they felt sad that they were not notified of this great event, they approved of the marriage. I finally had done something they felt was proper.

Chapter Twenty Seven

Deep Freeze

WE NEVER MADE IT TO California. Jeff concluded that it was too cold in Minnesota to settle down for good and decided that what he wanted to do more than anything in the world was to homestead on cheap land in northern New York. We would grow vegetables, raise sheep and goats, and have lots of children.

"Yes, Jeff," I said. "Sounds like a good idea."

In the fall of 1974, we bought a green VW bug, left our furnitureless apartment in Minneapolis, and drove northeast to Saranac Lake, New York, in the heart of the Adirondack Mountains. There we found an affordable second-floor apartment with two closet-like rooms, and a small kitchen, all placed in a row like a train compartment with the bathroom down the hall by the steps.

It was in Saranac Lake that, some weeks later, I found myself lying on a cold, narrow metal table with my feet in the stirrups. I was in a clinic and watching between my legs as the gynecologist cursed and sweat as he dug for the IUD (intrauterine device) in my uterus that refused to come out. The balding middle-aged doctor was angry at my exposed vagina and the white sheet that covered my trembling legs could not conceal his frustration. We were alone; there was no nurse. Between the horrendous cramps in my uterus, I couldn't help but think back to my abortion in Maryland when I was nineteen years old. At least this doctor didn't have sunglasses. I hated this gynecologist for his incompetence and his lousy bedside manner. I was petrified that I would bleed to death and never get off the metal bed.

I thought back to the Felliniesque episode almost a year before when I had this special patented IUD inserted in an abortion clinic in New York City. Twenty women all dressed in orange paper smocks tied at the back sat in beds arranged in a wide circle in a large room. The women were all sizes and shapes and of different ages, and were waiting to be wheeled in one after another to have an abortion. One by one, after the procedure, they would be returned groggy with anesthesia to the large room. I was the only one there for an IUD insertion. Those of us who were still awake chatted and laughed at our tacky orange paper dresses. The number 12 was hung on the bottom of my bed.

At last the painful half-hour reverse procedure was finally completed and the doctor showed me the bloody IUD. I got dressed and without a word, hoping my uterus was still intact, I left the gynecologist's clinic.

"All right, Jeff, I did my part. Now we can have as many babies as we want," I said to myself.

Jeff's plans of opening a leather shop in Saranac Lake to finance a farm were falling onto the back burner and it was too late in the year to begin homesteading plans. Instead he played chess in a bar called The Watering Hole, one of the thirty-one bars in town. "We can't eat scenery," Jeff said to me as the tourists packed up and the colorful leaves disappeared. Except for the handful of locals, who all owned pick-up trucks and worked for the town during the day and hung out in the thirty-one bars at night, Saranac Lake became a ghost town. One night I witnessed five men on bar stools fall to the floor in a drunken stupor like dominoes, one after the other.

I landed a job as a waitress at the Dew Drop Inn in the middle of town. One evening, there were only a few people in the restaurant. I felt a chill and I asked the proprietress permission to put a sweater over my waitress uniform. She responded with an emphatic "No." I looked at her in disbelief and in that instant my stomach contracted and clutched as if I had been punched. A strange feeling of nervousness followed, which in turn overwhelmed me with fear. Later that evening when I tried to explain to Jeff what I was experiencing, he dismissed my symptoms as something temporary.

The feeling wouldn't go away. The nervousness in my gut grew, and with it grew a sense that something was dreadfully wrong. I felt isolated and had fears that if anyone knew what I was feeling, they would lock me up in a mental ward somewhere in these horrid mountains. Once Jeff and I were at a party and someone passed around a marijuana pipe. I took a toke or two, hoping that some weed would calm me down. Instead I descended into a paranoid state that heightened the fears and sent me to an even deeper abyss. I begged Jeff to take me home and he did, but it took hours for the trip to wear off.

I couldn't concentrate. I couldn't work. I stopped eating and lost a great deal of weight. I went to bed with IT and I woke up with IT. I barely slept. I was in an acute state of anxiety before I knew such things existed. I thought I was going insane, and was afraid to tell anyone about it. I didn't know who I was, what I was doing, or why I was doing it. It was as if the floor had fallen out from underneath and left me nothing to stand on.

It was in the afternoon, after an attempt at a nap, that I crawled on all fours away from our mattress on the floor and into the hall for fear of waking Jeff up. I shuffled down the steps and climbed into our VW Bug.

"It's the gyno," I said to myself. "He did something to me and he has to fix it." I drove to the gynecologist's office. When I got there, the receptionist looked at me in bewilderment when I told her that I had to see the doctor right away.

"Do you have an appointment?" she asked.

"No, but I have to see him now! He took my IUD out the other day and something happened. Something changed. I feel awful. I have to see him now!" I screamed.

"What are you feeling? Are you bleeding?'

"No, I'm not bleeding. I'm feeling crazy. I can't sleep. I can't eat," I yelled again. I was shaking. The gynecologist was my only hope.

"He's not here right now," she said, "But here is the name and the address of the mental health clinic not far from here. I think they will be able to help you right away."

I didn't believe that the doctor was not in, but I left the office knowing that it was useless to talk to the receptionist. I got back into my car and searched for the mental health clinic, but I never found it. Perhaps I didn't want to find it because I was too afraid of the consequences. Visions of my mother on the floor in hysterics and running to commit suicide in the Hudson River intensified my need to keep my self-diagnosed insanity secret. In my ignorance, I was certain that I was losing my mind.

To alleviate my fearful state, Jeff decided to drive further upstate and visit Jack and Hailey Altman, a couple that he knew from his New Hope days. They lived in a tiny village called Hopkinton, not far from Potsdam, where Hailey worked as a secretary at the state university there. Jeff thought that seeing friends would make me feel better.

I began to hyperventilate in the car as if each mile north was trying to suffocate me. The Altman's were nice people. We had a nice dinner, played cards, and drank wine, which somewhat alleviated my anxiety. The next day, after another sleepless night, Jeff and I headed even further north to Massena, an industrial city on the St. Lawrence River on the border of Canada where Jeff decided to apply for work at the Alcoa Aluminum factory. The breathing was not as bad as the day before, but I remember feeling an emptiness, a numbness as we drove through the ugliest, flattest, bleakest terrain I had ever seen. I fell asleep in the car in the parking lot while Jeff had his interview. When Jeff got back, he opened the car door, sat down and said, "They won't hire me because I'm not big enough. They need big ironworkers here."

The Altmans had already gone to work the next morning when Jeff and I were fixing our breakfast in the kitchen. Jeff was sitting at the table outlining a vague plan of going back to Saranac Lake and getting a town job. I was standing at the kitchen counter attempting to pour coffee into a cup when my body became very still and rigid. I couldn't feel, move, speak, or hear. Jeff's voice became muted as it droned on. Hot coffee was spilling over the cup, onto the counter, and onto my shoes.

Chapter Twenty Eight

New York City

IT WAS THE CRASH OF the hot coffee cup onto the floor that shocked me back to where I was standing at the counter in the Altmans' kitchen. I picked up the sharp broken shards, put them on the table in front of Jeff and said, "If we don't leave this house and these mountains and go south to where there is a semblance of familiarity, I will die."

"South" did not really have a concrete meaning for me. I just knew that I had to get out of the bleak north.

It was the tone of my voice that spurred Jeff into action. It was a desperate plea for my life; an assertion that he had never before heard from me. Within twenty minutes we were on the road in the VW Bug with only our small weekend bags. We were heading south on the Northway without a real destination, improvising plans as we went. We reached the New York State Thruway, bypassing the exit to Saranac Lake and leaving behind all our belongings in the tiny apartment we rented. I never wanted to see Saranac Lake again.

With each mile south, the feeling of isolation, entrapment, and fear lessened and the blood started to return to my face. The seriousness of my condition prompted Jeff to make a few phone calls to friends, and within hours, Jeff had found work as a construction worker for a company in Ellenville. Jeff also called his German friend Klaus, who was now living with a beautiful German woman named Raina and her three children in New City, not far from Nyack. He asked Klaus and Raina if we could stay the night. We were greeted with warmth, a delicious home-cooked German meal, great wine, and a flaming fireplace. I slept better that night than I had in weeks.

Raina was an angel. I had several angels who helped me through my difficult years, but Raina was the first in a series on that journey from the frigid North. A fine artist, Raina was tall, thin with dark hair and dark eyes, eight years older than I. She had a warm smile and a giving, caring nature that drew me to her. Raina was a widow–her German husband, a pharmaceutical researcher, had died two years earlier, overdosing on drugs at work. Whether it was a suicide or an accidental death was never clear to me, but Wilhelm died, leaving Raina with three lovely children. Theo, the oldest boy, was eight years old; Paul, the middle boy, was five; and Nadine, was two when Jeff and I arrived on her doorstep in the early part of November 1974.

I stayed with Raina for a week while Jeff went to Ellenville to start his new job and find us a place to live. Raina and I became friends. I shared some of my fearful feelings with Raina; it helped to articulate how lost I felt. Raina recommended that I see a psychologist friend of hers and I had one forty-five minute therapy session. I revealed very little of myself, still fearful that there was something very wrong with me that needed to stay secret. The session touched the tip of an iceberg–or was it a volcano ready to explode? At least the doctor confirmed that I was not going mad; that I was suffering from an acute case of anxiety, and that anxiety was a warning for me to change something in my life. But what to change? What to do? I had no clue as to what I needed, and with no resources of my own, I continued to put one foot in front of the other and stay one step behind John, repeating the old mantra, "I'm doing the right thing."

I became more depressed. Irrational fears of going insane, of losing control, of suddenly stopping breathing, paralyzed me. I was fearful of getting help— mistrustful of the psychiatric profession. I was afraid of medication. I'd grown up in an apartment with parents who were physically and mentally ill, where there were cupboards full of medication that often created more pain and anguish. I refused to accept that I was suffering from the same afflictions my parents suffered. I kept my fears to myself.

Ellenville was conducive to depression. The town itself was depressed. It was winter and Ellenville was grey and dirty; I saw no colors around me that bitter season. It was cold. Our apartment on Route 209 in Ellenville was dark and nondescript. Jeff froze his hands every day at the construction job he hated and I got a job as an office worker for the Village of Ellenville assisting the Village Clerk. One of my tasks was to organize parking tickets that were handed out by the meter maids the previous day. Whenever I would recognize people's names, including mine, I would throw the parking tickets into the garbage.

Once we visited Phil Sigunick in his "white elephant" house in Cragsmoor where we'd all lived together the previous year. The day we visited was frigid. We opened the front door and were greeted by thick smoke floating about one foot off the floor. Choking and spitting, Jeff and I crawled through the hallway in the one-foot space until we reached the living room, hoping to find Phil still alive. There Phil sat in his old armchair, in front of a large oil drum he had "Rube Goldberged" into a wood stove. The stovepipe was precariously poked through a hole in the roof for ventilation and the leaky cut-out firebox was billowing smoke into the room. Phil didn't care. He was warm and for the moment, he was not hungry. His wife, the company and the lavish meals were gone. Phil was eating out of a box of Cheerios. Like the smoke that hung one foot off the floor, depression draped us all, and that winter in Ellenville was one of the darkest in my memory.

In the spring of 1975, Phil and Jeff's good friend from the Cragsmoor days, Josh Menton, who lived in New York City with his wife Erika, found Jeff a job at T. Anthony's on 445 Park Avenue at 56th Street, a high-end retail store where one could still buy quality luggage and superb hand-crafted leather goods. At that time, Erika was T. Anthony's head bookkeeper.

Overnight, Jeff went from a lowly construction worker in Ellenville to an elegant well-dressed gentleman/salesman for T. Anthony, where he opened the front door for customers and greeted them with the usual good morning, afternoon, and evening salutations. This was another world. Celebrities such as John Lennon, Michael Douglas, and Mick Jagger, to name a few, would come to buy luggage, and billionaire sheiks from the Arab nations would fly to New York just to buy a T. Anthony suitcase.

Jeff was not impressed by the parade of celebrities, nor was he enamored with catering to the wealthy. He was playing a role that made him uncomfortable. It wasn't long before Josh found Jeff a job working with him as a salesman for Kulicke Frames Inc., the most innovative and influential picture frame design firm in the United States. Kulicke was famous for designing metal welded frames, polished aluminum frames, and the beautiful "floating frame," where there is no visible frame and the artwork floats between two pieces of Plexiglass. Since the 1950s, Kulicke frames had been used for some of the best modern art in the most prestigious museums in the world. The frames were later modified for easy assembly and produced for the mass market, and Josh and Jeff sold them to high-end picture frame stores in the Metropolitan area.

For me, Jeff's sudden transition from Ellenville to New York City meant that I was alone the entire week and would see Jeff only on weekends when he returned home. To this day, I don't know what on earth I did with myself alone in Ellenville during the week. I've blocked that time from memory. Except for the town job, I saw no one. I made friends with no one and, having no transportation, I went nowhere. I sat alone in that dark, dingy apartment. Weekends when Jeff came home were filled with his weekly stories, his new fondness for the framing business, and the inevitable plans to move to New York City. I was terrified of the prospect. I was terrified of everything.

Within weeks, Josh, once again to the rescue, found us a small third floor apartment on East 78ᵗʰ Street between York Avenue and the FDR Drive. It was a lovely apartment by New York standards. It had one bedroom, a small living room, and a large kitchen that looked out onto a small public park across the street. It was light and quiet with very little traffic on our one-way dead end street.

It took me three months to venture forth on foot from the new apartment. Other than an occasional walk in the park across the street and playing cards in the evenings with Jeff, Josh and Erika in their apartment around the corner on East 79ᵗʰ Street, I went nowhere and was overwhelmed by city life—the noise, the crowds, the traffic. I was afraid to get on a bus to look for work. What if I flipped out in the street?

Jeff was of no help. He believed that psychologists and therapists were "quacks" and downplayed my need for help. Jeff felt that the irrational fears I was experiencing were of my own doing and that I had to somehow undo them, reiterating my own confusion about getting help. My dancing and theatre ideas were unnecessary frivolities. My parents were sick old people Jeff had no use for (he had no use for his parents either). He felt that Russians were generally not to be trusted and that my Russian background was superfluous.

I had no life force within me to argue his points. I became a shell of a human being, a mere shadow trapped by my fears. Was this the same person who had go-go danced through theatre, dance, and music lessons in New York City not so long ago? What had become of me? Who was I?

There is a Russian saying, "возьми себя в руки," translated loosely as "get your ass into gear." And one day I did just that. In the morning, I got dressed in the plaid skirt and jacket I got married in–it was a perfect secretarial outfit– walked down the three flights of stairs onto the street and, with my heart in my mouth, walked cross-town to Second Avenue. I got on a downtown bus and went on a job interview at Macmillan Publishing on Third Avenue and 53rd Street. I remember the bus driver driving downtown with his head out the window, sneezing all the way because he was allergic to one of the passengers' perfume. It made me smile, almost laugh out loud.

When I reached the Macmillan office building, the job interview was on the thirty-third floor. I panicked. I asked the guard at the door if he would ride up with me to the thirty-third floor. He looked at me as if I came from outer space and said, "I can't be riding no elevators with people. That ain't my job."

"But I'm scared of elevators," I cried out for everyone around me to hear.

"Girl, you better get unscared, cause you just might get that job," he said.

I hadn't thought of that. I walked back to the elevators and, with great trepidation, pressed the button "up". When I got off at the thirty-third floor, I felt the perspiration gathering on my forehead. I wanted to run back into the elevator and go home.

"Are you here for the Dictaphone-typist job?" asked a well-dressed young woman walking in my direction. "Come this way," she continued.

I felt trapped. I had seen the ad for the typist job in the want ads, but what the hell was a Dictaphone? I looked around the room and I saw women with earphones on their heads, typing away, and I surmised that they were listening to dictation through yes, a Dictaphone.

"Have you ever used a Dictaphone?" the young lady continued as we walked.

"Oh, yes," I answered. How hard could it be? Soon the woman sat me down in a tiny cubicle next to a few other young ladies in their respective cubicles who were "Dictaphoning." She gave me the little machine that looked like a tape recorder with earphones and told me that she would be back in a few minutes to check on my typing.

"Psssst. How do you work this thing?" I asked one of the girls next to me after one futile attempt to get it going. She got up from her chair and showed me the works.

"Tell the woman there is something wrong with this Dictaphone and she'll get you another one. That way you won't lose your time." (I was being clocked).

"I think there is something wrong with this Dictaphone. I couldn't hear very well," I said to the woman who was monitoring me. Without hesitation, she went and got another machine, buying me some time to hone my skills on the first machine. By the time I sat down to type my test, I was proficient. I smiled at my little friend. She smiled back and I got the job.

My survival skills held my life in balance for the three months that I worked for Macmillan. I was still frightened of the elevator and the bus; exhausted from the effort of overcoming irrational fears every day. But the mere fact that I was going out every day, concentrating on the mundane typing work I was doing, gave me time to regain my equilibrium enough to live day by day, hour by hour, sometimes minute by minute.

Chapter Twenty Nine

China Seas

IT WAS JOSH'S WIFE ERIKA who saw the ad in the *New York Times*. China Seas, Inc. a small, private fabric design firm was looking for a secretary/receptionist/typist. The best part: it was around the corner from where we lived on 76th street between First and Second Avenue.

I got the job.

China Seas was housed in an old warehouse building in the middle of 76th Street. I would walk up a flight of stairs where the door opened into a large, sunny open loft space with large windows, gorgeous authentic batik designs hanging on the walls, and a dark cherry wood floor. My desk, a slab of polished wood placed on top of filing cabinets with a worktable behind it, was tucked into one of the corners of the room. A goose-necked lamp created a warm light over my typewriter, another lamp near the phone. The production crew had desks similar to mine, situated directly across from me. At one end of the loft was a full kitchen with a large table always covered with a beautifully designed tablecloth upon which the employees prepared and ate their lunches. The shipping department was on the third floor, with a different crew of people milling around huge shelves filled with rolls of handmade batik fabric and beautiful designer fabrics that were screen printed at China Seas.

Inger McCabe Elliot, the founder and president of China Seas, Inc., maintained her office space on the other end of the loft space. There were exquisite oriental paintings hanging on the walls, antique Asian pottery standing on shelves, bright rugs covering the floor, and plush, comfortable armchairs surrounding her large desk. A former photojournalist for *Newsweek* and the New York Times, Inger discovered Indonesian batik in the 1960s and introduced authentic Javanese batik fabric to the American design market before finally opening China Seas, Inc. in 1972. During the 1970s and 80s when batik became very popular in the United States, batik motifs were copied, adapted, hybridized, and diluted by interior designers. Inger continued to import and sell "the real stuff," true batik as it had been painstakingly made for hundreds of years. In 1984, Inger published her first book, entitled *Batik: Fabled Cloth of Java.*

I loved working for Inger. Inger Elliott was a strong force in my life when I needed that the most. I remember her motto: "Know what you want and enforce this with much humor." She created a beautiful work environment and ran a tight ship. China Seas was a small importing and manufacturing company, competing with large interior design companies for production of batik and other innovative design fabrics. We were featured in *House Beautiful, House and Garden,* and *Interior Design* magazines, to name a few, and China Seas hobnobbed with some of the top interior designers in the business. It was a competitive business and there was no shortage of work. The employees all pulled their weight, enjoying the challenge; catching a break on the fire escape for a cigarette, some gossip, and some laughs.

I made friends. Nettie and Flora worked as production assistants and directed the production of the new screen-printed designs. Nettie was also the liaison between our 76th Street manufacturing loft and the China Seas showroom, located on West 72nd Street. Inger insisted that the employees take turns cooking lunch, and once a week the entire working crew from both floors sat at the large table in the kitchen and ate together. I brought the *borscht* and potato soup.

No one knew about the darkness, fear, and anxiety that plagued me. That was my secret. I buried myself in the massive and unending workload and in time, I was able to keep the demons at bay. . . for awhile.

It wasn't long before I graduated from the secretary/receptionist job to become Inger's personal assistant. I was learning about the textile and the interior design business very quickly and Inger was grooming me to go to Indonesia with her to choose original batik cloth, to see how it was made and help bring back samples.

Inger was married to Osborne Elliott, Dean of Columbia University's Graduate School of Journalism and former editor-in-chief of *Newsweek* magazine. Osborne Elliot had a shiny black limousine at his disposal that Inger borrowed to take her to meetings in the Fashion District downtown. The limousine was called for me when I began to go to meetings in her place.

"Could you please drive around the corner to East 78th street and beep the horn in front of my apartment?" I would ask the driver.

I would stick my head out of the backseat window and wave upstairs to Jeff if he was at home. I was having a good time again, but Jeff was not impressed.

The next shock came during a lovely evening playing "Hearts" with Josh and Erika after dinner. I was feeling well, relaxed. Jeff was dealing the cards and out of the silence announced, "What I want to do next is to set up my own retail framing business with Kulicke Frames in Minneapolis, where aluminum frames are still a novelty and I will be able to make a fortune."

I choked on the red wine, spitting and spilling the dark red liquid onto the cards, the table, and onto the floor.

"But I thought you hated the cold in Minnesota?" I managed to sputter.

He went on. He was determined that the move from New York City be made; that the move back to Minneapolis in June would be prefaced with a vacation starting in Calgary, Canada, driving west through the Canadian Rockies, then South along the Pacific Coast to San Francisco. California at last! Then we would turn east to Minneapolis to start the new retail business.

Panic and fear returned. Another move? For awhile I thought that he would change his mind, but within two months, Jeff had bought a pick-up truck, built a wooden makeshift camper which he fastened onto the back of the truck, and painted it red.

"You're going cross-country in THAT?" asked Nettie as Inger, Flora, a few other good friends and I stood in a line looking out the window at the red hippie pick-up truck that Jeff had parked outside of China Seas on my last day of work.

"You can always come back," Inger said quietly.

Holding back the tears, I descended the China Seas steps, crossed the street, opened the door of the truck, looked up at my friends, and waved good-bye.

I have had a few times in my life when I wish I could have pressed the Delete button, erased a part of my life, and replaced it with something else. As if I were trapped in a bad dream in which I tried to change the ending to no avail, I left New York City and China Seas, and moved back to Minneapolis with Jeff.

Jeff lured me with dreams of our new framing business, financial security, a house of our own, children: a successful and happy life. I felt I had to give my husband a chance; that my job was to support his dreams "for better or for worse," that my life was subordinate to his. I still did not have a voice of my own, any confidence, or even a true sense of self. Jeff was all I had. Or so I believed.

Chapter Thirty

Minneapolis... Again

JEFF'S DREAM CAME TRUE. HIS knowledge of setting up businesses paid off and Anderson Frames, Inc. on Hennepin Avenue became a household name in Minneapolis. With only two metal frames and three wood frames at great prices, people flocked to our shop to frame everything they had been hoarding in their closets. I worked the counter, took in the framing orders, and learned as much as I could about the art world and how to enhance art with mats and frames. The walls of our shop were bright with colorful graphics, posters, and original artwork, which we also sold at reasonable prices. We had art openings. We were busy.

Within six months of opening the business, we were framing art exhibits for the famous Minneapolis Institute of Arts and we framed Frank Lloyd Wright's collection of drawings for the Metropolitan Museum of Art in New York City with Jeff's custom inlaid wood frame. Jeff and I had the opportunity to fly back to New York City and to view the bowels of the Metropolitan where priceless art was stored, restored, and framed.

We rented a two-story Victorian home in South Minneapolis and bought a seven-year-old 1972 dark blue Mercedes Benz in excellent condition. I enjoyed its precision handling, plush seats, and outward gloss. I felt regal in the driver's seat. As I settled back into those deep cushioned seats, I was also settling into suburban middle class life, or so it seemed. The anxiety, out-of-control feelings, and depression I had managed to shove under the China Seas workload emerged once again with the move to Minneapolis. Despite all the busyness of setting up and learning a new business, there was an empty center, an ache that gnawed inside me and made me anxious. There was a darkness that shadowed my life, even through my surprise pregnancy which Jeff and I agreed was "a direct phone call from God." What happened to the new, more improved IUD I had inserted in New York City... again? For nine months, the obstetrician watched with amazement as the baby grew and the small plastic insert flattened against my uterus.

At midnight on April 3, 1979, Jeff and I arrived at the hospital. The nurses propped me up in a bed, showed me the button to push if I needed anything, and disappeared to take care of an emergency. For six hours, I dozed on and off, watched the clock and timed the labor pains by myself. Jeff had fallen asleep in the armchair beside me–so much for all the blowing and huffing and puffing he was supposed to help me with as my Lamaze labor partner. At six a.m., a nurse came to check on me and gasped. I was fully dilated.

At 6:30 a.m., our daughter Jessie Laura was born. The IUD came out seconds after she did. Several doctors on the floor rushed into the room to get a better look. They were astounded.

Later that morning, the nurses wheeled in Jessie, cleaned and bundled up in her hospital bassinette, which looked more like a big basket with a handle, covered by a large veil. At the same time, the kitchen help wheeled in my breakfast: French toast on a large plate with a large chafing dish cover to keep the food warm. For a moment, I was confused as to which one was Jessie and which was the toast. A kind of hysteria followed as I began to laugh at myself, the laughter soon turning into convulsive sobs of relief, accomplishment, and love for this tiny infant I had brought into the world.

Jessie was a beautiful baby with a shock of long dark hair, large brown luminous eyes, a long body with long aristocratic toes and fingers, and an olive complexion. There wasn't a red splotch on her. She was small–six pounds, eight ounces at birth–and her little body was perfect. She fit so exactly in my arms when I breastfed her, a time I remember as being one of the most peaceful in my life. Nursing Jessie gave me moments of needed peace and gave us the connection that is so profound, mother to daughter. Only I could nurture Jessie in this way. Bottles were out of the question. I was finally in control of something Jeff could not be a part of or dictate. He was envious.

All the good fortune, his daughter's perfection, and business success was not enough for Jeff. In early November, feeling the onset of winter and overwhelmed with the responsibility of fatherhood, Jeff packed his bag and left for California "to find himself," leaving me alone with a seven-month old baby. I was unprepared to be alone with Jessie. My anxiety level soared and I was petrified that somehow I could hurt her. Although breastfeeding came easily to me, I was not a "natural" mother; I was too uneasy. Diaper pins frightened me. I was afraid that I would stick her with a pin. While Jeff was away, I tripped and fell, and Jessie flew out of my arms in her plastic carrier. I watched her eyes for hours for signs of a concussion. In the middle of night, half asleep, as I was nursing Jessie, I saw what looked like sparks coming from her as she moved. In my delirium, I thought Jessie was on fire. I sprang out of bed and ran with Jessie to the sink before I realized that it was static electricity coming from the synthetic sleeper she was wearing.

Jeff had been gone for three weeks when the phone call came from my father in Nyack. My mother had a massive stroke and collapsed on the floor at home. She was brought by ambulance to Nyack Hospital, where she was in a coma from which no one expected her to emerge. I was packing to fly east when Jeff called home to tell me he was in the middle of a blizzard in Wyoming. Within twelve hours, his California trip aborted, Jeff drove home, and together we flew to New York City and drove to Nyack from the airport.

My mother died on December 7, 1979, a week after we arrived. She was seventy-two. I was sad because she passed without having the opportunity to meet Jessie. Perhaps meeting her granddaughter would have given her some joy.

That night many of my father's relatives gathered in our little stuffy apartment for the customary memorial service. They stood in the kitchen facing the Russian Orthodox icon which hung above the refrigerator, singing the sorrowful funeral hymns in Church Slavonic; the incense burner swaying softly in Father John Meyendorff's hand. As I sang with the relatives, holding eight-month-old Jessie in my arms, she started to gag from the inhaled incense. John grabbed her and ran down the stairs and outside, where she caught her breath in the cold fresh air. Later, Jeff did not cease to remind me that "instead of listening to Church Slavonic droning in my ears, I could have been lying on a California beach somewhere."

The week before my mother died, strange subliminal violent thoughts crept into my mind as I sat next to her bed in the hospital. I watched her helpless body rising and falling with every breath, aided by all the hospital tubes and mechanisms she was attached to. It was her helplessness that created the violent thoughts–thoughts that I would lose control and hurt her in some way. Of course, I immediately suppressed the thoughts; they were too hideous. But the questions arose. Where did these thoughts come from? Wasn't I also helpless when at age nine my mother lunged at me with bloody hands and arms? That day, I was frightened and ran away, taking with me sensations of fear, anger, and guilt that were suppressed for years. Little did I know then that suppressed sensations would inevitably rear their ugly heads when I least expected them.

I couldn't cry. I didn't cry at the two funerals that were held for her: one at the Lutheran church presided over by my brother Kurt, and the other at the Russian Orthodox cemetery in Spring Valley. I felt guilty for being unable to cry and for not feeling compassion or love. Why couldn't I help her more? Did she love me? Did she love my brothers more? Was it my fault that we did not have a relationship? All these questions would now be left unanswered.

Jeff flew back to Minneapolis and I helped my pale, weeping father move to an apartment on the second floor of his sister, my Aunt Tessia's house in Nyack. I felt sadness and guilt about my father. Who was going to take care of him now?

It was left to me to organize and clean out my parents' apartment on Washington Avenue. I threw out the wrapping paper in boxes and bags in the drawers and under the beds. I threw out the fabrics and furs and ribbons and threads from the bureaus. I threw out sheets that smelled like camphor and crying, and I threw out the bottles and bottles of pills and elixir and vodka. I kept one glass bookcase filled with Russian books and the art that hung on the walls, several photo albums, letters, old documents, the Russian *chachkas*. I also saved a tin box full of my mother's poetry. I stored everything at my father's new apartment. Within a week, I closed the door on 47 Washington Avenue, said good-bye to my father, and flew home to Minneapolis with Jessie.

As my mother had been very good at creating temporary nests for the family during the numerous moves from Estonia to America, and then again in Nyack, I too learned to create nests wherever I settled. Jeff and I moved seven times in six years. When I returned from Nyack, I immersed myself into life in Minneapolis. Even though Jeff continued to "pooh-pooh" psychologists and call them "quacks," I finally got the courage to start therapy. I would find myself sleepless or crying, and depression and anxiety continued to creep into my life. If nothing else, I owed it to Jessie to find some peace and to be a better mother.

The therapist sat and listened as I recounted my family history, beginning with my grandfather, the general adjutant to Czar Nicholas II; I thought I had to start from the beginning. By the time I got to the 1917 Bolshevik Revolution, the hour was over and the therapist asked me for seventy-five dollars. I left with more anxiety than when I had entered. It took me another few weeks to muster up the courage to see someone else. I was thirty-two years old when I heard the words for the first time: My parents and my early environment had something to do with my depression. In that moment, the light bulb flickered, a miniscule ray of hope emerged, and the painfully slow unraveling began.

During my last months of pregnancy, I had stopped working at the frame shop. Inspired by the fine art I had been framing, I started art classes at an old-fashioned second-floor *atelier* on Hennepin Avenue in Minneapolis. This *atelier* could have been placed anywhere on the West Bank in Paris. Light and airy and smelling of oil paint and turpentine, the art studio was filled with paintings, easels, brushes, charcoals, pastels, paints, and reminded me of my father's studio in the kitchen at 47 Washington Avenue. After Jessie was born, I continued painting in oil at home, and the art instructors from the *atelier* would do home visits and check on how I was progressing. Somehow, this comforted me. Later, Adam Satchett, a well-regarded watercolorist we met through our business, gave me lessons. I fell in love with the freedom of watercolor, a sharp contrast to the layering of oil paint. The painting made way for printmaking classes at the University of Minnesota's art department, where I drew and etched mezzotints on copper plates, and painted monoprints on paper. I was happiest when my fingers were oozing black or sepia ink or when my paint palettes were permeated with a mélange of colors. Painting eased my anxieties and Jeff liked it when I painted; it was something I could do at home and dinner would be ready on time.

I started dancing in the living room, working up a sweat in the mornings doing my Luigi's Jazz warm-up exercises. It felt good to remember my dance chops and put movement back into my body. The door to the theatre world, however, was still closed. Clawing back into the auditioning and performing scene would have compromised my role as the "good wife" which, I believed, still provided me with a sense of purpose and a safety net from the deep-seated fears and anxieties that plagued me.

A want ad caught my eye. The Hebrew Immigrant Aid Society (HIAS) was looking for Russian speakers to translate lectures for the new wave of Russian Jewish immigrants coming to the United States from Russia and Israel. During the 1970s, the Soviet Union temporarily loosened emigration restrictions for Jews, allowing nearly 250,000 Soviet Jews to leave the country and escape anti-Semitism. At first, many Russian Jews went to Israel, but most chose the United States, where they were treated as political refugees. This policy lasted for about a decade, until the early 1980s. HIAS placed Russian Jewish families and individuals in American cities with climates that closely resembled their cities of origin. Many Muscovite Jews were relocated to the Minneapolis/St. Paul region because of the similar climate.

I got the job. Before long, I was translating lectures from English to Russian on subjects ranging from dental hygiene–how to floss teeth (unheard of in Russia) to the use of deodorant (also unheard of in Russia), and what to expect at job interviews. The list of subject matter was endless and the Jewish immigrants were soaking up the information like "*pelmeni*" (dumplings) in hot broth. Aside from translating, I escorted people to dentists and doctors' appointments. I took them shopping and I began giving English lessons. I became a social worker for the Jewish immigrants, a liaison to their new world and they depended on me. At first, my Russian was a bit rusty. Over the years, I had spoken very little, but it wasn't long before I got the language up to speed. I enjoyed speaking Russian again, an unexpected gift to myself. I loved the job and I made friends. The Minneapolis nest took shape. As soon as I had eased into my new role, Jeff announced, "I want to sell the business and move back east, somewhere in the vicinity of Connecticut, Massachusetts, or New York. I will start a wholesale framing business. I can do that anywhere but I don't want to do it here. The winters are too cold."

"Go," I said. "I'm staying here with Jessie."

Jeff sold our very successful Anderson Frames, Inc. business to his main assistant, who couldn't afford it. It didn't matter. Jeff wanted out. The grass was greener back east and the quicker he could get there, the better. No money was put down–only a promise to pay monthly. I am embarrassed to say how little I was involved in our financial affairs. I always trusted Jeff with the finances, and this transaction was no exception. It was much later, when there were rumors of drug use by the assistant and the payments stopped, that I felt the brunt of Jeff's decision.

Years later when I traveled to Cuba, I happened to meet our landlord for Anderson Frames and Graphics at the Parke Centrale Hotel in Havana. He told me that he was unable to collect rent from the new owner. In lieu of rent, he took Robert Altman's etchings, valuable exquisite prints, some of which I still have hanging on my walls.

Jeff left for the northeast in search of a place to start yet another business and to look for a new home. Once again, I was left alone with Jessie, with the added weight of making a decision: stay in Minneapolis and break up the marriage, or follow Jeff to yet another unknown? I had created a nest, a life for myself that was hard to relinquish. I was angry. How many sacrifices must I make? For what? I was afraid. Was I ready to live alone as a single parent? I was confused. What path to take?

Jeff didn't make it any easier. He called me every night in his search for a home and business. "Please, come east, don't break up the marriage." He made promises. "This move will be the last one. I will build our dream house. I will create a successful wholesale framing business."

I wanted to believe him, but the seeds of doubt had been sown.

Reluctant as I was, I flew east and carried Jessie into the new maroon Chevy pickup truck (for which we had traded my beloved regal Mercedes), which Jeff had left for me at La Guardia Airport. Following directions, I drove north on the New York State Thruway. I was heading to our new home, to a house in New Paltz, New York that I had never seen and which Jeff had bought for $26,000.

Somewhere between the Newburgh and New Paltz exits on the Thruway there is an elevation stretch of road from where I could see the Shawangunk Ridge and its backdrop, the Catskill Mountains. When I saw those mountains, I turned to my two-year-old Jessie, who was asleep in her car seat and said, "You see those mountains, Jess? I will leave your father before I will ever leave these mountains."

That was 1981. It's 2016 and I'm still here.

Chapter Thirty One

Meyendorff Family History

THE HOUSE WAS BEAUTIFUL: A natural cedar that blended into the rustic setting. It had three bedrooms, a living room with a fireplace, a large kitchen with a porch attached, a garage that served as a workshop for Jeff, and a neighboring apple orchard that bordered our large back yard. The house was set on a quiet street, and I found it easy to fall into the role of a suburban housewife with all the comforts of the modern conveniences the house had to offer; another nest was built on 26 Rocky Hill Road in New Paltz.

The marriage was shaky. Jeff needed me to depend on him to feel complete, and he fed my perceived weaknesses. His continued unhappiness and ambivalence about how to generate a source of income for the family did nothing to allay my insecurities. All his schemes and grand ideas made me feel that at any moment my life would be disrupted again and my nest destroyed. Jeff searched outside of himself for fulfillment and he wanted me to share his search. I couldn't. I was no longer sure that I shared his dreams, and yet I had no dreams of my own. We were both stuck. And so we floated. . .

I begged Jeff to see a marriage counselor, but he refused to go.

When I packed two-year-old Jessie up and left Jeff in a moment of desperation, he closed the door of the garage, climbed into the car, turned on the engine, and tried to asphyxiate himself with the gas fumes. This was his second attempt at suicide. When we first met, he told me that as a teenager, he had tried to blow his brains out with a gun that misfired.

Jeff opened the garage door only minutes before he would have succumbed to the gas fumes. When his mind cleared, he called Raina, our German friend who lived in New City, about one hour south of New Paltz; I had left a note to say where Jessie and I were going. Jeff told me of his suicide attempt. He cried, begged me to come home, and promised to see a therapist. I had failed to save my parents from suffering. Must I fail with Jeff too? I had to heal the terrible tear in the marriage, to somehow help Jeff... The next day, I packed up Jessie and went home to try again.

Jeff stopped going to the therapist, but I continued to look inside myself to make the puzzle pieces fit, to find the source of my anxieties, and make sense of my complicated beginnings. Neither of us had an idea that while I was stripping the surface to get to the heart of my being, I was also setting the foundation to pave my way out of the marriage. It would take four more years, but I am forever grateful to Dr. Arnold Weiner at the mental health clinic in New Paltz for helping me find the courage to stand. . . and eventually walk away.

During this difficult time with Jeff in New Paltz, I tried to visit my father in Nyack as much as I could. I never knew my father as the handsome, vibrant man that my mother met at the masquerade ball in Tallinn, Estonia in the 1930s. I always knew him as the thin, sickly man who was in permanent pain and mental anguish. After my mother died, Papa had grown more helpless, his behavior childlike. Aunt Alina Teploff, my cousin, would often drive up from New Jersey to his rooms above his sister's apartment to take care of him, and for this I was extremely grateful. Later, when I found his journals, which he wrote in German, French, English, and Russian, Papa would berate Aunt Alina for playing bad bridge and for meddling in his numerous medications. At the same time, he waited for her visits. In his journals, Papa would also write about his physical pain and depression. His suffering was so vivid. I felt unfathomable sadness when I translated the following letter Papa wrote in French to his Haitian doctor, Dr. Jean Jacques:

Cher Docteur,

"I am writing to you because I know that you are a good doctor and very spiritual. Please help me to live my last weeks, months, years without torment. My headaches and my depression torment me to such an extent that I do not want to exist. I wait all day until the moment that I can take the Doriden² so that I can fall asleep. Sometimes I take Anacin in between. You told me I can take two Doridens, one Anacin, three Benadryl for the rash and Vitamin C everyday. I prefer to live one or two months with these little narcotics (even so they cause me to hallucinate) than to have torment for the rest of my life."

Despite his illnesses, Papa never lost his aristocratic flair. When social services sent a male aide to the apartment, my father decided that the man was his personal valet. He called him "человек," a discourteous expression for "servant" in Russian, a term straight out of a Chekhov play. In a memo from his journal he explained in Russian that his "человек" had been rude to him and that he would speak to him about this the next day. His rehearsal for his speech read as follows:

"I wanted to tell you 'know' that I fell sick. I have temperature 100.2. I have 'Tchess' (translated from the Russian "чесотка," meaning a rash). I have stomick pens and terrible head ach and you have consider with it and not to be rough (coarse) like yesterday."

When I visited Papa, I began asking questions about his past. Despite all the stories I heard in my childhood, I was curious to know more. Our conversations served as a distraction from Papa's pain and also helped me to thread the stories into a tapestry of a fascinating world, a world forever destroyed and vastly

....

4   Doriden is a hypnotic sedative introduced in 1954 as a safe alternative to barbiturates used to treat insominia. Unfortunately it was also addictive, with severe side effects. On the street, the combination of two Doridens and four Tylenols was called Dors & Fours, a Six Pack, or Loads.

different from the present. I pulled my father's suitcase from underneath his sick bed, the one he had carried across the Atlantic Ocean, dusted it off, and peered inside.

Nearly all of my father's twelve brothers and sister were gifted in the arts: fine art, music, sculpture, writing, and theatre. The St. Petersburg home on Vassilievskiy Ostrov, a fifteen-minute walk from the Winter Palace, was a center of activity with all of the thirteen children in residence. Under the supervision of my grandmother, the older children would be busy painting, playing musical instruments, singing, writing, and putting on plays while the little ones played checkers or hide and seek. Papa loved to draw. Every other Saturday, Papa's nine cousins visited the big house on "Первая Линния" (First Line Street). It was an idyllic childhood, the calm before the 1917 storm.

My grandmother, Elena Pavlovna, was a warm hearted, kind, fun-loving, educated woman who multi-tasked. How could she not with thirteen children? Everything was well-organized, as she was in charge of two households, summers in Kumna and winters in St. Petersburg. She had many interests, which she conveyed to her children. My grandmother was an excellent oil painter and would invite established artists to the home to teach painting to the children. She was very interested in beekeeping and went to many workshops to bring her knowledge back to her bees in Kumna. She loved flowers and took walks with her children, often bringing wild flowers and growing them in her nursery in the summer estate.

In St. Petersburg, my grandmother went to fine art galleries and museums and made crafts to sell at fundraising bazaars. For one such bazaar, she made several dolls, complete with costumes from several different nationalities and time periods. One anecdote that Papa shared about his mother: She was sitting with a guest in the drawing room and one of his older sisters came and told her that one of the youngest had cut her finger. Very calmly, my grandmother told the older girl where the bandages and the medication were and to take care of it. When the guest remarked about my grandmother's calmness, she said to the guest, "I have two hundred sixty fingers to be calm about."

In 1902, my grandfather Bogdan (which means God given) became the Adjutant General to Czar Nicholas II and had the privilege and responsibility of contacting the Czar day or night. Papa told me many stories about my grandfather. Once he was walking on Palace Square in St. Petersburg and Czar Nicholas II, not recognizing him from a distance, happened to be looking out of the window. "Who is that tall officer walking on the square and why is he walking and not in a carriage?" said the Czar to his aide. His aide replied that the man is Baron Bogdan Egorovich Meyendorff and he has a wife and thirteen children to feed. "Order him a carriage with horses immediately!" the Czar said. From that day on, a carriage was sent to the Meyendorff house to pick up my grandfather.

In 1905 when the Bolshevik unrests began in St, Petersburg, Bogdan decided to go to Estonia and take a look at the Kumna estate to make sure there was no violence or turmoil happening at the Meyendorffs' summer home. When he arrived, he found a group of Bolshevik partisans who were rounded up by the locals because they were accused of trying to do damage to the nobleman's home. The graves were already dug and the partisans were about to be shot when Bogdan stepped in and let them go, saying that he did not want any bloodshed on his property. In the end, this caused him to lose the possibility of a position as governor of the Reval (Tallinn) district as he was considered "too soft."

I was curious about my aunts and uncles, some of whom I never knew. Papa recounted some of the stories: One brother, Andrei, died in a hunting accident as a young man. He was sitting in a horse-drawn sled and reached for his gun, which was lying on the floor of the sled. Somehow his coat sleeve caught the trigger and the gun fired, killing him instantly. One of my father's older sisters, Anastasia, married Ilya Moukhanoff and they had three sons. In 1919, Ilya and two of his sons were shot by a Bolshevik firing squad in St. Petersburg. Sergei Moukhanoff, the third son, was more fortunate and was able to escape and eventually immigrate with his wife, Apka, to Argentina. Years later, Aunt Sandra, my father's twin sister, visited them in Buenos Aires and kept up a communication. One odd detail that I recently learned is that in 2011, Sergei and Apka died within fifteen days of each other in Buenos Aires. Facebook is full of South American Spanish-speaking Meyendorffs who are posting me on a regular basis. I think it will take another lifetime for me to research all these connections.

Uncle Pavel, one of Papa's oldest brothers, became a well-known painter in Russia and later in England. I recently learned that his painting of General Alexander Suvorov (1730-1800), sold at Christies in London in December, 2004 for $1250. Stella Arbenina, his wife, was a famous actress in Russia and Estonia, and later became a film actress in Germany and England. In 1917, as the Bolshevik Revolution unraveled in St. Petersburg and the city became a hotbed of arrests and murder, Uncle Pavel was imprisoned and nearly lost his life; their young children were sent to stay with my grandparents in Moscow to keep them safe. Little did Uncle Pavel and Aunt Stella know that they would not see their children for another three years. Those three years are the subject of Stella's riveting memoir *From Terror to Freedom,* which she wrote in 1923 when the family finally reached England.

Nikolai ("Nika") Meyendorff, another brother and a gifted artist, served in the Life Guards Horse-Artillery Regiment during the 1917 Revolution. He escaped Russia by evacuating from the Crimea via Constantinople. He lived in Vienna and then Paris, where he studied fine art at the École des Beaux-Arts. He settled in Belgrade, Yugoslavia with his wife, Nina. In the 1930s, King Alexander I of Yugoslavia commissioned Uncle Nika to copy every Byzantine fresco in his kingdom. It took Uncle Nika seven years to visit every single monastery in Yugoslavia and copy 800 frescoes. In the 1950s when Marshal Tito came to power in Yugoslavia, Tito decided to redo the frescos and had Communist artists copy Uncle Nika's work. The "politically correct" works were exhibited around the world. In the 1960s, Uncle Nika saw an exhibition in Vienna and recognized one of the works as his own.

While in Belgrade, Uncle Nika painted frescoes for twenty-three Orthodox Churches (including the Cathedral of St. Sava in Belgrade) and three royal palaces (one in Dedinje and two in Belgrade, including the old palace opposite the Russian consulate) and finished over forty separate icons. Uncle Nika drew outlines that were the beginnings of an *iconostasis* (the icon-laden wall separating the altar from the rest of the church) in the Russian Orthodox Trinity Church in Boston. Unfortunately, he was unable to finish the *iconostasis* before his death and his daughter, Elena Nikolaevna Meyendorff, my cousin from Salzburg, finished the work according to his outlines.

I knew and loved Bogdan Meyendorff (Uncle Bada), who immigrated to Paris after the 1917 Revolution and became a well-known miniature portrait artist in Paris, Biarritz, and New York City. (I have a miniature portrait of myself that Uncle Bada painted and gave to our family.) Uncle Bada was a character. My father and I reminisced about an incident that occurred on one of Uncle Bada's visits to New York City. He was well over eighty years old at the time and he was taking a stroll in Central Park in the early part of the day. Suddenly, he was attacked by a young hoodlum who demanded that Uncle Bada hand over his wallet. My uncle took his cane and hit the young man with such fierceness that the man ran away.

Uncle Bada was married to Aunt Katherine, nee Shidlovskaya, a member of a prominent Russian aristocratic family—the same Shidlovski family which served at Czar Nicholas II's Duma. Their son was my cousin Father John Meyendorff, whom I admired and respected highly. A professor and priest at the St. Vladimir Seminary in Westchester County, he was a leading theologian who died much too early, at age sixty-six of pancreatic cancer, in 1992. He and Father Schmemann were probably among the most erudite theologians of any faith during their time. When my mother died in 1979, Papa asked the Russian Orthodox priest in Nyack to perform the small funeral service (панихида) at our apartment. Because my mother was Lutheran, the priest refused to do this. Father John came without hesitation to perform the service. I shall never forget his generosity and his ability to erase the invisible borders between the two religions.

I was very close to my favorite Aunt Sandra (Alexandra), my father's twin sister, who left Estonia with my father and who lived with us at the Clarkstown Country Club, our first home in America. She often stayed and visited us in our various apartments in Nyack, and she took me under her wing and spent time with me. Aunt Sandra also was an accomplished artist and an excellent icon painter. In the early 1920s, she worked as a secretary for William Averill Harriman in his Moscow office. Harriman was a Democratic statesman, presidential advisor, and businessman, a diplomat who served as the U.S. Ambassador to the Soviet Union from 1943 to 1946. He later became the forty-eighth Governor of New York. Harriman was a high-profile politician who received special permission from Lenin to mine manganese ore in Georgia in partnership with a German company. For this reason and for other business reasons, he kept an office in Moscow.

When Stalin came to power, Harriman folded the business, closed his office in Moscow, and along with his American workers, returned to the United States. The Russians who worked for him, like my Aunt Sandra, were not as fortunate; they were forbidden to leave. Out of desperation, Aunt Sandra asked a fellow American co-worker if he would marry her and take her to America with him, but the co-worker's girlfriend would not allow this. As soon as the Americans left, Aunt Sandra was arrested and sentenced to five years (1928-1933) at the Solovki Islands prison camp, in the far north by the White Sea, for working with foreigners. In 1933, Aunt Sandra finished her five-year term and managed to reunite with her sister, Aunt Tessia and her family of seven children in Tver, Russia, carrying with her a seven-string gypsy guitar. It was then that my father sold a part of the Kumna estate and, with the money, obtained passports for Aunt Sandra and Aunt Tessia's family. Aunt Sandra never spoke to anyone about how she survived her prison sentence. She did share a prison song, which we all learned to sing. The following is one of the repetitive stanzas, which I translated:

Всех кто наградил нас Соловками	Everyone who rewarded us with the Solovkis
Просим приезжайте туда с сами	We ask you to come visit us
Посидите вы годочков три или пять	Stay there about three or five years
Будете с восторгом вспоминать	And you will have delightful memories

In the 1970s, when I was living in Minneapolis, Aunt Sandra died unexpectedly from complications from pneumonia. To this day, I regret not attending her funeral.

After the shock of the 1917 Bolshevik revolution in St. Petersburg, the Meyendorffs scattered in many different directions trying to save themselves and their families. As I mentioned earlier, my grandparents went to live with my Aunt Elena (Countess Elena Sheremeteva) on the Sheremetev estate near Moscow. At first they lived there in relative comfort. Then, as the revolution progressed, the Bolsheviks forced the family into a few small rooms with hardly enough to eat and no money with which to buy provisions.

My grandparents moved into the city of Moscow with my Aunt Maya, Aunt Nadya and Uncle Pavel and Aunt Stella's children, who had been sent there earlier to stay with the grandparents. All of them were preparing documents to leave for Kumna in Estonia, still an independent country. On March 30, 1919, when the documents had all been prepared, my grandfather died peacefully in his sleep. He was spared many of the horrors that followed the Bolshevik Revolution. His grave can be found at the very famous Russian Orthodox Novo Devichi Cemetery in Moscow.

By the time my grandmother got over the shock of losing her husband, war had broken out in Estonia, borders were closed, and their Estonian passports useless. Rations were extremely low and my grandmother, the two aunts and the two children all lived in a two-room shanty in Moscow. Aunt Maya wore out a pair of shoes running to the various commissions to inquire about their departure to Estonia. A year later, in August, 1920, by some miracle, all of them got permission to leave Moscow via train to Reval, Estonia.

In my childhood and adolescent years, I heard the name Kumna, the name of the family estate in Estonia, repeated hundreds of times by all members of the Meyendorff family. As I understood from my father, Kumna was the last vestige of peaceful and joyous times for all the Meyendorffs; certainly for my immediate family. It was the place where the surviving members of the family had lived in relative peace and calm before the next wave of displacement and terror arrived in the form of World War II.

I would have loved to be part of that life in Kumna.

On February 11, 1982, Jessie and I were on our way to Nyack Hospital to visit my father, who was diagnosed with pneumonia. I walked into the hospital with my little daughter, and was told that "Baron Meyendorff has expired." What? I could not comprehend...

Twenty minutes before we arrived, my father suffered a massive hemorrhage and died of cardiac arrest. Instead of seeing my father that day, I had to leave, carrying a plastic bag with his wallet, eyeglasses, and his faded, slack clothes back to his empty apartment in Nyack. When I walked into his rooms above his sister's house, which still were thick with his scent of medicine and something less definable–the odor of despair–I sat down on the sagging couch where he'd told me his stories, and I doubled over and wept. I had not cried when my mother died three years before; I cried now. I cried for the loss of my mother, the death of my father; the suffering Papa and Mama had experienced. I wept because I had never been able to tell them, as I could now, that I understood their sorrows and the resulting behavior that had mystified and repelled me. I cried because I didn't have a chance to tell them how much I loved and needed them.

Chapter Thirty Two

The Hudson Valley

BY CHANCE, I FOUND OUT that Svetlana Umrichen, the person I considered to be my second mother when I was growing up in Nyack, was teaching Russian language and culture at the State University in New Paltz, ten minutes from my home. I rushed over to the college to see her. After fifteen years of separation, it was a joyous reunion and we spent hours catching up. My meeting with Svetlana helped me overcome the grief of my father's death. It was also ironic that our reunion happened with my father's passing. Years ago, when I was an adolescent, he had forbidden me to go to Svetlana's house because of innocent encounters with boys–a painful decision for me. Now, I was filled with joy to have her in my life again.

I began to audit all of Svetlana's Russian language classes in New Paltz and became her informal assistant, soaking up as much Russian grammar, literature, and culture as I could. At the end of the semester, students performed skits in Russian and I helped with the Russian folk dancing recitals. We sang Russian songs, recited poetry. I organized a Russian Club at my house where Russian students from SUNY could visit and converse; I would make *borscht* and *zakuski*. I tapped into my rich Russian culture, and with Svetlana in my life again, I felt supported and loved. My strength began to return.

At that time, I had no idea that I would become a language teacher, but Svetlana, who held a doctorate in Russian Literature from New York University, instilled in me a love and a respect for the teaching profession. She made teaching fun, using games, poems, riddles, children's stories, and Russian literature to entice students to converse in Russian and to teach difficult grammar usage. Later, having spent years in universities and numerous language workshops to become a professional educator, I realized that Svetlana was by far the best teacher I had. We never lost touch again until her death in November, 2007.

I didn't have much time to get used to the modern conveniences in our red cedar fantasy house on Rocky Hill Road in New Paltz. Less than two years later, Jeff, Jessie, and I left our suburban nest and moved our meager possessions into a twelve by forty foot moldy aluminum trailer on Mossy Brook Road in High Falls, New York. Jeff had found a four-acre piece of land in Samsonville, situated under Mount Mombaccus at the southern end of the Catskill Mountains, and he wanted to buy it. Property taxes were low in the Town of Olive because of the New York City reservoir, and we could save money to build the dream house by living–for a short time, he promised –in the High Falls trailer.

When I saw the Samsonville land, which was wild and beautiful, it evoked the Adirondacks and my associated feelings of isolation and entrapment. I was afraid to live there, but I couldn't bring myself to put an end to Jeff's plans. He was edging so close to his dream. I blamed myself for being weak and fearful and hoped that something would change in me. I tried to make peace with the idea that we would be living in an aluminum trailer in High Falls, that Samsonville was a half an hour from anywhere. It all made logical sense–for John.

My mother had followed the Baron from Estonia to America, moving from apartment to apartment in Nyack, hoping for a kinder, more benevolent and peaceful world. Unknowingly, I followed my mother's footsteps, put on my blinders and followed Jeff, repeating the familiar mantra "I'm doing the right thing," relying on him to fulfill his promise.

The yellow trailer with white trim in High Falls looked like a dilapidated train car from a John Steinbeck novel. Inside, the trailer consisted of a tiny kitchen with a foldout dining table pressed up against a window directly behind the stove. The dining area spilled into the living area, where our futon doubled as a couch and bed. Behind the living room was Jessie's tiny bedroom, followed by a miniature bathroom with a pink tub, toilet and sink. There was another small room at the very end with a closet where clothes and shoes were kept. As in a train car, a narrow hallway connected all the rooms, which inspired Jessie to line up her stuffed animals and dolls on a daily basis. The one positive side of our new aluminum home was that the trailer was situated on beautiful property with a magnificent view of the Shawangunk Ridge. Jake and Angie, our neighbors and landlords, lived in a larger trailer perpendicular to ours several hundred feet away. I gave myself the name "Trailer Sally."

The winter of 1982 was one of the coldest in Hudson Valley history. After a snowstorm, the aluminum trailer froze and we could not open the front door. Jeff had to hammer his way out with an axe and a chisel. That day, I watched three-year-old Jessie, all bundled up, standing in the snow up to her waist, peering into the window of a neighbor's trailer to watch *The Smurfs* on their television. We did not own a television set. That spring all my shoes in the closet turned green from mildew, and my cookbooks in the kitchen blackened from mold. Our son Jarett was conceived on the futon in the living room. "Trailer Sally" was pregnant with her second child.

Having had an unfulfilling and unprepared hospital experience with Jessie's birth, I decided that giving birth was a natural ritual that should be celebrated. I wanted to have a home birth for my son. Our small trailer in High Falls was out of the question; there was not enough space and it was corroded and filled with mold. Jarett Ian, our son, was born on Mother's Day, May 8, 1983 in Dr. Larry and Jennifer Perl's birthing center in their home in Catskill, New York. I lay in a queen-sized bed in a lovely room with flowered wallpaper on the second floor of the Perls' beautiful Victorian home. The room was big enough for Jeff, Jessie, and Leanne Brevin, a friend from Minneapolis who was designated to be photographer and Jessie's caretaker if things got too intense for Jess. Larry Perl, the obstetrician, checked in on me periodically, and of course, the ever-caring midwife Jennifer was there and caught Jarett as he emerged and placed him on my breast.

I labored for six hours and in all that time, Jeff sat behind me, held me, inhaled and exhaled with me, inhaled and exhaled with me, and together we helped Jarett into this world. Jessie, at four years old, never took her eyes off the magical moment when Jarett emerged and was the first to cry out, "Mommy, I have a little brother!"

Like Jessie, Jarett was beautiful at birth: small, a little shorter than Jess, with a shock of long blond hair that he lost in his first few months. A few hours after the birth, I bathed Jarett, put on his first warm, cozy outfit, complete with a hat, and swaddled him in a blanket. While he slept, we ate chocolate cake and sang his first birthday song. It was indeed the best Mother's Day gift I have ever received.

I will be forever grateful to Jeff for sharing this passage with me.

It was an ordinary day of shopping in New Paltz for "Trailer Sally" and her two children. Our last stop was The Bakery on North Front Street. I parked the car and as I walked down the street with the kids in tow, I heard music coming from the second floor above The Handmade Store. It sounded like a combination of African and Hispanic music, with a rhythm that enticed me. I pulled my children into the building and dragged them up the stairs. The music intensified, arousing familiar sensations. I heard that irresistible beat. At the top of the stairs, holding both of my children's hands, my legs like weights, I stared at dancers springing across the floor, moving their arms, shoulders, hips, legs to Afro-Cuban music; they shone with sweat on their faces. I watched, tears rolling down my face. How long had it been since I danced so freely, with abandon, to music that stirred my soul?

Jeff grumbled something about the uselessness of dance classes, underlining the guilt that I already harbored about not being a good mother, but nothing was going to stop me from joining Brenda Bufalino's weekly Afro Cuban Jazz class in New Paltz. "Trailer Sally" donned her jazz shoes and tights and went to class. At first, my muscles burned; my bones ached, and I would hurry home to the miniature pink bathtub in the trailer to soak in Epsom salts. Little by little, class by class, memory muscles at work, my body became stronger, and I was able to keep up with the rest of the class. It wasn't too long before I started teaching my own jazz dance classes at the High Falls Firehouse, using Luigi's Jazz technique, which I had learned twenty years before in New York City.

I knew that the move to the bigger trailer on our own land in Samsonville in the summer of 1983 was going to be my final move with Jeff. Now it was up to Jeff to fulfill his plan of building our dream house and to continue his wholesale framing business, which he had resumed in a workshop in the village of Rosendale, a few miles south of High Falls. Of course, the new workshop had to be built on the land first to generate business and capital before the house could be built. And why not build a little apartment above the workshop as a little getaway/guest house for one person? "Trailer Sally" watched and waited as plans folded and unfolded and the business grew. The dream house remained a dream.

That summer, life seemed better. We dug out boulders to make space for a large garden. I canned and froze our garden harvests. Jeff excavated a root cellar to put the carrots, beets, potatoes, and turnips away for the winter. We had a sunroom built onto the trailer, heated in winter by a woodstove. The land was so private that the kids ran free without clothing all day long. I mowed the grass topless with a push mower; once or twice, the UPS man got an eyeful. We bought our first TV.

On a suggestion from a friend, I joined the Krumville Mountain Mamas women's softball team. I had never played softball in my life, but it sounded like a fun idea. Even when a very good-looking male coach showed up to whip us into shape, we couldn't win a single game. The Krumville Mountain Mamas were all young mothers with small children. The baby carriages would be lined up near the batting area. Jarett, who was about a year old, had to wait to be nursed if I got a base hit; sometimes it took forever, depending on who got up to bat. If Jarett became too fussy, one of the other mothers would nurse him. I still have the tee shirt with an imprint of a Victorian woman in a long dress with her hair up, holding a baseball bat.

When Jessie turned five, she moved into the master bedroom in the back of the trailer and Jeff and I moved our bed into the living room. Foot-long woodrats would crawl in from the cracks in the foundation and raid the garbage in the kitchen. Jeff would shoot them with a rifle from our bed.

As winter approached, my feelings of isolation grew. I remember driving home on County Route 2, after teaching my dance class in High Falls, counting every mile back to Samsonville: nine long miles uphill from Route 209. Memories of Saranac Lake haunted me. I would wake up in the middle of the night, hyperventilating and covered with sweat. Then, not too far from our property, a jealous lover set up a ladder, climbed up to the bedroom window of our friend Morty's house, and shot him in the face as he and his wife were lounging in bed.

I escaped the isolation by enrolling at Empire State College, an affiliate of SUNY New Paltz where I had flexible study options, no class schedules, and where I was able to design my own Bachelors degree. Going back to college had Jeff's stamp of approval, and he was willing to watch Jarett for a few hours during the day. Jessie was in kindergarten for half of the day at the Bennett School in Boiceville, the closest public school.

I called my degree Ecological Activism, prompted by my being incensed at seeing large amounts of garbage on the roads, garbage in our foods, and pollution in our air and water. Rather than being another cog in the wheel, I wanted to be part of a larger pro-active community to help clean up the environment.

My first assignment at Empire State was to create my own portfolio, a collection of prior life-learning skills and college credits which were to be applied towards my Bachelors degree. Out of the 128 credits I needed for my degree, I received 96 credits for my life-learning skills: my theatrical experiences (acting, directing, make-up, lighting and set design), my fluency in Russian, the dance and art classes, and the few credits I had managed to obtain at Rockland Community College in 1966-67. It took me six months to document and compile photos and newspaper articles to prove to the various college department heads that I had, in fact, obtained these skills. For the rest of my 32 credits, I read books such as *Ecology as Politics, Rules for Radicals, Oppression and Social Intervention,* and *The Dynamics of Non-Violent Action,* all leftist, socialist literature that made sense to me–a far cry from the right-wing conservative politics I grew up with in Nyack. I spent hours in the SUNY library, writing papers on the various philosophies and discussing my ideas with my mentor, David Porter, who was grooming me on how to become a revolutionary in the United States. In 1966, I had been flunking out of Rockland Community College out of boredom and lack of interest, but now I was stimulated by the intellectual student world in which I found myself. I was ready for a revolution– if not in my personal life, then perhaps I could help create change in the world. The trailer in Samsonville became more distant. It was not the place I wanted to return to.

I had not yet found a home.

Chapter Thirty Three

Russia

LIFE CHANGING EVENTS ARRIVE WHEN we least anticipate them. Just as my deepest wish to go to Russia was rising from my subconscious, the opportunity to go to the land of my heritage also surfaced, as if from nowhere. In the summer of 1985, Charles Reeves, to whom I gave private Russian language lessons in New Paltz, started his own travel agency to Russia and asked me to accompany him as an assistant tour guide. He had assembled a large group of educators from all over the United States who were going to Moscow and St. Petersburg, staying one week in each city, and he needed help. Moscow! St. Petersburg! My Russian blood rose – the cities of my parents' earlier days, the large manor house in St. Petersburg where my father had lived as a boy. I had heard so much about Russia, knew that my paternal side was pure Russian. As displaced as I had been–born out of context in a DP camp in Germany–I felt a force, a pure magnetism pulling me "home."

Yet there were obstacles to my traveling there. How could I leave my children for two weeks? Would Jeff take care of Jessie and Jarett without making me feel guilty? Was it worth the guilt? What about my anxiety? What if I got a panic attack in Russia?

Desire–need–won out. There was no question–I could not miss this opportunity to go to Russia. Decisions were made quickly, travel plans formed, and within weeks, I found myself at JFK Airport in front of twenty-five educators bound for Moscow.

On my first night in Moscow, I walked across the huge expanse of Red Square with the medieval Kremlin Wall on one side, the GUM shopping center on the other, and the lit-up multicolored St. Basil's Cathedral in the background. I had not anticipated the beauty, the fairy tale quality; I wanted to stop every passerby and tell them what it meant for me to be in Russia where crowds of people were speaking my native Russian language. I felt proud of my heritage and fortunate for my fluency in Russian. I could immerse myself into exotic Mother Russia: the mysticism, the uniqueness of the Eastern and Western cultures, the history, the beauty, the ugliness, the politics, the drama. I'd come home.

In Moscow, there was the Bolshoi Theatre, the museums, the restaurants, the cafes, the streets that hold so much history. I couldn't step into a Russian Orthodox Church without welling up in tears–I heard Papa singing in his pure tenor voice, the liturgical music in the choir. The familiar scent and smoke of the incense, the candle-glowing icons, the bells' chimes all summoned me to my religious roots. Here in Russia, the guilt I associated with the Orthodox religion was gone, and only the beauty remained. And Mama–I saw her in the theatres and cafes of Moscow, the city she loved, reciting the poems of Pushkin, Lermontov, and Ahkmatova. I managed to visit the grave of my grandfather, Baron Theofil Meyendorff, in the Novo Devichi cemetery in Moscow. I stole away from my tourist group one afternoon to visit Mikhail Bulgakov's apartment, where he wrote his famous novel *The Master and Margarita*. The apartment had become an informal shrine to him with graffiti and hundreds of signatures from all over the world on the walls. I added mine.

One night, after a long day of sightseeing with the tourist group, I returned to my room at the hotel in Moscow and I couldn't fall asleep. The more I tried, the more alone and disconnected I started to feel. *Where am I? What am I doing here? Who am I?* Just as in Saranac Lake, I felt the floor, my foundation, slipping from underneath me. I slid into that amorphous dark of shifting fears. Would I be carried off in hysterics to a mental hospital in Moscow? The thought terrified me and made my mind spin out of control. Why was I feeling so alone? Was the "displacement" within me? Shaking, I got out of bed and forced myself to move.

I danced. For an hour, by my bed in my postage stamp-sized room, I danced to Luigi's Jazz exercises, the rhythms playing in my head. Exhausted and soaked with sweat, I then soaked in a hot bath, crawled into bed, and promptly fell asleep. The next morning, I awoke feeling well and rested. I had won a battle with my demons and felt better than I had in months. I was able enjoy the rest of the trip. Every morning, I woke up and danced for thirty minutes before venturing out into the Russian streets. Underneath, perhaps, lurked the dark unease that could surface later, but at least for the time being, I could dance it away.

In St. Petersburg, the palaces looked like wedding cakes, and the canals that ran through the city from the Neva River gave the city its reputation as "Venice of the North." St. Petersburg held a particular interest for me because it was where my father and his family had lived. I took the entire tourist group on a pilgrimage to see the Meyendorff manor on Pervaya Liniya, on Vasilievsky Island, not far from the Winter Palace. I pictured my father as a child in the large yellow house, running in the hallways with his twelve brothers and sisters. Across the street was the White Russian Cadet Academy where Papa and his brothers went to school as young men to learn how to become proper Russian officers. At the Winter Palace, I looked up and saw the window where Czar Nicholas II stood when he noticed my grandfather walking across Palace Square and ordered horses and a carriage for him.

1985 was an interesting time to visit Russia. That year, Mikhail Gorbachev became General Secretary of the Communist Party and introduced Glasnost, which meant openness in association with freedom of speech, and Perestroika, which meant economic restructuring. These two concepts profoundly affected the social, political, economic, and cultural climate of the time, loosening the leash on the Russian masses, giving them more freedom to welcome foreigners and to speak openly for the first time in decades.

I was an enigma to the Soviet Russians. Most of the people I spoke with could not believe the fluent Russian coming from an American who had never before been to Russia. Some people were suspicious; some were eager to hear my story. Most people were excited about my Russian aristocratic background and even told me that my particular accent evoked the enunciation and accent of the highborn in pre-revolutionary Russia. Many acknowledged the loss of the *intelligentsia* and the rich Russian culture that was suppressed by the 1917 Bolshevik Revolution.

In St. Petersburg, my ability to speak Russian well also got me into trouble with the Communist authorities. As my group was comprised of educators from many American states, the teachers were eager to see a Russian school, enter a classroom. This proved difficult because most children were on summer vacation, but I found a children's camp outside of St. Petersburg, that, according to my information, we could visit. I coordinated a small group and we undertook the journey. The Russian counselors and the children came out to greet the Americans with bread and salt, a traditional Russian greeting. To the children, we might as well have been from a different planet. Americans! They sang to us and we all learned the chorus section for the popular children's song "*May There Always Be Sunshine.*"

Пусть всегда будет солнце	May there always be sunshine
Пусть всегда будет небо	May there always be blue sky
Пусть всегда будет мама	May there always be Mama
Пусть всегда буду я	May there always be me

The children gave the American teachers drawings and poetry to take home with them. The Russians and the Americans spent the day crying and laughing with each other – a profound and spontaneous experience of East meeting West.

Later that day, when we returned to St. Petersburg, I was called on the carpet by the infamous Intourist Agency. I was greeted by a large Russian woman wearing big black boots.

"How dare you go outside the legal radius of the city with foreigners?"

I told the woman that I had no idea that I'd broken a rule; that I was told we could go. She was furious with me. Before I turned around to leave, I mustered up my courage and said, "I come from America, where we do not have boundaries within cities. People in America are free to travel wherever they please." The woman stood there dumbfounded and silent.

Between 1986 and 1987, there would be three more two-week trips to Russia. By then, I was leading the tours alone. The first group consisted of students from the private Friends School in Baltimore, Maryland. On a Saturday night,

I decided to take the young people to a Russian Orthodox Church for the night service. Ancient grandmothers (бабушки) dressed in black with kerchiefs on their heads were prostrated in deep prayer on the church floor. One of the young men in the group turned to me and said, "I would give anything to change places with one of these woman, to feel the depth of their faith in God." The boy was sixteen years old.

The second group I escorted was made of patrons and playwrights of the Manhattan Theatre Club. I shared many a straight vodka with the famous playwright Terrence McNally and John Novi, proprietor of the Depuy Canal House in High Falls, New York. The third group was a combination of students and adults from different areas of the United States. The group became a part of an all-night candlelight vigil in front of the famous Angleterre Hotel, which was slated to be demolished by Soviet authorities the next day. In addition to being one of the more historic hotels in St. Petersburg, it was there that Sergei Esenin, one of my favorite Russian poets, was found dead at age thirty, an apparent suicide. Esenin's poems were posted on the building on large sheets of paper and also on tiny pieces taped to the fence surrounding the hotel. It was a Russian-style demonstration: people huddled in groups, held candles, recited and shared Esenin's poetry, hoping that their vigil would save the hotel. The Americans fit right in. The next day, I heard the explosion from my hotel as the Angleterre fell to the ground. I shuddered in response to every blast.

After my trips to Russia, I had a difficult time returning to the United States. It took me weeks to settle into the Western, materialistic culture. Poverty in America, the richest country in the world, became vivid to me. There were no bums, no panhandlers, no cripples on Russian streets. Everyone had jobs, no matter how menial. One day, I became very anxious during a mundane grocery shopping trip to ShopRite in New Paltz. I stood in front of the toilet paper section and burst into tears. There were too many choices: umpteen brands with degrees of size, softness, and color. In Russia, apart from the luxuries of the hotel, one was lucky to have toilet paper at all.

I thought in Russian. I dreamt in Russian. In my dreams, I visualized churches painted sky blue with outsized hanging bells and golden cupolas. I saw cupcake palaces and wide boulevards and squares filled with people all speaking in Russian. My Russian roots were taking a deeper hold upon my subconscious–and my heart. To paraphrase the immortal Russian author Vladimir Nabokov, a fellow White Russian émigré, "How deep did the tentacled ache go?"

On my final trip, I made a profound decision. I changed my educational path to follow my subconscious, switching my goal of attaining an Ecological Activism degree to a Russian Language and Culture degree and pursuing a language teaching profession. My mentor, David Porter, was astounded. By changing my degree, I would have to redo much of the work I had already accomplished and begin anew with the new Bachelor's program, taking proper Education courses at SUNY New Paltz. My decision was unprecedented at Empire State College, and David often showed his other students my self-imposed workload.

In the summer of 1986, I finished my three-week student teaching program, the last component of my Bachelor's Degree. I was fortunate enough to be accepted into a New York State approved student teaching program at Smith College in Massachusetts, where I did my student teaching in French since there was no summer Russian program in any of the middle schools near Northhampton, Massachusetts. I loved being at Smith College. There was a refined atmosphere at the Ivy League college. I enjoyed living in the dorms. I rode my bicycle going to my student teaching program or to ballet or African dance classes. Jeff and the children came to visit and slept in my dorm room with me. As we slept in the same room, I knew Jeff and I dreamed very different dreams. The marriage was crumbling.

I'm not sure when or where Jeff met Kiyoko, a beautiful Japanese girl living in New Paltz, but it wasn't long before he began taking Japanese language lessons from her. In his usual way, Jeff suddenly became enamored with everything Japanese. The byproduct of his infatuation with Japan (and Kiyoko) was that our family began dining in fine Japanese restaurants and learning to eat with chopsticks. Sushi and sashimi were exotic foods we learned to enjoy, except for Jessie who never got the hang of chopsticks and hated all types of fish.

Conversations centered around Kiyoko, and it soon became apparent to me that Jeff had deeper feelings for her–feelings he did not deny. When I asked him if he was sleeping with her, he said he was not. I wondered why Jeff was holding back, if he was telling me the truth. Why didn't he sleep with her? Why not let his emotions fly?

He couldn't. Jeff was in conflict. He couldn't let his emotions get the better of him. His feelings for Kiyoko did not fit in his personal rigid logic. I was angry at him for not being honest. Perhaps he knew that I would leave him in an instant if he slept with Kiyoko; that I was waiting for an excuse to fly.

And then he twisted the knife in his usual logical fashion. We were lying in bed in our makeshift bedroom in the trailer living room. Jeff turned to me and asked, "Would you give me a divorce so that I could marry Kiyoko? The green card would allow her to stay in the United States and she could then make a living here. Of course, after she obtained the green card, I would divorce her and marry you again."

I looked at him in disbelief, let his words sink in for a moment, and answered, "No. That's not happening."

Jeff had played his last joker card.

It was winter. It was cold. "Trailer Sally" became very ill and lay motionless on the big bed in the living room. Jarett and Jessie were also sick and the three of us were huddled together under the blankets. Jeff was somewhere with Kiyoko taking Japanese lessons. "*Kunichiwa* to you," I thought.

One day, I mustered every ounce of strength I had and called Sally Reid, our medical practitioner at the Rhinebeck Health Center. I told her there was no way I could drive to Rhinebeck; that something was terribly wrong. About four that afternoon, Sally came to the trailer with her medical bag and stethoscope in hand, checked my lungs, and diagnosed me with pneumonia, the illness which had led to my father's death and killed his twin sister, my Aunt Sandra. I felt I must make a life change, or die. Six weeks of recovery–plenty of time to realize that the time had come to move on and leave Jeff. I took this recuperation time to plan my exit from Samsonville. I said nothing to Jeff.

After I was back on my feet, I continued my jazz dance classes in High Falls. One evening, during class, I stopped dancing and took the needle off the record. I turned to the class and asked if anyone knew of a place–an apartment or house for me and my two children. I was leaving my husband and we needed a place to live. To my surprise, someone from the back row, someone I did not know, said she was vacating a beautiful house in Stone Ridge that belonged to the veterinarian Dr. Andre Ross; the student and her husband were moving to Maine. My legs became weak. The blood rushed to my face. This was my chance.

The next day, I went to meet Dr. Andre Ross, a small, elegant, grey-haired woman with kind, generous eyes. And the house was indeed beautiful, with a bedroom for each of the kids, an attic space with a claw-foot bathtub upstairs for me, and the Vly Ridge as a backyard. This was my dream house come true. I had no money and no job, but Andre, my new angel, noticed my desperate need, accepted me as her tenant and trusted that I would come up with the rent. Within a month, Jessie, Jarett, and I were settled in at 2013 Atwood Avenue in Stone Ridge. Jessie was seven, Jarett was three, and I was thirty-nine years old. I was free... sort of. Perhaps the Displaced Person had at last found a home. Or had I just lost one?

Chapter Thirty Four

On My Own

WE WERE PROMISED ONE OF the kittens and we came to take a look, having been forbidden by Jeff to have any pets. This turned out to be more difficult than we anticipated, since the kittens were hidden in a crawl space under my friend's unfinished house. Jessie, Jarett, and I crawled, barely wedging ourselves into the shallow crawl space; we inched along on our bellies, and mewed for the kittens, but none appeared. We couldn't find any of the babies, but just as I climbed out and stood up, a grey, striped blur ran between my legs, stopped and looked up at me. We called this tiny kitten "Mitsi," short for Dimitri Mourkovich, the name of my first grey cat in Nyack. Mitsi became our beloved cat and lived with the children and me for eighteen years. I traded a husband for a grey-striped, lovable, affectionate male cat.

Jeff initiated the two-year separation agreement, during which he watched and waited like a predator for me to fail, to give up my independence and come back to him. He would stop by the Stone Ridge house and plead with me to come home. In his presence, I could feel Jeff's vise-like grip, and it repulsed me. He couldn't understand my revulsion; I couldn't tell him what I felt. I could see that he continued to hope...

Jeff organized a trip to Disneyland–anything to keep us together. I agreed to take this vacation for the sake of the children. On the flight over, my gold antique wedding band snapped in two, permanently broken. Wasn't that symbolic enough?

During the "holiday," Jessie was the only one ecstatic to be there. Jarett, who was three years old, didn't comprehend much, but to a seven-year-old little girl, the fantasy rides, the huge roller coaster, the giant Mickey Mouse and the poufy-skirted Snow White were a great distraction and delight. To me, they added to the ludicrousness of this outing.

To make ends meet, and to maintain my independence, I cleaned houses, and taught Russian wherever they would hire me: Gifted and Talented programs at BOCES in New Paltz, after-school programs in the Phoenicia and Woodstock elementary schools, and summer and evening programs at Ulster County Community College. These programs led to working on weekends teaching Russian for the SUNY New Paltz Language Immersion program and teaching workshops on language acquisition at BOCES in New Paltz. I finally landed a full time job teaching Russian at the Mountain Laurel School, a Waldorf elementary school in New Paltz. There was never enough money, but it didn't matter. I was on my own, determined to survive.

In the summer of 1987, Svetlana urged me to apply to The Russian Institute at Bryn Mawr College, a three-week gratis program for Russian teachers to enhance their Russian teaching skills. The program was too good to pass up. I applied and was accepted.

Again I found myself in an Ivy League college and enjoying my studies, an intensive, innovative program taught by the best professors in the field. All aspects of language and culture were covered: music, literature, poetry, art, drama, and of course, methodology. I loved the program and excelled. As always, Jeff cooperated and took care of the children while I was away.

On February 9, 1988, Jeff and I were legally divorced on grounds of incompatibility. I obtained sole custody of the children, although visiting rights were unrestricted. Jeff pleaded poverty and paid me $300 a month for both children's upkeep, with the explanation that he, too would be taking care of them. I didn't argue. I just wanted out.

In the summer of 1988, I decided to go to a SUNY New Paltz study abroad program in St. Paul Valery University in Montpelier in southern France, on the Mediterranean Sea, to obtain a French language teaching certificate. At the time, I had only a Russian teaching certificate, and I wanted to broaden my horizons and become more employable. To my surprise, Jeff decided to accompany me with the children to Paris and offered to drive me to Montpelier from Paris in a "Deux Chevaux" Citroen, a small two-cylinder car that looks like a Rolls Royce. Jeff planned to continue to Spain with the children for a month's vacation while I went to the university. Jeff would not let go, and used the children as a means of staying close. My baby steps towards independence were not taking me far enough. I succumbed to his plan, but there was a slight difference: this time, Jeff was following me.

When we got to the hotel in Paris and I opened up the suitcase, the bottle of champagne that Jeff had bought in New York to share with me had burst. My clothes were dripping wet and smelling of bubbly pink alcohol. Did he really think he could lure me back with champagne? And why did he buy champagne in New York? Paris was all wrong.

After seven hours of driving in the small Citroen from Paris to Montpelier with two children and a suitcase that smelled of alcohol, Jeff dropped me off at the student dorms at St. Paul Valery University. (The children were great. They were very patient and I loved being with them.) I looked forward to being on my own and settling in to my new life as a French student.

On his way to Spain, Jeff stopped in Biarritz, France. It was becoming clear to him that Jessie and Jarett had enough of sitting in the car. He took them to the beach, where Jessie was stung by a jellyfish. The only person who spoke English and could help Jessie was a twenty-year-old maid at the hotel where they were staying. Her name was Celine. One year later, Celine would come to the United States, marry Jeff, and become his third wife, setting me free.

Within a week, Jeff and the children returned to Montpelier from Biarritz, having abandoned the idea of going to Spain. Jeff rented a small efficiency apartment near the sea and he and the children stayed for another two weeks before flying home. Was Jeff watching over me or was he already thinking of Celine? Did it really matter?

I was still at the University when I received an invitation from a British acquaintance I had met a few months earlier at a social gathering in Stone Ridge. He asked me to meet him in London. I must have told him that I was going abroad to study and he looked me up. I had completed my studies and received my French language certification. The children were safe at home with Jeff, and I had another week before school in New Paltz began. I was free. I accepted his invitation.

I arrived in London with a deep Mediterranean tan, wearing a white miniskirt and a little summery blouse. England was freezing. Robert invited me to go to the Isle of Skye in Scotland, where it was even colder. I had to borrow clothes from his family to survive. There was no stopping now. Although I found Robert to be a rather uptight person, we managed to spend a lovely week in a beautiful hotel on Skye and returned to London, where it was still chilly and damp. The fatal blow to our miniscule germ of a relationship came in a pub in London when I told Robert that I would have difficulty living in England's climate–it was too cold and not sunny enough. The next day, I found myself at Heathrow Airport. No great loss; it was time to go home.

In late summer, upon my return from France and London, Tom Stratten, a fine artist and a good friend, took me to a jazz dance class in Woodstock. Lynn Barr was teaching. She noticed my dancing and we spoke after class. Ours was an immediate attraction. I invited Lynn to come over to my house in Stone Ridge and we sat all night on my couch, drinking wine and sharing our experiences and adventures. We were like two little girls at a sleepover, laughing, crying. I learned that she, too had a difficult childhood, but unlike me, Lynn had a husband who took care of her every need. I was in awe of her life, her beauty, and her talent, and fell under the spell of her compelling personality. That night Lynn changed the direction of my life, and for this I am forever grateful to her.

Lynn began her modern dance career at seventeen with the Paul Sanasardo/ Donya Feuer Studio for Dance, the same dance company that Pina Bausch, the famous German choreographer, joined when she lived in New York City. Pina later formed her Tanztheatre company in Wuppertal, Germany. Lynn's choreography, although steeped in Martha Graham's technique, was very much influenced by Pina's unique combination of dance and theatre. Later, Lynn became a dance soloist with the Philadelphia Lyric Opera Company and with the New York City Opera at Lincoln Center. Later, she gave up both jobs to live with her husband, the musician Albee Barr, in a cabin that they purchased in West Shokan, New York. Lynn and Albee commuted between West Shokan and

New York City because Albee's musical career as composer, arranger, singing coach, studio musician, and club musician took him to the city to work. Albee's success as a musician enabled Lynn to concentrate on her dancing career and not have to work at a menial job. They had no children. Albee and Lynn were very much in love. They shared a blissful marriage for fifty years until Albee's sudden death from cancer in September, 2011. Then everything changed.

When I met Lynn, she had formed her own Lynn Barr Dance Company and toured the Metropolitan area with her productions "The Women" and "Mystos." Over the years, I watched Lynn's career unfold with her stunningly choreographed "Il Circo de la Vita" at the McKenna Theatre in New Paltz and her guest appearances as choreographer in Europe. Over the years, Lynn's dance company performed at the New Dance Group Theatre, St. Marks Church, and Judson Church in New York and at the Kaatsbaan International Dance Center in Tivoli, New York.

I started taking Lynn's modern dance classes in Woodstock and became enamored of her unique theatrical and dramatic choreography. I was drawn to her passionate commitment to modern dance. Our friendship deepened. It was in one of Lynn's classes where I met Ann Zanchetti, an exquisite dancer and choreographer and an original member of Lynn's dance company, and Lucinda Knaus, a talented fine artist. The four of us formed a deep friendship that has lasted to this day.

Every other weekend, Jeff would take the children to Samsonville and I boarded the Adirondack Trailways bus in Rosendale, bound for New York City where I would take five or six dance classes over the weekend. I was determined to get my dance chops back and become a modern dancer. Lynn and Albee let me stay on the couch in their penthouse apartment on 24th Street and Tenth Avenue which she and Albee shared with Phyllis Arbury, an elegant elderly woman I grew to love.

Penthouse A, as we called it, became my home away from home. After the dance classes, Lynn, Albee, and I would often go to a movie, a play, or attend a concert or dance production if it was cheap or free. Sometimes Albee played the piano for famous singers in clubs on weekends and Lynn and I would eat pasta with tomato sauce and arugula salad and drink cheap wine in the best inexpensive restaurants in New York. Lynn and I "played." We reverted to being little girls without responsibility, whose young lives were protected, safe, and intact. I never slept better than I did on Lynn and Albee's couch in Penthouse A. For two days, every other weekend, I had no children to take care of, no work to do, and no financial worries.

By the end of the weekend, my muscles ached so much that I could hardly get off the bus in Rosendale and drive home. But I was determined to catch up. The need to succeed in the dance world was prompted by thoughts of my mother, who never had the opportunity to shine as a poet and an actress in America. My father was trapped by his illnesses. I was not going to let this happen to me. I was going to make it. I was going to be a dancer, and I pushed myself.

In the early 1990s, Lynn started teaching modern dance at SUNY New Paltz and formed the Study Abroad dance program under the auspices of the college. There were Study Abroad programs for language students, why not for dance students? For fourteen summers, Lynn traveled to picturesque, medieval Urbino, Italy for three weeks and choreographed modern theatrical pieces for dance students from all over the world. At the end of three weeks, her students performed her pieces in Urbino's ancient piazzas and on stages in several Italian cities. Over the last four years, SUNY's funds for study abroad programs began to dwindle, and Lynn's dance program was moved to less expensive Prague, the capital of the Czech Republic, where the students danced on the Charles Bridge and outside the Smetana Museum.

During the summer sessions, Lynn needed help, and Annie, Lucinda, and I took turns being her assistants, reaping the benefits of a vacation abroad. Sometimes we all managed to go together. With Jeff's cooperation in watching the children, I was able to go to Italy three times as Lynn's student and as her assistant. Once I went to Italy as a courier, the person who accompanies a package on a flight. My round trip fare to Italy was free, and I surprised Lynn by showing up at the piazza in Urbino. Unheard of these days.

As Lynn's assistant, I was able to stay in the beautiful and inexpensive dorms at the University of Urbino, which looked out onto fields of sunflowers and grapevines as far as the eye could see. In Prague we stayed in an historic hotel in the center of the city. Often we shared the room and sometimes even the bed. Lynn was very generous.

Lynn and I did some serious "playing" in Italy and Prague. After the dancing day was over, there were the restaurants and wine; there were the trips to Venice, Florence, and other famous cities where Lynn gave dance workshops; trips to beaches on the Adriatic Sea. Once, after the three- week dance program was over, Lynn, Annie, and I went to the island of Ischia. I thought I had "died and gone to heaven." We loved our little-girl carefree roles and we lived every moment. For me, this freedom was a temporary escape from my hardscrabble existence as a single parent and a schoolteacher in public schools in upstate New York. For Lynn, it was a way of life.

It was in Italy on my forty-third birthday that I realized that I could never be the professional dancer I had hoped to become. Although I had started dancing in my teens, I did not have the years of ballet technique to form a strong base for dance. Luigi's Jazz technique and the few ballet classes I had taken in New York City were not enough. I was killing myself on the dance floor trying to keep up with the young gorgeous dancers who flocked to Lynn's programs in Italy and Prague. I had the energy and the spirit and the theatrics of a dancer, but that was not enough. Dance would always be an integral part of my life, but I could not make it the center of my life.

It also became clear to me that if Lynn and I were to maintain our friendship, I could not continue being her modern dance student. I had reached my peak. I had to find my own artistic path, a path where Lynn and I could share our respective talents and expertise and possibly even collaborate on creative dance/ theatre projects. That path for me was theatre.

We were on a flight home from Italy and I remember turning to Lynn in the seat next to mine and saying, "Within six months, I will be in a theatre production. I hope you will come."

By the early 1990s I had accepted a Russian teaching job at Arlington High School, a public school in Lagrangeville, New York because I could not make ends meet teaching Russian at the private Mountain Laurel school in New Paltz. At that time, Russian language was being phased out of public schools; the Cold War was over and we were no longer enemies with Russia. It was fortunate that I was also certified to teach French. I was transferred to Arlington Middle School in Poughkeepsie to teach French. I was driving one hour each way to school from Stone Ridge, dropping Jessie off at Marbletown Elementary School and Jarett at the nursery school at the college in New Paltz and picking them up on the way back, a grueling schedule.

Yet I was determined not to miss any opportunity to win a role in theatre. I was trying to meet my commitments at the school and still make it to auditions. One night, I found myself, as required by my job, at the Open House at Arlington Middle School. I was sneaking looks at my watch, waiting for the moment that I could escape from the students and their parents and drive thirty miles to audition for a play at the library in Marlboro, New York. I covered the distance at rubber-burning speed, but by the time I pulled, tires squealing, into the Marlboro Library, it was dark. The library's lights were out; there was no one to be seen. The audition was obviously over. I was devastated.

Then I saw several people emerging from the dark building and walking down the steps. I jumped out of my car and called out, "I'm here to audition for the play. Is it too late?"

One of the group, a beautiful woman whose blonde hair glowed under the street light, stopped and said, "Yes, it's late." Then, seeing my disappointment, she added, "But I suppose you can audition right here." She held out a script at an angle so the streetlight illuminated the pages. "Can you see the words?"

The blonde woman was Sigrid Heath, a talented director and actress. She soon became an important liaison for re-establishing my acting career. Right there under the streetlight, she gave me the role of Sheila in the play *The Boys Next Door*, by Tom Griffin. The play is a comedic commentary on four learning-disabled men who live in a group home in the Boston area, and Sheila, who also has mental disabilities, is the girlfriend of one of the men. I loved becoming Sheila and I played her to the hilt. Lynn and Albee attended the opening night.

After a hiatus of twenty years, I had fulfilled the promise I made to myself: to become involved in a theatre production within six months. I was on my artistic path. The cage door flew open and I flew out, wild for my freedom and eager to soar.

Chapter Thirty Five

Life is on Boil

CASSANDRA CAME TO LIVE WITH the children and me in Stone Ridge when she was eleven years old. Her mother Christina, a good friend, was chronically ill from hypoglycemia, a food disorder related to anorexia and bulimia, and could no longer take care of her. I had met Christina–Teeny, I called her–through the High Falls Coop where we both shopped and worked to get our food discounts. Teeny was born in 1957 in Newcastle-Upon-Tyne, Northumberland in England and was raised by her aristocratic English grandmother, The Lady Serena Mary Barbara James, daughter of the Earl and Countess of Scarborough. Later Teeny married an American man, became pregnant with Cassandra, and moved to the United States. They lived in a large beautiful farmhouse in Accord, New York that I remember was always very cold; the size of the house made it difficult to heat properly.

Teeny and I philosophized about our aristocratic families, about food, and about our husbands while Cassandra and Jessie, who were a year apart in age, played together. Teeny and I became friends, a friendship which has flourished to this day. I knew that Teeny was on a very strict diet–her interpretation of the macrobiotic diet–to treat the potentially fatal condition of hypoglycemia. I did not know the extent and the danger of her illness. I'm not even sure I knew what hypoglycemia, anorexia, and bulimia were at the time. To struggle to stay alive, Teeny spent many hours of the day cooking food for herself that she could keep down. She was having difficulty with her marriage. Her husband Blaire Miron worked in New York and came home on weekends. Taking care of Cassandra alone in the absence of her husband was adding to Teeny's stress and exacerbated the food disorder. In 1989, out of desperation, Teeny went back to England alone to attempt to heal herself, and Cassandra came to live with me and my children.

Jessie, Jarett, and I welcomed Cassandra into our home and I became her "second Mom." She slept in the spare bedroom next to Jessie downstairs. Jarett was upstairs in the attic with me. On weekday mornings, we would all pile up in my old Nissan Sentra and drive to New Paltz singing along with Sting or *Les Miz* tapes. I dropped Jarett at the SUNY nursery school and Jessie and Cassandra at the New Paltz Middle School before continuing on to Poughkeepsie to teach. In the evenings, the children played well together, did their homework. Little Jarett was subjected to coming-of-age parties when Jessie and Cassandra first got their periods. I would fix them their favorite meals complete with special desserts. Although I know it was hard on Cass to be without her mother, she adapted as well as she could, going to her father's house on weekends and to England during the summer. I was supposed to get a monthly check from Blaire Miron for Cassandra's upkeep, but the money came sporadically, if at all.

I remember one incident when we were all home because it was a snow day. We were so happy, listening to music, playing the piano, the children building forts with blankets and pillows under the dining room table with Mitsi, their mascot cat, dressed in doll clothes. We watched the heavy wet snow fall on the power lines, making them hang dangerously low. We heard a crack and within minutes, the kitchen and the living room were filled with smoke. The microwave crackled and smoke poured out of my stereo system. I called 911. We were still in our pajamas. I took my scrunchie off, shook my hair free, and said to the girls, "Get dressed, comb your hair, put on the mascara and lipstick, ladies. In about five minutes, there's going to be about fifty handsome firemen all over this house!"

I was right. In ten minutes, there were at least six handsome firemen in the house trying to stabilize the house from the tremendous jolt of electricity it had received from the falling electrical wires outside. The hair brushing and make-up were not enough of a distraction to deter the firemen from doing their job, feeling all the walls in the house for a possible fire. Fortunately, I only lost my microwave and my stereo. Everything else was fine.

In 1990, not being very successful in healing herself, Teeny returned from England, only to pack up and go to Florida where she had a warm place to stay. I remember when Teeny came to my house to drop Cassandra off again. She was emaciated, her skin was yellow, and she smelled of decay. She still appeared to be malnourished and unwell, but with the on-going and continuous support of a Philadelphia-based macrobiotic counselor who specialized in helping people with hypoglycemic-related disorders, she applied his more balanced and appropriate diet to help heal her condition. Miraculously, it worked. Teeny is working on her memoirs and her journey to health is well-chronicled for people suffering with anorexia, bulimia, hypoglycemia, and related food-disorder diseases. A year later, Teeny returned from Florida and came to live with the children and me. She was feeling much better, and although she was still back and forth to England, she was a tremendous help to me when my life went into high gear. Teeny was one of my angels who came to me when I needed her the most.

There is a Russian proverb, "Жизнь кипит," which roughly means, "Life is on boil." In 1991 my life started boiling. I was taking care of children, teaching in public school, finishing up a Masters degree, dancing weekends in New York City, taking dance classes during the week, spending summers in Italy or Russia, participating in summer Russian teaching programs, rehearsing for plays, singing Russian gypsy songs in a Russian ensemble and completing an English as a Second Language eight-week intensive teaching certification program. I used to cry while I vacuumed the dusty corners of the house.

I survived by taking twenty-minute cat naps in the car between events.

And. . . I had boyfriends.

I walked the short distance to the New Dance Group Studios on 38th Street just down Eighth Avenue from Port Authority to take my usual Friday night "hot" jazz dance class with Jorge, one of Alvin Ailey's dancers. I got there to find out that the class was cancelled. Seeing the disappointment in my face, the director, Roy, suggested that I take a ballet class on the third floor. He said there was a new ballet master teaching.

"But I'm not a ballet dancer."

"It doesn't matter. He's Polish. You'll love him," he said.

Obviously Roy had no idea of how distant Poland was from Russia, but it didn't matter. Eastern Europe was Eastern Europe.

I walked into the studio with trepidation. I was not good at ballet. My thoughts as I walked up to the ballet barre: *It's good for me; every dancer has to take ballet; I will become strong.* As I started the movements, I looked up from my feet, which I knew would never be ballet feet, and took a good look at the teacher. Oh my God! A Rudolf Nureyev type: the body, the slanted eyes, the blond hair, the Eastern European accent, the smile. . . I couldn't concentrate. My body wouldn't cooperate. I was dead weight across the floor. It was the worst ballet experience I ever had.

After class, I picked my self-esteem off the floor and walked up to this beautiful man. I remember saying something in Russian just to be cute, apologized for my inability to do ballet, and thanked him for the class. To my surprise, the most beautiful man in the world answered me in broken Russian. My body turned to jelly, my mind raced. Was this man really speaking to me? He quickly changed from Russian to heavy accented English, and before we knew it, we were talking, laughing, still half-dressed and sweaty and still in the third floor ballet studio. Neither of us wanted to leave; both of us emotionally starved. He suggested continuing our conversation at the nearest restaurant. What did I have to lose?

Marek Zyks and I never took our eyes off each other as we became acquainted over pasta and wine that night. I promised to return.

From then on, every other weekend on Friday nights, after ballet class (my ballet technique much improved), Marek and I would travel by subway to his sister's warm, cozy, Polish decorated apartment on Avenue X in far-away Brooklyn. We would be fed delicious Polish food–kielbasa, potatoes, pierogies–drink wine, and make small talk until we could escape to Marek's small candle-lit room with a mattress on the floor with the pillows and blankets inviting us in. Here we made passionate love through the night until our exhausted bodies embraced into sleep. In the morning, a long hot shower together, breakfast, more dance classes in Manhattan, returning to Brooklyn for more lovemaking until Sunday, when I left for home on the bus, my body and mind satisfied. I was in love.

Every other weekend turned into every weekend when Marek bought a car and drove up to see me in Stone Ridge. He loved being in the country, loved being in my house, and loved discovering the little upstate towns outside of the city. He loved me. Although Jessie never warmed up to him (Jessie never liked any of my boyfriends), Marek took time for the children. He played soccer with Jarett in the back field behind our house and took walks with the children and me. At night, we had our romantic time in my beautiful attic bedroom.

I introduced Marek to people who could help him launch his dance and choreographic career in New York. I introduced him to Lynn Barr, who had a large network of artistic friends, and I introduced Marek to the famous Polish political poster artist Jan Sawka who, like Marek, came to the United States for political and artistic freedom and to earn money with his artwork. Sawka lived and worked in High Falls with his family, and I was in awe of his talent and his work. These introductions opened opportunity doors for Marek, and we found ourselves often going to concerts and galleries, meeting interesting people in New York City and the Hudson Valley. Life was good.

Marek was married to an attractive blond Polish woman and had two beautiful daughters who lived with their mother in Krakow, Poland, a fact I knew from the beginning of our relationship. Marek told me that the marriage was over; that there was little communication between him and his not-yet-divorced wife; that he missed his children and hoped that someday they would be able to come to the States. I believed him because I wanted to believe him. Truths and falsehoods become mere flickering shadows in the light of passion, and Marek and I continued to love in the moment, avoiding the shadows.

In the summer of 1990, Marek took a trip to Poland on "business" while I participated in a six-week Russian teacher exchange program at the Herzen State Pedagogical Institute in Leningrad (St. Petersburg was still officially called Leningrad in 1990), sponsored by the American Council of Teachers of Russian, based in Washington D.C. This was a great opportunity for me to live in Russia and expand my skills as a Russian teacher, and I was thrilled to get back to Russia. The trip was sanctioned by Jeff, and confident that the children would be fine staying with him, I left Washington D.C. on June 28, bound for Frankfurt, Germany and then on to Leningrad.

The Herzen Institute is one of the largest universities in Russia. Named after writer and philosopher Alexander Herzen, it was established in 1797 by Emperor Paul I, who modeled the university's architecture on the palaces along the Moyka Canal. Like so many majestic and dignified buildings in Leningrad, it had fallen into disrepair. In 1990, restoring old buildings was not a priority in the economic depression that had seized Russia at that time.

Chapter Thirty Six

From Russia With Love

I WAS LIVING IN THE dorms of the Herzen Institute, just behind the huge Kazan Church on Nevsky Prospect in the center of the city. When my group moved in, the Institute building looked like a set for an Alfred Hitchcock thriller: no electricity in the halls, glaring naked light bulbs in the rooms; large, wide decrepit staircases and balconies, and a dirty white stone façade that cast strange shadows on the interior walls. The bathroom in my room, which I shared with one other girl, had a perpetual flood on the floor. We called it "Домик на Болоте" ("House in the Swamp"), the title of a Russian fairy tale. Another Russian saying I remember from our experiences at Herzen: "Кошмар и тихий ужас," which means "A nightmare and a quiet dread."

Russia in 1990 was not a user-friendly country. It was easy for me to fall into an anxious state and I jazz danced every morning on a landing near my room to ease the anxiety that would rear its ugly head. I was always exhausted for lack of sleep during "white nights," a time when the sun never sets and darkness never falls. Even at two a.m., there is a dusk light before the sun comes up again. I missed my children–six weeks seemed like such a long time. I missed Marek. Making an international call home was almost impossible. I had to go to the Balkan Hotel, which was far from Herzen, and book the phone call, usually two days in advance. When I returned, I would be hopeful that the lines were not all busy. If they were, I would have to start the process over again.

The cafeteria food was less than satisfying. All meals were stuffed with cabbage and radishes as fillers and cucumbers were served three times a day. If you didn't like cucumbers, you were in big trouble. The Russian people were standing in line everywhere in Leningrad for lack of food and products, which kept the Herzen student population eating at the cafeteria. I remember having to buy a pair of socks. First, I stood in line to choose the necessary socks for which I got a receipt. With the receipt, I stood in line to pay for the socks, and then I proceeded to stand in another line to receive the socks. "Hurry up and wait" was the buzz phrase for six weeks. Then there were the shops and restaurants only for foreigners, where Russians were not allowed to go. I tried not to go in them. I was incensed at these social deprivations that forced Russians to live in this oppressed state. It was demeaning and unfair.

It took about two weeks for my sense of survival to kick in, and like everyone else in Russia, I started to adapt to the circumstances. My life in Leningrad started to flourish. There were excursions to museums, palaces, trips to Novgorod (an ancient city near Leningrad), and excursions to the old orthodox wooden churches in Kizhi, an area north of Leningrad. There were films and theatre performances and a trip to the home of my favorite Russian poet, Anna Ahkmatova. Often on Sundays, I went to the Russian Orthodox Church around the corner from the Herzen to light a candle for my parents and my dear Aunt Sandra, my father's twin sister. I felt closer to my parents when I lived in Russia. I took a group of my colleagues on a pilgrimage to see the Meyendorff house where my grandparents lived and where my father was born. This became a tradition whenever I visited St. Petersburg.

Early one morning, I got a knock on my dorm door. My brother George came to visit. At that time, he lived and worked in Moscow, and decided to take the overnight train to Leningrad to see me. I was overjoyed. For a whole day, we walked and talked about our past—about our parents, our history together and separately, our sadness, our guilt, our present lives. Our friendship deepened. George wined and dined me, plied me with champagne, and later that night, after a scrumptious dinner at an expensive Georgian restaurant, complete with caviar, smoked fish, and many shots of vodka, George took the overnight train back to Moscow. I would see him again in Moscow.

Of course there were the classes at the Institute that kept me busy: Russian literature, contemporary politics, grammar and conversation, and a class of boring phonetics, which I regularly skipped. Within the teacher group, I made a lasting friendship with Molly Dane, a young woman from upstate New York. Life was still good . . . and then it got better.

I noticed Sasha right away: a tall, good-looking Russian man with long blonde hair down to his shoulders. A hippie in Russia? I was intrigued. We were two weeks into the program when Sasha brought his group of singers and dancers called "Slavyane" (Slavs) to Herzen Institute for a cultural exchange evening. His guitar playing was extraordinary–an excellent musician. That evening, we exchanged a few words and the next day, Sasha picked me up at Herzen to show me the sights. It was July 10. I had one more month.

Sasha and I began our friendship walking arm in arm and talking. He was amazed at my ability to speak Russian well, having lived in the United States for most of my life, and I was intrigued that he could live a bohemian life in Russia. I loved spending time with a Russian musician and artist. Sasha showed me areas of Leningrad where westerners never tread. I was taken to the bowels of the city, to the most extraordinary out of the way parks and canals, taken inside palaces, opera houses where the famous opera singer Feodor Chaliapin sang; he took me to *ateliers* where fine artists sat in front of easels and painted–all off-limits to tourists. We drank tea in artist cafes and had "tomato sandwich on black bread" picnics on boats while floating on the beautiful Fontanka River. At four a.m. with the "white light" sun just coming up, we would gaze across the Neva River at the Fortress of Peter and Paul and watch the drawbridges rise to let the big ships through. "Как в сказке" ("Like in a storybook,") we proclaimed. Sasha showed me Dostoevsky's St. Petersburg: raw and dirty and brilliant, and I felt a part of the fabric of the city, my father's city. I had come full circle.

We were often accompanied by Igor Malanchuk, a handsome young man, the booking agent for Slavyane and a good friend of Sasha's. Molly Dane, my friend from the Herzen group, completed the foursome. In fact, we became the quartet of "колдуны" (Russian slang for "wizards") because we knew that our friendship and our adventures in Leningrad were unique. I must add that there were no political or financial motives to our adventures; that all of our adventures cost little or no money. None of us had any. Sasha and Igor were poor students and Molly Dane and I were poor Americans. We stood in lines for food and drink, sometimes cooked in the kitchen of the Cultural Institute where Sasha and Igor lived. Or we ate at the Herzen Institute cafeteria, where Molly Dane and I shared our food coupons with the boys. Cabbage, radishes, and cucumbers went a long way.

The four of us were all married or in relationships, a "safe" environment which kept our emotions moving in slow motion, albeit steadily to inescapable romance. Sasha was married to one of the singers in his music group, who was diagnosed with multiple sclerosis. Because of her illness, that summer she did not travel to Leningrad to sing and dance in the group and stayed home. As Sasha explained, he was now "прикован" or "shackled" in Russian. He felt trapped by his wife's illness in the small Siberian village where they lived. Igor was on the brink of a divorce, Molly Dane had a husband in New York she did not live with, and I had Marek. I was forty-three years old, Sasha was twenty-nine.

It was July 21, my forty-third birthday, when my colleagues from Herzen and our little quartet gathered in the upstairs lobby for a few drinks–champagne, cake, beer. Some friends brought gifts: an Anna Ahkmatova poster, a poster tube (hard to get in Russia), roses and daisies. I was touched by Sasha's gift, little Siberian woven slippers that today hang as keepsakes on my living room wall. Later, Sasha and I huddled by the tape recorder listening to Nina Simone and Peter Gabriel tapes. He brought his guitar and sang me a beautiful Russian song which was popular at that time, "Я хочу быть с тобой" ("I want to be with you"). I remember a few of the lyrics:

В комнате с белым потолком	In a room with a white ceiling
С правом на надежду	With a right to hope
В комнате с видом на огни	In a room with a view of the lights
С верою в любовь	With a faith in love.

We kissed for the first time and although we both held our emotions in check…it was getting harder. Sasha and I were falling in love.

RETURN TO KUMNA

The next day Molly Dane, my roommate Susan, and I took a six-hour overnight train from Leningrad to Tallinn, Estonia. It was difficult to leave Sasha, but a good opportunity to take a step back to see a clearer picture of my feelings for him. In my heart I knew there would be no holding back when I returned.

As Leningrad was relatively close to Estonia, I had planned to visit Kumna, the old Meyendorff family estate that my paternal grandmother, my parents and my two brothers had fled in the face of war in 1941. I wanted to see for myself the place I had heard so much about, to relive the family history, to bring home real memories. I was told by my father that when the Meyendorffs left Kumna, the Soviets maintained headquarters in the main house; that they'd nearly destroyed the building by burning the little Russian Orthodox chapel the Meyendorffs had built in the attic. I had few expectations of what I would find.

At that time, there was only one emotional force that could pull me away from my new love: the past, the ancestral estate of Kumna, where the ghosts of my forebears might still be in residence. I longed to see the ornate wooden house, with its generous wings that had welcomed family and guests for generations and from which my father and mother and my two brothers had been so rudely ousted.

Following my brother George's directions, my friends and I took a one-hour train ride south from Tallinn to Keila, the little town near Kumna. As the train traveled across the Estonian landscape of fields and forest, seemingly untouched by time, I felt my anticipation rise. I watched the field workers gather hay, and the old plow horses pull their loaded wagons. It was as if time had stopped and waited for my return.

We got off the train, aware that we had not eaten in several hours. We settled our coats on the warm grass and enjoyed a picnic breakfast of rolls and thick jam, then rose and started walking. How to find Kumna from here?

We saw a blanched Lutheran church, and as the bells tolled, I entered and found an old man, perhaps the groundskeeper, who wore work clothes. His leathered face could have betrayed a high age such as a hundred, but who knew how long he had labored there? I asked him in Russian, "How far is the old estate, Kumna, that was once the property of the aristocratic Meyendorff family? Baronessa Meyendorff was my grandmother."

"Ahhh, the Baronessa Meyendorff. A kind, generous person. Those were different times," he answered.

His eyes closed as if he was retrieving the past. When they opened, I saw one eye was milky with cataracts, which gave it the appearance of a cold blue marble. He nodded and said, "Kumna," as if he had been expecting me, or someone else, to request the way to Kumna. He told us it was very near, but the road was overgrown and we would have to walk through high weeds for a bit and cross a stream that had long ago been dammed but was now free. He pointed to the east, where the sun had risen; it was almost high noon. Shading my own eyes with my right hand, I walked on. I led the others, proceeding at a quickening pace...

"Mourka, slow down," Susan called after me. But I couldn't. I didn't care that the side branches had thorns that caught in my skirt and scratched my bare arms. Bees buzzed round the flowers and insects hovered near me, but I was unafraid . . . I pushed on through the high grass and then, without warning, my feet slipped. I was in deep mud. The old stream that had been dammed and was now running free had created a narrow channel and the earth around it was soaked, oozing black mud. . . and sucking at my every step. But I thought I could see the carved wooden peaks of the main house rooftop. I almost ran out of my shoes. They squished at my every step, releasing the water that soaked the soles . . .

But nothing mattered. I was running now, as something inside me had always wanted to run... I was running "home." I recognized the house from the painting of Kumna that we had hanging on our wall in Nyack when I was a little girl. There was the circular drive, now almost obliterated. I ran faster along the near-invisible drive to where it led, the listing wooden steps to old veranda. The estate wore its age and dilapidation well–what Kumna had lost in function, it had gained in mood and the romance of ruin.

The shutters listed and a bird flew from the eaves, screeching at my approach. How long had Kumna belonged to the birds? Swallows swooped from inside the house, surrendering at once to my entrance.

The main door was boarded, but the side door, which I instinctively knew led to the kitchen, swung open on rusty hinges that squeaked as I pushed my way inside.

While it had been hot outside, indoors was cool and shaded gray-green. The grand old wood cooking and heating stove with its many burners and wide belly sat as if waiting for someone to put on the kettle. The long harvest table also waited, with enamel tin plates and a white chipped cup. The table also seemed to expect me... us, guests–or the family.

I gasped and was silent. My friends caught up with me and also fell silent. This was no place for chatter. There was a sacred silence. The ghosts of the Meyendorffs were indeed here. Even their shoes and boots were here, no longer lined up by the door, but scattered, separated... A dog bowl still rested on the floor. Someone had left in a great hurry, decades ago, but the departure could still be felt.

I ran through the house. It was large and gracious with long floor-to-ceiling windows. It was inhabited now only by birds and, from the look of the dotted droppings, mice. As I explored the wings, my pace slowed. The bedrooms felt haunted– the floral wallpaper was faded, the porcelain corner stoves gaped open... Gradually, the chill of past winters overtook me and I descended to the cellar, alone, and there, sat on an old crate and hunched over, hugging my own shoulder. I shook and only later realized I was crying.

No wonder my parents agonized, my father chronically ill, my mother disturbed and agitated. How could they be forced from here and not suffer? For the first time, I truly felt their suffering.

Sasha was waiting for me when we returned to Leningrad, and I flew into his arms. My gentle beautiful Siberian man–what a gift! Sashenka! Sashenka! That night, with Igor's connections and a set of keys, the Quartet of Wizards managed to attain entrance to an abandoned spa somewhere near the Neva River. It was dark and quiet when we walked in. We lit candles, sat on beautiful blue and white tiles on the edge of a warm pool and shared bread, cheese, and wine. Igor and Molly Dane disappeared to another pool of water nearby. Sasha and I took off our clothes and slid into the warm clear water, letting our bodies touch for the first time, clinging to each other, not wanting to let go.

Later, I went with Sasha to his friend Ruslan's apartment to listen to them play their guitars and sing Russian songs. We sang together. The "white night" sun was just pushing away dusk when Sasha and I made love for the first time, giving in to our pent-up desires, knowing that we had little time . . .

For the next two weeks, I stopped going to classes at the Herzen to share every moment I had left with Sasha. We became inseparable, and our Russian life together took on the romantic, passionate intensity characteristic of two people in love who would, in all probability, never see each other again. Sasha promised to come to Moscow to see me off...

Before I left Leningrad, I broke my iron-clad rule to not buy anything from the *Beryozka* store, the store where only foreigners could shop, and I bought Alexander Solzhenitsyn's contraband books and gave them to Sasha as a gift: *The Gulag Archipelago, One Day in the Life of Ivan Denisovich, August 1914,* and *Cancer Ward*. In turn, he gave me his book of Alexander Pushkin's poetry to always keep by my bed, to read a poem each night.

On August 7th, the American Council of Teachers of Russian group left Leningrad by train to spend a few days in Moscow before our departure for Washington D.C. I was so distraught about leaving that I left all my clothes hanging in the closet at Herzen. When my brother George took me for a farewell dinner to a restaurant in Moscow reserved for diplomats and embassy personnel, I arrived in a tee shirt and jeans.

The next day, as promised, Sasha and Igor arrived at our hotel in Moscow to see us off, having scraped up enough money for the train from Leningrad. For two days, Molly Dane and I hid the boys in our hotel rooms until our tearful departure from Sheremetyevo International Airport on August 10. I was devastated to leave Sasha.

As always, it was difficult to re-enter the affluent material world of the United States, not knowing if I would ever have the opportunity to again return to poverty-stricken Mother Russia and the dilapidated estate in Estonia. If it weren't for Jessie and Jarett, I might have stayed in Russia that summer of 1990.

Like water, I took the shape of the vessel in which I found myself and made Russia home. Russia blended my history, my childhood, my family—necessary roots to rebuild and regain my emotional strength and confidence. I fell in love with a wonderful, kind, sensitive Russian married man, and although we were not destined for each other, I am thankful for our meeting.

Upon my return from Russia, I attempted to break off my relationship with Marek, knowing full well that we, too, were not destined to be together, but I wasn't strong enough. Marek was hard to resist and he did not want to let me go. We stayed on our collision course. We were going the distance.

Six months later, I got a call from JFK International Airport. To my great surprise, Sasha and Igor had just alighted off a Russian Aeroflot flight and were waiting for me to pick them up at the airport. Where did they get the money? How did they get visas? When I signed a formal invitation for Sasha and Igor to come to the United States, nowhere in my wildest dreams did I think this would become a reality, given the cost of airplane tickets and the complications of Russian bureaucracy. But here they were. I grabbed a bunch of bananas and a bag of oranges (unheard of in Russia) and with my mind racing, I took off for JFK.

Sasha and Igor entered my life in the United States and our worlds collided. How could I feel differently about Sasha on American soil? But I did. For two weeks, I showed Sasha and Igor the sights: New York City, the mountains, the lakes. We visited Molly Dane, who was as surprised as I was to see our two wizards. Sasha and I had a wonderful time together, but we could not recapture the Russian moment. With Marek in the picture, I couldn't make love with Sasha. I had moved on. Sasha's friendship survived, but our romance shattered.

Two weeks later, Sasha returned to his wife in Siberia and Igor "jumped ship" and did not board his return flight home. For two years, he stayed in the United States illegally until his marriage to a friend of mine procured him a green card and legal status. But that's another story...

Chapter Thirty Seven

Mourka...The Play

IT WAS SPRING, 1991. MAREK and I were relaxing in my deep, claw-footed porcelain bathtub upstairs in my attic space in Stone Ridge; candles were lit, wine was poured. It was our weekend together. I don't remember if it was the first or the second glass of wine that gave Marek the courage to tell me: His wife and children were coming to the United States to live with him.

"When?" I asked.

"Next week."

He might as well have punched me in the stomach. The news took my breath away. All I could do was put my head in my hands and cry.

I waited for him for days, weeks, months. Having procured a role in Lynn Barr's production of *Il Circo de la Vita* at the McKenna Theatre in New Paltz, Marek would come to Woodstock to rehearse and on the way, he returned twice to my house. He couldn't stay away. Then, during the performance, with his wife in the audience, I watched my beautiful Polish ballet dancer dance out of my life as I stood in the back of the theatre, tears streaming down my face. It was over.

My amorous affairs with Sasha and Marek took a toll. I felt depleted, but gave myself no time for self-reflection, nor did I want to wallow in self-pity. To ease the pain, I immersed myself into the theatre world. It didn't matter that I was holding down a full-time teaching job; that I was taking care of children; that I was finishing my Masters Degree. I was going to do it all.

Tired of finances always being a problem, curious, and hoping for a miracle, I put an advertisement in an elite national magazine. The ad read, "Russian Baroness seeking a gentleman to underwrite her theatrical career." I was not sure about my part in the bargain; I would make that decision upon the encounter. I got several letters, many from men of European descent. I answered one, an American gentleman from Philadelphia who seemed the most compatible, and we made arrangements to meet in a bar in New York City. A large man in his late fifties, well-dressed, with a round pocked-marked face and glasses sitting on the edge of his nose greeted me as I approached. My heart sank. To be polite, I stayed for conversation and drinks. As the afternoon wore on, he obviously enjoyed my company and was already speaking about financial arrangements and travel plans. I, on the other hand, was fighting an alcohol haze that was distorting my first impression of him, creating images of a life well-lived, having my theatrical career underwritten, and never worrying about finances again. A sugar daddy? After the third glass of wine, it was tempting. Before my departure, the man offered to buy excellent seats to a Broadway play of my choosing. He assured me that there were no strings attached. How could I resist? I hadn't been to a Broadway play in ages. I accepted, my curiosity getting the best of me.

I chose Terrence McNally's play *Master Class*. The man did not enjoy the play as much as I did, and when it was over, the inevitable hotel room conversation popped up. "Just for a drink," he said. Feeling in control of the situation, I was determined to finish this game on my terms, the thought of possible danger never entering my head. In the hotel room, it was soon apparent that it wasn't "just for a drink" as he started to make amorous advances towards me. Visions of life on easy street disappeared as I put my hat and coat on and shut the hotel room door behind me. I remember him screaming some kind of obscenity. The angels were watching.

In 1992, after I finished an ESL certification program at BOCES in New Paltz, Sigrid Heath cast me as The Murdered Woman in her adaptation of Luigi Pirandello's classic *At The Gate*, which opened at the Byrdcliffe Theatre in Woodstock. Every night for a month, half naked, covered only by a silk maroon colored robe, I cascaded, writhed head first off of a raked bed located center stage, slid down a ladder, and danced onto the stage, laughing in a deliberate hysteria. In my entire acting career, this was by far my best entrance onto a stage.

The play took Woodstock by storm with rave reviews, and I established myself as a sought- after actor in the Woodstock circles, which gave me more opportunities to perform. Sigrid and I became close friends and I revered her talents as a writer, director, and actor. It was then that Lynn Barr planted the seed for me to write and produce my own play based on my history and life experiences. In 1993, over lunch in Kingston, I approached Sigrid to co-write and direct my one-woman play. I insisted on paying her a meager fee out of my teaching salary for her professional services, a fee way below what she deserved. To my great relief, she agreed.

For a full year Sigrid and I collaborated on the play, meeting after work and on weekends. Each week, we laughed and cried together as I opened my soul to Sigrid–the history, the coming of age, the artistic and travel adventures, the marriage, the lovers. Sigrid wrote it all down, using her theatrical skills to transform my story into a play. Together we moved the play from the written page to the stage, rehearsing into the wee hours of the night.

Sigrid and I incorporated music and movement into the play. There was Russian gypsy music, classical music, Aretha Franklin, and the Peppermint Twist. There was a choreography set by Lynn Barr with music that incorporated all aspects of my life: church bells that I recorded at the Nyack church, African drums, jazz, R&B, and the Russian Orthodox Liturgy. Anderson Studios in Woodstock set up the technical components, including projection of videos and photographs onto a large screen on stage. Bart Friedman filmed all the videos. Zachary Jacobs was the lighting designer, Teeny helped with the costumes, Albee Barr arranged the music, and Phil Sigunick, my artist friend from Cragsmoor, designed a stunning poster. The one-woman show, appropriately named *Mourka*, was one of the first multi-media productions in the Hudson Valley.

On October 20, 1994, *Mourka* opened to a full house at Town Hall in Woodstock for a three- weekend run. I remember calling Sigrid the day of the opening and telling her that I couldn't go through with it, to cancel the opening. I was terrified. I remember Sigrid saying, "Just tell the story." And I did.

Chapter Thirty Eight

Eastern Europe

DURING THE TIME THAT SIGRID and I were writing and rehearsing my play, I met Nicholas Jaromev, a Bulgarian (I was working my way through the whole Eastern bloc). I was forty-seven years old and Nick was a handsome Bulgarian in his late fifties. I met him at a party in Krumville, not far from Stone Ridge. Nick greeted me at the door and we proceeded to drink wine and dance together through the night. During one of the dances, he picked me up, turned me upside down and lifted me so high that one of my boots scraped and left a black mark three feet long on the pristine white ceiling. That should have been an omen of what was to come, but instead, we laughed and kept dancing.

Nick had a strong chiseled face with a dark complexion, a mustache, a short beard, silvery hair and dark mischievous eyes–the antithesis of blond, fair Marek. He lived in a rustic cabin in the woods just north of the Krumville Inn on Route 2 with an incredible view of Mombaccus Mountain. The cabin reminded me of wicked Baba Yaga's house built on chicken legs in the Russian fairy tales. Nick worked as an engineer at Ulster County Department of Public Works in Kingston, where he designed and constructed roads and bridges. At work, he had a reputation of being a character. There were stories too numerous to mention here . . .

Nick left Bulgaria in 1976. He escaped the oppressive communist dictatorship in power at that time by walking across what was then the country of Yugoslavia.

He reached Trieste, Italy, where he spent a year in a refugee camp. He lived and worked in Italy before he immigrated in 1981 to the United States, a country where he never felt comfortable. In fact, he hated the American culture and insulated himself as much as he could in his cabin, his own little kingdom.

Nick was as gentle and nurturing as he was barbaric, wild, crazy, and tough. An alcoholic, he lived his life to the fullest and I fell for the fervor, comedy, and drama that his life entailed. I was on the rebound from Marek and heading for another rollercoaster ride.

There was never a dull moment with Nick. He was a great cook, but he would shoot squirrels and catch snapping turtles, make a stew out of them, and tell me that I was eating chicken. A few times I entered his kitchen and he would be butchering a deer, his kitchen covered in blood. Nick and I snowshoed in the winter, picked mushrooms, fished for our breakfast, had great dinner parties, gardened, got high tasting his home made wine, and took trips to Montreal, his favorite city. Once, two of his Macedonian friends arrived drunk at his door and stuck a huge hunting knife into his dining room table in front of me, for fun.

Nick loved it when I played his old piano. When I played Chopin's *Prelude in E Minor*, Nick cried. It reminded him of when he first came to the United States. A stranger in a strange land, he lay alone on his bed, listening to someone in his apartment building in New York City playing that piece over and over.

At age fourteen, Jessie hated Nick, and Jarett, at ten years old didn't disclose an opinion. But on the occasions that we were invited to dinner, they ate his food, squirrels and turtles notwithstanding.

After my show closed in Woodstock, Nick and I took a trip to Bulgaria to meet his half brother, his sister and his mother. In Sofia, Nick invited a number of his friends to a fancy restaurant where a live gypsy band played. Nick and I slow-danced, the two of us alone on a wooden stage–a scene straight from Mihalkov's Russian film *Burnt by the Sun*.

We went to Pliska, a small village where Nick's mother and sister lived, where there were no paved roads and milk was delivered by donkey cart. Nick took me to Vitosha, a mountainous vacation resort for Bulgarians near Sofia. We slept in bunk beds in a small dirty room in a dilapidated, frightening hotel. The toilet was a hole in the ground (similar but even more ghastly than the ones in Russia). The night we stayed there, drunks were yelling; there were sounds of shattered glass. I couldn't sleep. I was petrified. The next day, we took a hike on the mountain, walking through fields of red poppies and white daisies, looking at Sofia from a distance. It turned out to be a magnificent place, and for the time being, the horrible night was forgotten.

On one of my Italian dance trips with Lynn, Nick insisted on accompanying me. Nick and I decided to visit Istanbul, Turkey first, and then go to Italy from there. I wanted to take a romantic voyage by sea from Istanbul through the Bosporus to the Aegean Sea, circle the Greek islands, and then cross the Adriatic Sea to Italy. Nick insisted that we take a train through Greece, Bulgaria, and Serbia to Austria and then south to Italy. The timing could not have been worse. It was 1995 and the United States was bombing Serbia.

At the first stop after the Bulgarian-Serbian border, Nick and I were taken off the train, our suitcases and bags flying as we descended the steps onto the platform. I had just taken my shoes off, propped my feet up on the table in front of me and settled into our beautiful sleeper compartment when we heard the yelling, "американцы, американцы!" The border patrol in Serbia had purposely kept our American passports and now we were traveling without legal documents. It was a trap. On the platform, we stood and waited for a train back to the border, where we were promptly arrested, separated, interrogated, and held in empty cold rooms for ten hours. Nick was robbed. I was incensed and told the tall Serbian official, dressed in a camouflage military uniform and reeking of alcohol, in three different languages that I was an international star, that I was to perform in Italy and that Italian officials would be searching for me very soon. Everything fell on drunken deaf ears.

After what seemed to me a very long time, I saw an old Muslim woman shuffling past my room. She wore a black veil and kerchief. All I could see was her eyes. She looked in on me pacing in the room. She put one finger to her covered mouth as if to say, "Quiet," and shuffled into the drunken Serbian official's office. I heard her speak to him; they argued. My guess was that she was his mother. Soon after their conversation, the Serb in camouflage walked into my room and handed me my passport. Nick and I were reunited, and after what seemed to us to be an exercise in American harassment, they let us go. What stopped them from throwing us into the woods and killing us? Was it an angel disguised as an old Muslim woman? I will never know.

They put us on a rattling old train with uncomfortable wooden seats that stopped at every village to pick up the local peasantry with their chickens and goats. I remember asking myself why my life couldn't be as simple as the peasants' as my anxiety level rose to an all-time high after the arrest. Now we were bound for Nis, the nearest large city, where we could get on a different train to Vienna and then onto Rimini, Italy, where I was to meet Lynn. In Budapest, I had twenty minutes to run to the post office to send Lynn a telegram, saying that we were safe, but would be arriving later than we thought. I was never so happy to see Lynn as when we finally arrived in Rimini early the next morning.

After our return from Italy, Nick's alcoholism became more apparent. He began to drink more and his nurturing instincts deteriorated into criticism and verbal abuse. He was a nasty drunk; his unhappiness, discontent with the world, and his fear of intimacy surfaced. I did not and could not fill his expectations, and my thoughts of being the one to make a difference in his life disintegrated. Arguments between us escalated. Driving up Route 213 to Nick's house, I began to feel anxious, never knowing what to expect. I wasn't heeding my warning signs and I began drowning my anxieties in alcohol.

The first time Nick hit me in the face, it was outside by his garage; my glasses went flying, hit the ground, and shattered. I didn't see him for weeks. Nick begged me to return, calling me on the phone, chucking pebbles at my bedroom window on his way to work in the morning, screaming my name, begging forgiveness...

It was hard to know if I loved Nick or if I needed him. Maybe both–the need to be nurtured and taken care of still strong in me. The little girl was afraid to be alone. Hoping for a change, I put on my blinders and crawled back to Nick.

For a while Nick stopped drinking and we were fine.

It was late when I got a ride to Nick's house one night (my car was being repaired) and to my dismay, there was a bottle of wine standing on the table. I drank and watched Nick as he drank, his mood escalating from "glad to see you" to petty criticism, to jealousy, and then to verbal condescension and abuse. At first, I tried to laugh it off, but the abuse was getting stronger. He insisted that I was physically deformed because I never could have an orgasm with him (he had no clue about a woman's body), accused me of sleeping around; his accusations became more absurd by the moment. I tried to go to sleep and ignore him, but he was relentless. He wanted to hurt me.

I got dressed and asked him to take me home. He refused. I told him that I would walk home. He slammed me against the door. I ran out with Nick in pursuit. He got into his car and told me to get in; that he would take me home. Nick drove drunk and angry, speeding around curves, the car hitting a side rail. I thought this was the end. I begged him to stop. He wouldn't. Finally, I opened the door and was about to jump when he screeched to a halt, hit me in the face, pushed me out of the door onto the asphalt, and drove away.

In the dark, I stood up slowly, tears of relief running down my face. I was alive. It was three a.m. as I slowly began the four-mile walk to Stone Ridge on Route 213. I was not afraid of the animals that I heard rustling in the woods. I was afraid of men driving in cars. I was afraid of the police, and I was afraid that Nick would come looking for me. Whenever I heard a car coming, I hid behind a tree. When I got to the farm near my house where there were no trees, I ran past it to safety on the other side. At home, I barricaded myself inside the house, putting furniture against the doors. I owned no keys. I called Igor Malanchuk, who lived in West Shokan at that time, and asked him to drive down and stay the night. I was petrified that Nick would return. He never did.

I freed myself from my marriage, set my life on the front burner, and turned up the heat. I achieved a tremendous amount in a short time, both in the educational and artistic fields, and suffered through self-imposed emotional upheaval. I paid a high price for these life experiences. Just as my mother was absent from my life, I was absent from my children's' lives when they needed me most.

Chapter Thirty Nine

Absent

IT WAS 1990, A TYPICAL night at home in Stone Ridge and I was tucking seven year-old Jarett into bed when, without any prior indications, he announced, "I want to go live with Dad." I was shocked. I asked him if there was anything wrong at home. Was anything wrong with the way I treated him? I was never secure with my abilities as a mother. Jarett assured me that everything was fine. I left his room in tears, questioning the motive for his announcement. Was I really a good mother? When Jessie and Cassandra started menstruating, we had a party commemorating the occasion. Was there too much female energy for him? Did Jarett come up with this decision by himself, or was it with a prompt from his Dad? Did Jeff feel he could give Jarett a better home? How often would I be able to see him? What should I do? Jarett did not pose a request; he made a statement. I was convinced that Jeff had influenced Jarett to come live with him; Jarett was too young to make an important decision like this on his own.

Allowing Jarett to go live with Jeff was one of the decisions I have regretted most in my life. The recriminations go on and on in my mind. I should have fought to keep my two children together. I should have been more in control. But what if Jarett really wanted to live with his dad? I didn't want to come between him and his father and have Jarett hold this against me. And wouldn't the responsibility of only one child be easier on me? I wouldn't be losing Jarett; I would see him regularly. It was not an easy decision and I resented Jeff for creating this conflict. What I didn't realize at that time was the effect the separation would have on Jessie, when Jeff showed his blatant preference for Jarett. He made a choice between his two children. For this I have never forgiven him.

Jessie was beautiful, tall with long dancer legs: a beautiful spirit, always smiling, laughing, a happy child. Jessie was more open emotionally than Jarett, but her strong will and high energy was often difficult to harness. She loved her little brother and with her natural giving quality, she helped take care of him. School was not easy for Jessie. In kindergarten, she was diagnosed with a learning disability; she was not as organized as other children her age. Jeff and I were upset with this diagnosis and sent Jessie to the private Mountain Laurel School in New Paltz, where there was more freedom for Jessie to learn at her own pace. Even at a young age, because of her vulnerabilities, it was apparent that life's challenges would be difficult for Jessie to navigate. And Jeff was not about to complicate his life with Jessie's vulnerabilities. He preferred the easier child.

Jarett was easy. Good-looking, shy, with a shock of blond hair, Jarett was always well-behaved. Although he had a few good friends, Jarett was quiet and kept to himself. School came easy to him. He excelled in all subjects, particularly in math. He played sports very well. There were never any major problems. His single idiosyncrasy was that he hated to lose at games, particularly card games. He would cry and throw down his cards. He was competitive to the point that he could not bear to lose. What this could indicate on a deeper level, I was not to learn until the future, when more serious issues arose.

The land and workshop in Samsonville sold and Jeff moved to New Paltz, where he set up a candle business on Route 32 in the village. When Jarett went to live with his father, Jessie, who was eleven years old at that time, began to shift between our home in Stone Ridge and her father's home in New Paltz. Whereas Jarett had his own room in Jeff's house, Jessie slept on a cot in the living room. She was a biweekly weekend guest. Because of Jeff's address in New Paltz, Jessie was able to attend the New Paltz schools, and be closer to her new school friends. Later, when Jeff moved to Rosendale for a short time before his departure for France, Jessie stayed with her friend Danielle in New Paltz and used her address to stay in the New Paltz district.

As Jessie began to drift in her teenage years, her self-esteem floating on thin ice, I did not give her the support that she needed. At home in Stone Ridge when we were together, I was often overtired and stressed, and Jessie and I would argue. I could barely drag Jessie out of bed to go to school. Her grades at New Paltz High School, which weren't great to begin with, plummeted. I remember the one and only time I slapped Jessie in the face, and Jessie, who towered over me, promptly slapped me back. I didn't like her group of friends in New Paltz. I didn't like that Jessie was smoking cigarettes. I was losing parental control; I was losing Jessie. At that time, I did not realize to what extent I was adding to her sense of abandonment and insecurity, leaving the subject raw and gaping.

I was busy with work, finishing a Masters Degree, attending workshops, having affairs, and taking trips to Russia and Italy for weeks at a time. On the weekends Jessie would go visit her father, I went to New York City to take dance classes and have fun with Lynn. I was also living on the edge of shadows, a darkness that continued to invade my subconscious, and I stayed busy to keep the demons at bay. I was terrified of violence.

In the 1990s, when I was working as a French teacher at the Arlington High School near Poughkeepsie, there was a domestic violence incident that sent me running to my psychologist, Dr. Arnie Weiner. A sixteen-year-old boy, a student at Arlington, shot his parents and two siblings, and this incident left the community in shock. The day after, psychologists, social workers, parents and teachers were asked to be on hand with the student population to talk and console children who were deeply shaken by the incident. There were no classes. Although I seemed calm and was able to talk to the students, I was terrified. My mother's violent acts and my out-of-control feelings crept into my mind again. Who is capable of performing such a heinous act? Anyone? Was I capable of an act of violence? A cold terror gripped my heart and I feared the return of more extreme symptoms, recalling the depression that had seized me in the past. Arnie was able to put my fears to rest, citing the mental imbalance the boy had suffered and his particular family situation. I had nothing to fear.

When Jessie was fifteen years old, she met a young man at a walkathon at Mohonk Mountain House in New Paltz and fell in love. He was a handsome, polite person and I liked him. I was happy for Jessie as she walked around in a bliss cloud enjoying her romantic moments with him. Sadly, the romance lasted only five months, and Jessie was devastated. The loss of him on top of her feelings of abandonment was too much. Jessie went into a depression and would not be consoled. It was a dark time for Jessie, and I had very little time and energy for her. It was 1994 and along with teaching four days a week at the Marlboro School District, I was busy launching my one-woman show, an overwhelming project that pushed my creative energy to the edge.

There was an incident with Jessie that haunts me still. I was sitting in the car in the New Paltz High school parking lot, waiting to pick Jessie up from school. As I struck up a conversation with an acquaintance, I heard Jessie screaming, "Mommie, Mommie," a great smile on her face as she came running to meet me. She was about four feet from the car when she tripped over her own feet and fell, skidding on the asphalt, notebook, books, and paper flying, her head inches away from hitting the car. I watched as if in slow motion: Jessie falling, her eyes changing from excitement to fear as she reached for me and I was unable to stop the fall. I felt such deep sadness as I picked up Jessie, tended to her scraped knees, and put her in the car. I feel the sadness of that moment still.

In 1999, Jessie received her high school diploma–barely. Because she had failed an English class, Jessie was not able to graduate with her class in 1998, something that Jessie has since regretted. After graduation, she worked at odd jobs, not knowing what she wanted to do with her life. Jessie's insecurity made it difficult to pass the numerous drivers tests she took and she never obtained a license, which left her dependent on others. Jessie's favorite times were her birthdays and Christmas when she could regress and become a child again, a time when she felt safer and more comfortable. And so the two of us continued. Putting one foot in front of the other, clinging to our separate lives, we repeated the familiar mantra, "We're doing the right thing. . ."

In 1996, Jeff married Celine, the young woman he had met at the hotel in Biarritz, and in his usual style of "the grass is greener," became a Francophile. He decided that France was the place to be and he wanted to live there with his new French wife and he wanted to take Jarett with him. Jarett had just finished the eighth grade at New Paltz Middle School and would be continuing his studies in a boarding school in France. This decision sent a ripple through Jessie and me for different reasons. Jessie was devastated because her father and brother were moving further away from her, and I was angry because Jeff was taking Jarett further away from me.

Once again, Jeff was forcing me to make a decision based on his logic and practicality without considering the emotional impact this move would have on Jessie and me. Legally, Jeff could not take Jarett out of the country without my consent, and I fought Jeff's decision. Although the experience of living abroad could be interesting for Jarett, I did not want him living so far away and I did not want Jeff to be the sole influence on his life. I think Jarett was ambivalent about going to France, but he would go for the ride.

Phil Sigunick, our mutual artist friend in Cragsmoor, offered a solution. Rather than deny Jarett his experience in France (he could always come home if he was not happy there), we set up an escrow account that Phil would manage. The account would ensure that Jeff paid for telephone calls between Jarett, Jessie, and me and that there would be enough money for Jarett to fly home at every opportunity: holidays, school vacations, and summer vacations. With this legalized document, in the fall of 1996, I let Jarett go to France. But even as I kissed him goodbye, I felt tears spring to my eyes. It felt too much like a real goodbye. Would I ever fully be his mother again? Was I doing "the right thing?" Was I losing both of my children? I had too many doubts as I watched him go, his face turned away from me as he ran toward an unknown future.

For two years, thanks to the escrow account, Jarett came home for the summers and for long school vacations and I received many adventure-filled phone calls and emails from him on a weekly basis. In the spring of 1998, the year the soccer World Cup was held in France, Jarett returned home. I remember Jarett bringing home a bottle of red wine with a picture of the Eiffel Tower and a soccer ball on the label. Jarett was fifteen years old and speaking French very well. He had gotten a taste of independence, going to a boarding school near Aix-en-Provence, playing soccer with his colleagues, riding motor scooters, going to cafes, having girls as friends. Jarett kept his grades up despite the fact that everything was taught in French, but he continued to excel in math, the subject that was the easiest for him. France was a good experience for him.

Upon Jarett's return, I noticed sadness, a grief about him I hadn't seen before. Jarett was very close with his new three-year-old half sister, Alina, and leaving her was difficult. Because Jarett kept his emotions to himself and didn't speak to me about his feelings, I could only surmise that Jarett's insecurity about losing people close to him stayed deep in his heart. Perhaps this is why Jarett felt he had to maintain a perfect disposition; perfection would cut his losses. Perhaps this is why Jarett, as a child, had a difficulty in losing at card games. Jarett created a very tight, unattainable world for himself and grew more silent.

While working at Jeff's still-existing candle and votive business in New Paltz, Jarett took the high school GED equivalency exam and applied to Ulster County Community College (UCCC) in Stone Ridge as an advanced placement student. Except for a philosophy teacher whom he admired, Jarett did not enjoy his time at UCCC. He felt out of place because he was younger than most of the students and he found the courses dull.

Jeff was running out of money in France and decided to return to Minneapolis, where he would set up yet another candle and votive business, leaving Celine and Alina in France. He took Jarett with him. I wasn't happy about Jarett leaving again, but had no say in the decision. Jarett wanted to go. There was not much holding him here and it gave him a good excuse to quit UCCC. While in Minneapolis, Jeff introduced Jarett to the futures stock market and Jarett became intrigued. At first, he paper-traded, read books, and learned as much as he could about the business of trading futures. Later he ventured out and started trading on his own. I was impressed with how successful Jarett was at this tricky business. Unfortunately, on September 11, 2001 when the World Trade towers came crashing down, Jarett lost all his profits–a substantial sum. He was eighteen years old.

It was a lonely time for Jarett in Minneapolis. He had no friends. All he did was work and trade. Jeff and Celine attempted to keep their long distance marriage intact, but it became increasingly difficult. Once, when Jeff flew back to visit his family in France for a week, he left Jarett alone to operate the business on his own. It was during that week that Jarett had a bad car accident. He was not hurt, but the car was totaled. Jarett's stress level was rising. Not long after the accident, during Celine and Alina's visit to Minneapolis, the long distance marriage came to an end. Jarett remembers Alina sitting on his lap in the workshop, the two of them listening to their parents' last argument together.

Jarett's perfect young world was crumbling. He was disillusioned with relationships after watching his parents' break-ups, disillusioned with the political world as the United States invaded Iraq, disillusioned with the educational system not meeting his needs, disillusioned with the world.

At home with me again, Jarett became more uncommunicative, which made it difficult to reach him and I felt an emotional distance between us.

I felt that I had lost Jessie and now I was losing Jarett.

Soon after Jarett's arrival home from Minneapolis, he found an apartment in Rosendale and lived there for two years with three cats that a girlfriend had left with him. There he wrote three extraordinary poetry books that he combined into one called *Vision of the Word*, which he self- published in 2008. The books, written in a unique rap rhyming style, were part of Jarett's healing process–as he put it, "to share his story of finding himself, piece by piece, through these turbulent years."

I will indulge the reader with one of Jarett's poems, one of my favorites:

FINDING NEVERLAND

If one listens to the music of a breathing heart

One can envision the perfect rhythm of spirit.

Meditative healing apart from this world of division

That breaks the illusion of separation.

Uplifting the mind to a higher kind of precision.

Behind closed eyelids there lies a sanctuary.

A home on wheels of dreams and ideals

That we carry around concealed

From the material habitants of the external world.

A unique den hidden away from the lies of men.

A location of energy we can tap into for rejuvenation.

I hold an invitation to visit my safe haven

Reserved for the deserved few.

. . .Take my hand and I will show you. . .

The poem was a gift at a time when we both needed it. I love the poem, but the words "safe haven" haunted me. Would I ever find mine?

Chapter Forty

Falling in Love

I DIDN'T WANT TO LIVE on Main Street, Rosendale. I had been living in a beautiful house in Stone Ridge with the forests of the Vly Ridge behind me. Why would I want to live in a small town? On Main Street, no less? Dr. Andre Ross, my wonderful landlady and friend had retired from her veterinarian profession. She had to sell the house for financial reasons and I was pressured to find a place to live. I could find nothing in my price range that came close to the comforts of our house in Stone Ridge. It was my friend Teeny who was staying with me at the time, who noticed the ad in the *Woodstock Times*: For Sale by Owner, a yellow Victorian house with pink and yellow trim on Rosendale's Main Street. Teeny said: "Why not take a look?"

It was August, 1996. I bought the house in ten minutes. I fell in love. It had everything: four bedrooms upstairs, a living room, a dining room, a small kitchen, wood floors, beautiful wallpaper, three fireplaces, a large old kitchen sink, a claw-foot bathtub, a small yard that I could turn into a vegetable garden, a porch on the front of the house, and a Romeo and Juliet porch on the second floor overlooking the backyard. With the staircase going up to the second floor, it was like the little dollhouse I used to play with when I was little. The house was even featured in a 1992 issue of *Victorian Homes* magazine. I gave the owner, Roger Hirschman, a check for $300 as the binder. The check was not good; I had no money. I told Roger to put the check and the house on hold for three days. I needed five thousand dollars as a down payment.

With great trepidation, I picked up the telephone and called my brother George. I had never asked him for anything and now I was calling to ask for a five thousand-dollar loan. George and his wife Karin agreed to loan me the money, and I have been deeply grateful to them for giving me a step up into the "adult" world of homeownership. I was on air. Finally, my own home, my own nest.

It was pouring the day we moved from Stone Ridge to Rosendale. Because they were pressured to leave their rental, the people who bought the Stone Ridge house were moving in as quickly as we were moving out, creating a tense, muddy, chaotic situation. The movers didn't know whose furniture and boxes were whose. Their dog, barking and always underfoot, was leaving muddy pawprints everywhere. Our cat Mitsi escaped into the woods. He would have none of the dog and the chaos. I was worried about him, but didn't have a moment to stop and search for him. In Rosendale, the beautiful wood floors in the house were barely visible for the furniture, the boxes, and the muddy boot tracks. It was a mess.

The last thing to be moved was the piano. I was not leaving my piano. To push the piano straight through the front door, the moving van had to park perpendicular to Main Street, blocking all traffic from both sides. For twenty minutes, I walked from car to car, apologizing and assuring people that their wait would soon be over. Nobody complained.

At last the ordeal was over. I bade good-bye to my drenched group of heroic friends who volunteered to help, promising a huge house-warming party in the near future. I made makeshift beds for Jessie and Jarett, tucked them in and, with my heart pounding, drove back to Stone Ridge to search for Mitsi. I was ready to traipse all over the mountain for him.

It was quiet at the old house. I got out of the car and called his name several times. There were a few panicky moments when there was no response but then, there he was, running to greet me from under the bushes with his distinct familiar meow. Mitsi was waiting for me to return. We were both overjoyed to see each other as I scooped him up into my lap and drove him to Rosendale, our new home.

At first, I was afraid of the small French Godin coal stove situated in front of the fireplace in the living room. Roger, the previous owner, showed me how to use it. The air intake had to be just right or the flame would go out and create a carbon monoxide leak. I took meticulous notes, but it still frightened me. The coal stove and the backup propane stove in the dining room were the main source of heat. What if I did something wrong and the house caught on fire? What if I didn't light it properly and it leaked carbon monoxide and killed us all? I remember many a night sitting on the couch, staring at the coal stove to make sure it was working properly. I would fall asleep on the couch, afraid to go upstairs to bed. I was alone and head of the household. There were no men in my life to help lug the coal up the stairs from the basement and keep the home fires burning three times a day. The chores were all mine: chopping wood into small pieces to start the coal stove, cleaning out the ash, shoveling snow, digging the garden, cooking, cleaning. I took on the responsibilities with a new feeling of independence, a feeling of fulfillment of being on my own. I was forty-seven years old.

Sometime in January, 1997, when I least expected it, my life changed in a most extraordinary way. Miklos Rudnay, an acquaintance I had met through Nick, the Bulgarian boyfriend, was standing in the express line of the supermarket in Kingston waiting to pay for his shopping as I walked past. I stopped to say hello and mentioned a Russian music performance that I was going to be in at the end of January. He gave me his phone number to let him know more about it. Little did we know that this brief encounter in the mundane Grand Union, surrounded by our weekly shopping, would lead us into a fairy-tale love affair and a long fulfilling marriage.

Two years before, I had met Miklos when Nick invited him to his house for dinner. Nick and Miklos worked together as engineers for Ulster County Public Works in Kingston. I remember Miklos sitting at the dinner table that night, a good-looking man with a dark complexion and a soft-spoken baritone voice. We ate and drank red wine altogether. I liked him. I met him once again when he came with Nick to my house where we shared a pasta and red meat sauce dinner in Stone Ridge. I remember showing him around the house. I knew very little about Miklos. I knew he rented a house in Hurley and that he had a wife who lived in Hungary. His daughter Sofia was attending Bard College and his son Greg was attending UCCC and living at home. One thing was certain: Miklos, a family man, was not someone to start a relationship with. The red flag was up.

"Handsome Hungarian son of a bitch," Nick said with a tinge of jealousy. "I feel sorry for him. He's in big trouble with immigration. His wife doesn't want him to come back to Hungary and his working visa has expired. He's stuck and needs someone to marry him for the green card."

Trying to be helpful, I called a few of my single girlfriends to see if they would help Miklos out. One friend came close, but although they enjoyed each other's company, she balked at the idea of marriage. Lucky for me.

Three years later, on that cold day in January, seeing Miklos on the express line of the Grand Union, I couldn't help notice how handsome he was. I wondered if he was alone and if his problems with his wife and immigration were resolved.

Later that month, my friend Lynn called and told me that I must see a film called *The English Patient* which was playing at Upstate Films in Rhinebeck. She told me that I must not see this film with a woman; that it must be seen with a man—the film was too romantic. I didn't have a boyfriend at that time, nor was I looking for anyone, so my choices were slim. I heard the film was about a Hungarian, so I thought of Miklos. His phone number on a slip of paper was somehow shining up at me from my dining room table. I heard through the grapevine that he had obtained a green card through the immigration lottery, but I knew nothing about the wife. What happened to the red flag? Had I learned nothing from my experience with Marek?

I called Miklos and listened to his low baritone voice on the answering machine. It sounded very sexy. Red flag number two. I left a message.

It was snowing the evening I drove to Kingston to meet Miklos and drive with him to the movies in Rhinebeck. On the way, I remember feeling an odd sense of excitement combined with a sense of peace, a feeling that something out of the ordinary was going to happen…

I don't remember the exact moment I fell in love with Miklos. Was it when we kissed in the car at the Holiday Inn parking lot after seeing *The English Patient*? Was it two weeks later, when we kissed for the second time at the Russian New Year extravaganza where I sang with my Russian ensemble group? I remember Svetlana, my second mother from Nyack, came to the event. She walked up to Miky, introduced herself and said, "Mourka is the girl for you." Then she turned and walked away. Or was it several weeks later when we first made love on my couch and he forgot his watch on my dining room table? I don't remember. That I was in love with his beautiful innocent brown eyes, his sensuous lips; his strong masculine body, and that low sexy Hungarian-accented voice, was a certainty.

It was risky. There were issues. Although his wife was still in Hungary, Miky was reeling from his wife's rejection of him. Eastern Europeans hang onto their marriages, no matter how bad, for the sake of the children. He felt like a failure. He was working three jobs to make ends meet, as an engineer for Ulster County, a taxi driver for Kingston Cabs, and for a short stint, at a Chinese restaurant in Kingston, cutting vegetables. He was single-parenting and paying for Sofia's education at Bard. To relax, Miky drank hard liquor and smoked cigarettes. It was a difficult time for him.

Still, I kept showing up. At first there were little "ciggie" meetings at his house in Hurley (eight minutes from my house) where we would share ten minutes and have a cigarette together, often with his son Greg. The "ciggie" meetings became more frequent, and sometimes would happen in the evenings when he was sitting in his parked taxicab in Kingston or Woodstock, waiting for a ride. We would sit in the taxi and talk. I would put a coat over maroon satin pajamas that I bought from Victoria's Secret especially for those occasions. I liked smoking in maroon satin pajamas.

I saw through the liquor and the cigarette smoke. I saw a tender, loving man overwhelmed by his responsibilities, struggling to stay above water financially and puzzled that he had to face these difficulties alone. I asked nothing from Miky. I didn't try to fix his problems, and for the first time in my life I wanted to share my love and caring unconditionally. I had nothing to lose and everything to gain.

Before either of us knew that writing was a healing tool, Miky wrote. He wrote about his broken marriage, his financial situation, his sorrow, his drinking, and through the writing, he slowly eased himself out of his depressive alcoholic haze. He opened himself up to new possibilities and to the knowledge, that he too, deserved a fulfilling life.

It was March 30, and I was on my way home from a rehearsal with Sigrid Heath in Woodstock. We were preparing for another production of my one-woman show for the Cuneen Hackett Theatre in Poughkeepsie in April. It had started to snow and Miky, who was on a flight from London, having visited his sister, was expecting me to pick him up at the airport.

While standing at a stop sign in Hurley, my car got hit from behind by a drunk driver who promptly drove away from the scene of the accident. Fortunately, a fireman with a beeper saw the incident and called the police and the ambulance. The impact from the drunk's pick-up truck was strong enough to make me throw my head back, leaving me with a headache and feeling dizzy. My car was totaled. When the ambulance arrived, they had to practically cuff me to make me get in.

"But I have to be at JFK Airport in three hours!" I yelled. "Someone will be waiting for me!"

They would hear none of it, and I got carted off to the hospital.

That night, I could have called a myriad of people to bring me home from the hospital, but I called Miky's son, Greg. As we drove through what now was a full-fledged blizzard, Greg, sensitive to my feelings for his father, asked me if I wanted to go home to Rosendale or if he should take me to their house in Hurley. It would have been my first overnight at their house.

"Your house," I said.

Still with a headache and my body sore, I undressed and crawled into Miky's bed and I waited, my mind racing. *Would Miky be happy to see me? Did I do the right thing by coming here? Maybe I shouldn't have come.*

Miky had gotten a message in the airplane from his brother-in-law (the miracle of communication before cell phones) that the person who was to pick him up was involved in a car accident and would not be at the airport. At four a.m., after a six-hour harrowing bus ride through the blizzard from Port Authority and an even more harrowing taxi ride from Kingston, Miky reached his house, still in suspense, not knowing how or where I was.

I heard the front door open and heard his footsteps coming down the steps into his lower-level bedroom. I looked up and saw the relief on Miky's face as we fell into each other's arms. We were safe. We were in love. My soul mate, my angel had arrived.

After that night, Miky and I saw each other as often as we could, traveling between our respective homes. For nine months, he kept the house in Hurley to make it easier on his children, Greg and Sofia to accept the seriousness of our relationship and the new circumstances that would inevitably arise. The wife was a different story.

Every year for the month of August, Miky's wife Magda would come to the United States from Hungary to renew her green card status. And every year, at that time, for the sake of the children and with hopes that his wife would stay, Miky would break off any current girlfriend relationship and return to the house. Magda knew of my existence, but as the other girlfriends had vanished, she thought I would disappear. August, 1997 was different. When Magda arrived, much to her surprise, Miky stayed with me in Rosendale for the entire month. The middle-of-the-night phone calls, tears, and screaming tirades of guilt-laden speeches began. She couldn't believe that Miky would leave her. Magda wanted her secure independent life in Hungary, subsidized by her husband, and she wanted him home once a year when she arrived to the United States. Her gig was up. Miky had had enough and their marriage skidded to an abrupt end.

On New Year's Eve, 1997, Miky and I picked up the remaining few dust balls from the corners of his house in Hurley and drove the last of his possessions to our little Victorian house in Rosendale. At midnight we drank champagne and celebrated our life together. Miky was officially moved in.

We were now a family with four children. Sofia finished her Bachelor's Degree in Biology, and because of immigration problems, she returned to Hungary in the fall. Greg, who was also attending Bard College, moved in with us in Rosendale. Jarett was in a boarding school near Aix-en-Provence, and Jessie finished high school and was working at the ShopRite deli in New Paltz when she met her boyfriend Colin. It wasn't long before she moved in with Colin and his family, who seemed to accept them living together. Although I was not enamored of the relationship, I was happy that Jessie had someone in her life.

With all of our imperfections, Miky and I fit together perfectly. According to Teeny, even our Chinese astrological numbers were perfect, which is rare. Miky worked as an engineer for Ulster County and I was in between jobs, teaching jazz dance and picking up odd teaching jobs. A year later I landed a full-time job as a French and English as a Second Language teacher in the Newburgh Public School District. Having secured that position, we both earned close to the same salary, shared all the expenses, and Miky was able to quit all his side jobs. We took turns cooking and slowly made needed repairs to the house. We started a vegetable garden and I planted flowers around the house. To my relief, Miky became the coal stove director and I, his assistant. We traveled well together and took many exciting camping trips in the United States and in Europe; I hope someday to publish my travel journals filled with our numerous adventures. We drank red wine in the evenings to relax. We were in love and I was never happier. In 2005, Miky's divorce went through and on a spring-like afternoon on January 28, 2007, Miky and I were married by two local judges in a gazebo at the edge of Williams Lake, ten years after we met at the Grand Union in Kingston.

Chapter Forty One

The Roadrunner

IN 1998, WHEN I TOOK the full time teaching position in Newburgh, I was determined that my job would not get in the way of my creative projects. I was not yet finished proving to myself and to the world that I had talent and that I could be successful as an actress. Never mind that I was performing for adolescents five times a day, five times a week in the classroom. That didn't count. I had to perform on stage, be recognized and be applauded.

I didn't lose any time. In November of 1998, two months after I started teaching in Newburgh, I opened my one-woman show, *Mourka* at the Gilgamesh Theatre, Theatre 3 on W. 46th street in New York City for a short run. I remember walking down the institutional green-colored corridors of my school, reciting my twenty-five-page script for a performance in the evening. I received a stunning review in the newspaper, *Новое Русское Слово*, the Russian equivalent of the *New York Times,* which brought me large Russian audiences.

In May, 2004, my show was produced in New York City again at the Solo Play Lab on 36th Street. In between, I read my play in every theatre and performance space in the Hudson Valley, as well as for a New York's Channel 13 Public Broadcasting. My story was published in a compilation of émigré stories called *On the Other Side of the Planet*, edited by Mark Popovsky, a well-known Russian writer who also immigrated to the United States.

I performed in several plays for Performing Arts of Woodstock, including the part of Kate in *All My Sons* by Arthur Miller and Zlata in Eve Ensler's *Necessary*

Targets. I started my own production company called "A Company of Two… or More" with an excellent actor who played the main role, Joe, in *All My Sons*. We performed two-character one-act plays at parties and gatherings in people's homes, using the living room of the house as a stage and the existing doors as exits and entrances. Our repertoire included Anton Chekhov's *The Bear* and Edward Albee's *Counting The Ways*. We did several of these "parlor" performances in the Hudson Valley until my relationship with my partner soured and my wonderful idea was scrapped. I loved bringing live theatre into people's homes.

In 1997, I became the lead singer in a Russian musical group called *Mourka and the Tsigane* (Russian for Gypsies) and sang Russian folk and Gypsy songs with my cousin Nikita Gorsky, who had started the group with several of his musician friends. Nikita Gorsky was by far the kindest, most generous person I had ever had the privilege to spend time with. We had grown up together in Nyack, then lost track of each other until he called me to sing in the choir at the Russian Orthodox Church in Pine Bush, New York. Not too long after, I joined his music group and we were booked often, performing the spirited Russian and Gypsy music.

We sang for weddings and Russian gatherings in clubs and restaurants in the Hudson Valley and in New York City. We sang locally at MaMA, a cultural center in Stone Ridge, and at the Rosendale Café. With Albee Barr playing the piano and with his access to a recording studio in New York, I recorded a cassette with twelve songs called *Russian Gypsy Songs and Romances*.

After three years of singing at what I called "wallpaper gigs" where people talked and ate through our performances and didn't pay attention to the music, I began to tire of the same repertoire and longed to sing more sophisticated Russian music. I was ready to push myself to another level, but the repertoire I wanted to sing was too difficult for Nikita and the group.

In 2000, I was asked to perform at Mohonk Mountain House's summer festival in New Paltz. Mohonk was paying two thousand dollars for the gig. I realized that for that sum of money, I could attract professional musicians to accompany me at this festival and give me the chance I needed to move forward musically. I happened to have a flyer on my dining room table announcing a Russian concert in New York City. I looked closer at the flyer and noticed it was sent to me from a group called the Ensemble of Russian Music, based in Brooklyn. When I called the phone number on the flyer, I had no idea who these musicians were. I only knew that they played authentic Russian instruments: the four-string *domra*, an older cousin of the *balalaika*; the *bayan*, an accordion with buttons instead of a keyboard; and a contrabass *balalaika*, a three-string stand-up bass. With these instruments, how bad could the musicians be?

One spring afternoon, with my music in one hand and a bunch of lilacs in the other, I arrived in Brooklyn to meet the musicians and to rehearse. Little did I know that when I walked through the door of the Brooklyn apartment, I would be rehearsing with some of the best Russian musicians in the world.

Tatiana, an internationally acclaimed *domra* solo artist was all business when she greeted me at the door and took my flowers into the kitchen. The other two musicians were Evgeny, Tatiana's husband, a renowned musician who played the *bayan* and arranged all the music for their concerts, and Vadim, an accomplished contrabass *balalaika* player who played with the some of the best musical groups in New York. At first, intimidated by the level of musicianship surrounding me, I could barely squeak out a few notes. As the evening progressed and the group warmed up to me, I grew bolder, and with nothing to lose and everything to gain, I started belting the songs one after another. In the end, the group agreed to do the concert with me. When Evgeny walked me to my car and I opened the door, he leaned over to me and said quietly, "I like the way you sing."

Those words echoed through my mind for a very long time.

One of the most difficult tasks that I had to face was to tell Nikita, my cousin, whom I loved so much, that I had moved on and wanted to sing with another group. I wrote Nikita a long letter thanking him for giving me the opportunity to sing and explaining my need to move on to another level of music. He understood. He respected my musical abilities, my need to progress and he let me go without anger or guilt. Our friendship was saved and flourished as I continued to sing in the Russian Orthodox Church choir in Pine Bush.

On August 3, 2009, I received the shocking news that Nikita had suffered an accident. He had blacked out and fallen backwards from a scaffold while on an electrical engineering job in Baltimore, Maryland. He died instantly. The tremendous tragedy shook the Russian community and the Russian

Orthodox Church in Spring Valley overflowed with family, relatives, and friends at his funeral. I am still filled with great sadness at the loss of my cousin and friend Nikita.

My new career as a Russian singer blossomed beyond my expectations with the Russian Instrument Ensemble. I arranged concerts for us at universities and colleges in New York and New Jersey. We played locally at the Rosendale Café. We had concerts in private homes and I sang at the annual Petroushka Ball at the Plaza Hotel and at the Harvard Club in New York City. We also performed for a Russian party on a boat that sailed around Manhattan with the World Yacht Club. We had a blast. I generated a great deal of money for the group, and in turn, I had the opportunity to sing with the best Russian musicians in the metropolitan area. Tatiana, Evgeny, Vadim, and I became great friends and I was able to sing the repertoire I had always wanted.

Years ago, when I cleaned out my parents' apartment in Nyack, I saved a box of old 78 rpm records that sat among my own records collecting dust for years. When I began performing Russian music, I dug into the box and discovered beautiful Gypsy romance songs dating back to pre-revolutionary Russia. Among them were Klavdia Shuljenko recordings from the Soviet Union. Klavdia was an extraordinary singer who started singing in jazz, pop and cabaret bands in the late 1920s in Moscow and rose to fame in the late 1930s. From the number of recordings my mother had, it was obvious that Shuljenko was her favorite. Because of this connection and because of Shuljenko's ability to tell a story through her songs, I fell in love with her theatrical style and incorporated her music into my repertoire. The ensemble and I learned ten of her songs and I sang them for the first time at the Rosendale Café, transforming the café into a high style 1930s Russian salon.

Looking back at this time in my life, I don't know how I managed to teach public school and still keep up with my creative endeavors. I was exhausted and overwhelmed with my busyness, but I was afraid to stop, and on some level, all this was taking a subconscious toll. I couldn't relax. When I least expected it, subliminal visions of violence would enter my mind and a shudder would work through my body. I would cry easily and fall into short bouts of depression. These dark moments pursued me all my life. I didn't know what they were; I didn't want to know. I buried myself in my work at school, the theatre, the music, and my life with Miklos. Miky used to call me the roadrunner. We used to laugh at the image of the roadrunner running at full speed, then running out of road, leaving the roadrunner hanging in empty space for a second before plunging down into the unknown.

Chapter Forty Two

Finding Home

I KNOW THE FEELING. IT starts with the first moments of consciousness in the morning, before the reviewing begins, before the first morning stretch. It starts in stillness in the stomach, a flutter that escalates to anxiety which spreads simultaneously down the legs and up the arms, causing tension in the body before it travels into the drowsy mind. When the first thoughts come into play, the nervousness perpetuates a sense of fear, then terror, accelerating to dread, signaling consciousness and the beginning of a new day. Nothing has changed. No healing miracles have happened in the night; no medication to help me through the day. I'm trapped in a black hole. Call it what you will–depression, darkness. I call it hell.

One hot summer day in August, 2009 while Miky and I were on vacation in Maine, I crashed. Shivers went through me and shot an icy chill through my nerves and settled in my heart. In an instant, I found myself in a deep self-loathing depression, a place I had never been before. It happened fast, just like that time in the restaurant in Saranac Lake when anxiety gripped my insides and I spiraled into panic. In 2009, whatever foundation I thought I had crumbled; demons arrived at my doorstep and demanded acceptance. I thought I had found a home in Rosendale and my life with Miky, only to realize that safety was still an illusion for me.

My most difficult journey was still before me.

Displacement was not external. It was deep within me, planted by my displaced parents and taking the shape of reprises of terror, fear, of images of violence that sabotaged and paralyzed me. Day by day, week by week, month by month, year by year, very slowly, my journey took me inward in search of love, understanding, compassion, and forgiveness–in search of home.

I went to the source. I journeyed to that part of Russia where my mother was born and lived happily until her mother's early death. Mama was seventeen years old when the Civil War broke out and her family was forced to leave and move back to Estonia. My mother left her spirit in Russia and I needed to find it.

I retraced my mother's footsteps in the resort city of Taganrog in southern Russia. I felt her spirit around me when I walked down the huge white marble steps that led to the Sea of Azov. I walked the Taganrog streets and imagined the place where she first fell in love; where she flirted near the banks of the sea; where Anton Chekhov, her favorite writer, was born. It was here, where I felt my mother's presence on every corner, that I began to see the thread that runs through my history. Three generations of women, exhausted from the effort of spending their lives searching for love and meaning, created a downward spiraling pattern for the next generation. My mother's attempted suicides, her headaches, depression, and anxiety, her inability to fulfill her creative passion in the new American world, her turning to alcohol and drugs for relief–all these stemmed from the loss of her mother and her home. This thread looped around me as the depression and fear were passed down to me as a harmful inheritance, leaving me with emotional instability and a void to fill. To change my mother's destiny, I bullied myself through life and in so doing, I took time away from my children when they needed me most and perpetuated the pattern of insecurity, instability, anxiety and depression.

I started to write and I heard a tiny voice encouraging me to go forward with every sentence, paragraph, and chapter. Sometimes I wondered where the words came from. How did they link together to create those memories, thoughts, and ideas? How did they replace layers of displacement, disappointment, and fear with love, understanding and forgiveness for my mother, my father, my children, and for myself?

I am a work in progress, with meditation and yoga as necessary companions that nurture and comfort me through difficult moments. I am grateful for my creative energy, which allows me to see beauty and participate in the world of theatre, music, dance, and art. African dance classes give me energy; the drums, beating a primitive rhythm, remind me that life need not be so complicated. Tennis, a sport that combines gladiator combat with chess, is challenging, but I'm addicted. The mended safety net surrounds me; the emotional foundation now sturdy. I have found my home.

I crossed the ocean with a ship full of refugees escaping war-torn Europe, and as my Meyendorff ancestor before me, I held onto a suitcase packed with my history: the adventures, the passions, the fears and the elations. I moved, was displaced physically and emotionally over thirty times while living in the United States, and everywhere I went, I dragged my suitcase with me, not wanting to let go, knowing that someday the contents would spill out and overflow.

ACKNOWLEDGEMENTS

I believe in angels, and mention in my writing several that saw me through difficult times. I could not have explored the violence, the anguish, the pain, and the suffering that both of my parents and I experienced over the years, had I not found home in the safe haven of my love for Miky and his love for me. I give a million thanks to Miky, the angel who supported me when words did not come easily on paper, who listened to my chapters first, before the edits, for feeding me and loving me without conditions.

I thank my children Jessie and Jarett for loving me despite my imperfections, for being patient until I could find my way back to them. When I finished my chapter "Absent" and read it back to myself, tears rolled down my face, and I began to sob. It was hard to breathe–the depth of sadness and grief that I felt pushing down on my chest was overwhelming. In that moment I knew what I wanted to do. Still sobbing, I got into my car and drove the eight miles to Jessie's house, wrapped my arms around her and apologized for being absent emotionally through her difficult times. She understood and forgave me. A new honesty emerged in our conversation–a new start to our relationship. Still sobbing, I then drove to where Jarett worked and apologized for letting him go and perhaps setting the stage for when his world turned upside down. I felt such love for my children, and the love was returned to me. Our healing had begun. Jessie and Jarett have taken on the challenges of their lives, healing their past to uncover a more fulfilling future.

I shudder to think what would have happened if I didn't get help from Debby Frankie Ogg. Debby, psychologist, spiritual healer, interfaith minister, who healed herself from a fatal form of cancer, became my wise woman angel. With Debby, my difficult journey home–back to myself– began, and this time I was ready to go to stillness. This time I was ready to stop everything to make that search deep into my soul and find out what I had been running from all my life. This time the pain was too intense. Although I begged for medication, I am grateful to Debby for her insistence that I could heal without it. With her guidance, I found other tools to relax and find tranquility. Debby restored my spirit and saved my life.

Kripalu yoga, which focuses on breath and movement as a life force, helped me regain my day-to-day balance and taught me how to manage stress. I was fortunate to meet Tanya Robie, my yoga instructor, another angel, who touched me to my core in my first yoga class. Tears welled up in my eyes and fell on my yoga mat the first time Tanya massaged and tucked my feet into a blanket as the class prepared for "*savasana*," the resting pose where I could let go of tension and wave after wave of negativity and darkness. I never left.

My gratitude extends to my supportive and patient team, without which the task of writing my memoir would have been much more difficult: my brother George, who retraced his steps and helped me piece together our family history; Nina Shengold, for taking on the monumental task of copy-editing the memoir; and Doug Motel, the computer wizard, who launched the book into cyberspace. I must acknowledge and thank my good friend Sigrid Heath for co-writing my one-woman play *Mourka*, and for setting me on the path to memoir writing. I thank Eva Tenuto, Executive Director of TMI Project, who created a space for me to write, to perform my stories, and to begin my memoir.

Laura Shaine Cunningham, acclaimed novelist, playwright, journalist and good friend became my mentor angel, and with her invaluable help, I realized that chapter by chapter, I was creating a book. Without Laura's help, this memoir could not have been written. Laura gave me the confidence to keep working week by week, day by day and sometimes hour by hour. I learned to write better under her patient tutelage, found my own voice and discovered joy in the writing process. With Laura's support and her faith that I had a good story to tell, I was able to recreate my adventure, relive the lighter and darker moments and set them down on paper. I am in deep gratitude to Laura for believing in me.

EPILOGUE

I read somewhere about a Chinese poet who noticed many centuries ago that to recreate something in words is akin to living twice. Recreating the lighter moments of my life was adventurous and pleasurable; recreating the darker moments was excruciating and had me running to Debby for resuscitation and life support. I relived my children's pain, my parents' pain, and in the last chapter, I relived my own pain and faced my darkest self. I saw the tunnel coming and there was no stopping the collision with the truth.

My efforts extended beyond writing. I researched family archives and read memoirs and journals written by my parents and other relatives. I read other people's accounts of their time period and nationalities. I reconnected with family and people from different parts of the world, people I had not seen or heard of in years. There were meetings with my children, Jessie and Jarett, my husband Miky, and Debby in my living room where sensitive parts of the memoirs were read out loud and then discussed. Had I known how much work, laughter and tears it takes to write a memoir, would I have begun?

No revelations took place, no bells went off the day I finished the first draft of my memoir. For a few minutes, after I wrote my final sentence, I just sat there and reveled in the knowledge that for three years, I was able to sit for hours in my leather chair by the wood stove, a place which I dubbed my "Winter Palace," and do something which only a few short years ago, I would have thought was impossible: write my story.

APPENDIX

MEYENDORFF FAMILY HISTORY

The Meyendorff genealogy can be traced back to Swedish Vikings who migrated into Novgorod in the early part of the twelfth century. In Stockholm's Town Hall, the family names are written very clearly, so the genealogy is easy to read. One of the first family crests is that of the Meyendorff family. In 1180, many of the Meyendorffs migrated to Germany and some to the Baltic States: Latvia, Lithuania and Estonia.

Pope Clement II (1005 –1047), a Meyendorff from Germany, was Pope from 1046 until his death at age 45. He was the first in a series of reform-minded popes. One of his more criticized reforms was the ban on the use of "simony," the payment of money for sacrament to the church as a way of getting ecclesiastical preferences and benefices. Clement II declared that only God could give forgiveness and absolve one's sins. Because of his beliefs, it was widely suspected that he was poisoned with lead sugar on his way to the Vatican in Rome. A toxicological examination of his remains in the mid-twentieth century confirmed the centuries-old rumors that the Pope had died from ingesting lead sugar. It is not clear, however, whether he was murdered or the lead sugar was used as medicine.

Baron Georg Walter Konrad von Meyendorff (1795-1863) made a journey from Orenburg, in south Russia, to the country of Bukhara (now known as Uzbekhistan) in 1820. This trip was supported by Emperor Alexander I after a Bukharin envoy made several trips to St. Petersburg between 1816 and 1820. The main purpose of Meyendorff's trip was to discover land that the Russians had very little knowledge about and to open up a new trade route with these underdeveloped southeastern countries. Baron Meyendorff was in charge of compiling the geographical and the statistical records of the countries that they were passing through. With him went Herr Volkonsky, a well-known Russian aristocrat, and Semosryf, both lieutenants on the staff. A journal about this trip was written in French by Baron Georg Meyendorff, compiled by Dr. Carl Hermann, and translated into English by Captain E.F. Chapman.

Baroness Olga von Meyendorff (1838-1926) was a widow with two children who, according to some historians, had an affair with Franz Liszt. In any case, they were very good friends and shared many interests, especially music. In 1872, Liszt composed an Impromptu and dedicated it to the Baroness. A book was published including their full correspondence, *The Letters of Franz Liszt to Olga von Meyendorff 1871-1886.* These letters are a part of the Dumbarton Oaks Collection bequeathed to Harvard University by Mrs. Robert Woods Bliss in 1969.

Georg Otto Wilhelm Meyendorff, or Egor Federovich Meyendorff (1794-1879), my paternal great-grandfather (his two names reflect the Baltic and Russian aristocratic names; I will use the Russian name), became Adjutant General for Alexander II. For the last thirty-four years of his life, he was also president of the Church Council of Lutheran Churches in St. Petersburg, and was in charge of building the St. John Lutheran church on Bolshaya Konnushennaya Street in St. Petersburg. Before the revolution, Malaya Konnushennaya Street bore the name Meyendorff Boulevard in honor of Egor Federovich.

As a young man, Egor and his brothers took part in the war of 1812. In a conversation with their mother, General Kutuzov, a famous Russian general in the war of 1812 with Napoleon, said," Я не настолько стар, чтобы не иметь права назвать себя другом ваших храбрых сыновей." ("I am not so old that I do not have the right to call myself a friend of your brave sons.")[3]

Egor was also a friend of Alexander Pushkin, and after Pushkin's death in a duel with Dantes, Egor's influence was largely responsible for pardoning Pushkin posthumously and restoring his honor as Russia's most prominent poet.

In the early part of the nineteenth century, my great-grandfather lived in the Republic of Estonia, part of the Russian Empire from 1720. There was an existing law that if an Estonian married a Russian Orthodox woman, their children would become Russian Orthodox. Egor Meyendorff married Russian Olga Fedorovna von Briskorn (whose first husband was Yakov Alexeevich Potemkin) and they had seven children. Olga's dowry included Kumna, the family estate in Estonia near Reval (now known as Tallinn). Egor was a devout Lutheran, and it disturbed

From Elena Nikolaevna Meyendorff in Salzburg

him that his children would become Russian Orthodox. He thus commissioned a statue of Martin Luther (made in 1862) that stood on the large family estate. Years later, the Soviets took down the statue, melted it, and used the bronze to make a statue of Stalin. There is now a large, albeit different, monument of Martin Luther standing near Kumna, the family estate in Estonia.

My great-grandfather on my grandmother's side, Count Pavel Shuvalov, was an infantry general, ambassador to Berlin from 1885-1894; he was also a member of the Russian State Council and became the Foreign Minister of Russia. His friendship with Otto von Bismarck, the German ambassador in St. Petersburg, was largely responsible for keeping the peace between Germany and Russia for many years before the inevitable World War II. Countess Shuvalova's brother, also named Pavel, was head of the Moscow police and was assassinated by revolutionaries in 1905.

The Meyendorff Castle is in a small village now known as Barvikha, not far from the center of Moscow. In the beginning of the nineteenth century, the castle belonged to a General Kazakov, who gave it to his daughter Nadezhda as a wedding gift when she married General Verigin. Nadezhda requested that her father reconstruct the castle in a romantic, medieval style from her childhood fairy-tale books, which her father promptly did. When Verigin died, Nadezhda later married Baron Mikhail Felixovich Meyendorff (a fifth cousin to me) for his title. The Baron, in turn, married Nadezdha for her money. Baron Meyendorff added a few towers and surrounded the castle with brick, and this strange, Gothic-style castle became known as the Meyendorff Castle. Czar Alexander III visited the castle in 1888 and my grandfather, Bogdan, visited the castle as part of Czar Nicholas II's entourage in 1896. There is a plaque in one of the towers commemorating these visits. In 1903, Baron Felixovich Meyendorff accepted a position as first secretary of a diplomatic mission to Denmark and he and Nadezhda moved to Copenhagen, never to return.

After the 1917 Revolution, rumors have it that Lenin stayed and worked here. In 1935, the castle became a sanatorium, and Mikhail Bulgakov, an author and playwright famous for writing the novel *The Master and Margarita*, stayed here and was treated for an ongoing kidney disorder. Andrey Makarevich, lead singer of the rock group Time Machine (Машина Времени) also spent some time here.

During the Soviet years, the castle became a Young Pioneer children's camp, an orphanage, and a hospital before it fell into complete disarray. In 2001, Vladimir Putin took notice of its strange Gothic architecture and had the castle restored. It is now an event destination and conference center for high government officials from all over the world.

Irine von Meyendorff, a distant relative and a well-known film actress during World War II in Germany, visited my family when they were living in the Displaced Persons Camp in Uchte, West Germany in 1946. My brother George remembers a very beautiful woman climbing out of a fancy, shiny green Fiat with gold trim and coming up to the apartment to visit our parents. Irine's family escaped the Bolsheviks in the Baltics and went to Germany, hiding their jewels in the infant's crib. Because of Irine's extraordinary beauty, a producer from the German film company Universum Film Aktiengesellschaft (UFA) spotted her in 1935 and made her into an instant film star in a film called *The Four from Santa Cruz*. Despite the fact that Irine abhorred the Nazi regime, she continued her successful acting career with her innate acting talent. Her rebellious nature and aristocratic background were at odds with Nazi ideology. Her first husband, Heinz Zahler, was Hermann Goehring's personal physician, and she tried to persuade him to overdose Goehring with codeine, to which he was addicted. This he did not do, deciding to let the course of history take its toll. Once, Irine confronted Goebbels when he made sexual advances towards her. Goebbels was quoted as saying, "Unfortunately, Fraulein von Meyendorff seems rather cold." After that incident, Irine got fewer and fewer acting roles. In 1961, Irine married the famous English actor James Robert Justice, abandoned her film career in Germany, and moved to England. She died in England in 2001.

ULK FAMILY HISTORY

My mother's brother, my Uncle Zhenya, his wife, their daughter Helgi and their adopted daughter Silvi had their own miraculous escape story. In August, 1944, my Aunt Lyalya, as I called her, took the two children and left Tallinn, Estonia by ship in a convoy to Konigsberg (now known as Kaliningrad). From there they took a train to Vienna, then filled to the brim with refugees and retreating German troops. Luckily, Aunt Lyalya was fluent in German and would not take "no" for an answer as she pushed, pulled, and shoved the children and herself on board.

When Aunt Lyalya left the country with the two children, Uncle Zhenya, the director of a peat briquette factory in Tootsi, Estonia, stayed behind to tie up loose ends. (Peat was an important fuel in Estonia.) My uncle was told by the "Sonderfuhrer" (high German command) to sabotage or destroy the factory so it would not fall into Soviet hands. Uncle Zhenya, who could not in his good conscience destroy the basic heating fuel in his country and put people out of work, got the German officers drunk that evening, so they would not notice that their orders were not followed. Before the officers sobered up the next morning, my uncle managed to leave Estonia by train with the last of the retreating German army.

Years later, on Easter, 1944, the "Sonderfuhrer," an Austrian by birth and a man with an enormous sense of humor, visited the Ulks and the Meyendorffs at their apartment in Vienna. My brother remembered him as a fun-loving, jovial man who understood and forgave my uncle's transgression in not bombing the peat factory in Estonia.

My cousin Silvi's adoption into the Ulk family is necessary to mention to reiterate the extreme hardships that people endured during World War II. Silvi was born in Gatchina, Russia, south of St. Petersburg to Finnish parents, Eva and Juhani Burklund. Silvi was the youngest of their five children. In the spring of 1942, with World War II at their heels, the parents decided to flee Russia and go to Estonia with the two youngest children, Silvi and her brother Yalmari. On that journey west, both parents died; the mother from starvation and the father from gangrene, having stepped on a mine. Silvi and Yalmari were picked up by the retreating German army and were deposited into an orphanage in Tallinn. In December, 1942, my Aunt Lyala, knowing that her family was leaving Estonia forever, decided to take at least one parentless child with them. The orphanage was full of children, and she was at a quandary about whom she should choose. She saw Silvi crying uncontrollably in her crib, picked her up, and took her home.

On September 5, 2016, two weeks before publication of my memoir, I received an email from a reliable source in Estonia that Nicholas "Koka" Andreev, the young man that my mother Rita was in love with during their school years in

Tallinn; the "Koka" that she writes about in her journals, wrote his own memoir. It was translated from Russian to English by his daughter and is entitled, *A Moth On A Fence*. "Koka" mentions the love affair between he and my mother in his book and how utterly devastated he was when the affair ended. Is this discovery a germ for a new novel? Perhaps...

Made in the USA
Middletown, DE
18 September 2017